Mao's lost children: stories of the
rusticated youth of China's cultural
revolution

MAO'S LOST CHILDREN

STORIES OF THE RUSTICATED YOUTH OF
CHINA'S CULTURAL REVOLUTION

D1537170

STORIES OF THE RUSTICATED YOUTH OF
CHINA'S CULTURAL REVOLUTION

MAO'S

LOST

CHILDREN

Edited by Ou Nianzhong and Liang Yongkang

Translated by Laura Maynard

MerwinAsia
Portland, Maine

MERWIN

ASIA

Distributed by the University of Hawai'i Press

Library of Congress Control Number: 2015946970

ISBN 978-1-937385-67-5 (Paperback)
ISBN 978-1-937385-68-2 (Hardcover)

Printed in the United States of America

The paper used in this publication meets the minimum requirements of the
American National Standard for Information Services—Permanence of Paper
for Printed Library Materials,
ANSI/NISO Z39/48-1992

Contents

Contents

Contents

INTRODUCTION

Most people in the West would probably associate the heyday of Communist China with the leadership of "Chairman Mao" (Mao Zedong), the Red Guards' reign of terror, and the Cultural Revolution of 1966–1976. Many have only the vaguest awareness of these events, but another and extraordinary event occurred which they may not have heard of at all. On December 22, 1968, Chairman Mao declared: "Educated youth, go to the countryside to receive re-education from the poor and lower-middle peasants: it is a must." Between 1968 and 1980, 15 million middle-school graduates from Chinese cities were sent to live and work in the countryside, a "rustication" of what amounted to nearly 10 percent of the urban population of the time. In general, their experience was to prove an extremely harsh one. They were known as *zhiqings*, a portmanteau word from *zhishi qingnian*, "educated youth." This is the first book to appear outside China in which so many have recounted the experience of rustication in their own words.

Such an enormous social upheaval prompts a number of questions, the first of which is: Why did it happen? Rustication really began in 1953, only four years after the Communists had seized power. Between 1962 and 1966 nearly one and a half million young people were sent to the countryside, but the main impetus was undoubtedly the Cultural Revolution. The original aim of rustication had been twofold. The ostensible one was to develop the rural and frontier areas of the country, and thus provide work for the numerous secondary school graduates who were otherwise unemployable. But the government's hidden and more important aim was to save money: the welfare benefits it provided in the cities, such as education, rationed food, employment and other privileges, did not extend to the countryside. Since the nation's most populous, prosperous and fertile regions lay to the east, the main areas of rustication were in the far north, such as Heilongjiang and Inner Mongolia; Xinjiang in the northwest and Yunnan in the southwest; and on China's southernmost island, Hainan.

By the mid 1960s, a generation was growing up which was the first to have been born in the People's Republic: it had known allegiance to none other than the red flag, and was widely imbued with Communist ideals and a spirit of collectiveness and self-sacrifice. In the power struggle that was developing between Mao and his rivals, many members of this younger generation formed "Red Guard" groups to support his leadership and revolt against a system of education they regarded as elitist. They took to the streets. From a movement against bourgeois intellectuals, the Cultural Revolution grew rapidly into a revolt against all forms of authority. Its aim was to smash the "Four Olds:" Old Customs, Old Culture, Old Habits, Old Ideals. The Red Guards attacked anyone whom they regarded as insufficiently Maoist: government and party officials, their own teachers, their own parents—and each other. Mao's dominance was sealed, but he and his associates had unleashed a monster that was out of control. Violence, looting, and purges became widespread. Those who were associated with the old Nationalist regime, and their children, were publicly denounced and turned out of their homes and jobs. Millions of people were affected, public buildings were damaged, historical sites destroyed, private property confiscated. Schools were disrupted, universities closed, factories reduced to part-time operation. Anarchy paralyzed the country.

The government now had to find a way to dissipate the threat posed by the Red Guards, who were at least 4 million strong, and to divert their energies. Rustication, a process that had been happening for the past thirteen years, provided a ready answer. The appeals to young people to embrace it soon took the form of a concerted campaign, with the slogan "Up to the Mountains, Down to the Countryside," and its political rationale was made more explicit. First, it would bridge the three major differences between the two Chinas—between the urban and rural worlds, between workers and peasants, between mental and manual work. Mao saw rustication as a way for intellectuals to undergo "re-education," to connect with the world of physical labor and appreciate social realities. Second, it would help to defend the country against what were perceived during the late 1960s and early 1970s as two major external threats: the Soviet Union in the north and the American imperialists in the south.

Why did so many young people sign up for rustication? For the Red Guards and their sympathizers, the reason was simple ideological fervor: it was a way to fulfill their revolutionary ambitions. And there were several good reasons to love and obey Chairman Mao which may not be apparent to Western liberals. Chinese politics have not been characterized by a strong democratic tradition, and before the Communist revolution, life for the masses was hardly a bed of roses. They were poor, at the base of a feudal system that allowed them to be exploited by landlords, capitalists, the bourgeoisie, and foreign imperialists. But Chairman Mao presented himself as a man of the people, a savior, a father figure who was nevertheless a rebel against old-fashioned authority and the stifling weight of tradition. He was a compelling writer and orator, whose style was vivid, pithy, and direct. He promised a better life for everyone, the resurgence of China as an egalitarian, socialist nation. It was a powerful message.

Even those who were not necessarily swayed by Mao were still drawn to rustication as an opportunity for excitement, romance and adventure. It promised independence and an escape from the monotony of home life, and the promise was strengthened by the idealized depictions of the borderlands that appeared in the films and literature of the government's propaganda machine. There was a third, more mundane, reason for embracing rustication: the need for food, shelter, and income. On the state farms, a basic level of security known as "the iron rice bowl" was guaranteed, but even the rural villages and communes seemed to offer a better prospect of these things than a life of urban unemployment.

There were two other good reasons for embracing rustication. The first was a desire to conform, to accompany those many friends and long-standing classmates who had already undertaken to go. And the second was that rustication soon became a pre-condition of employment back in the cities and of enrollment at colleges and universities: nobody would be willing to offer a job or place to a candidate who had come straight from school. But there were other, and more sinister, reasons. One was to escape the stigma of coming from a "bad," that is, ideologically deviant, family. If one's parents had been identified as rightists, rustication seemed to offer a way to expiate this hereditary sin, though in practice it seldom succeeded. The second reason was straightforward coercion. The state media bombarded the populace with propaganda and songs urging youngsters to join the movement. From July 1968, these were reinforced by workers' propaganda troupes, which were dispatched to schools and local communities. Moreover, teachers and military representatives resorted to all means—study groups, one-to-one talks, even threats—to make the students sign up. The latter were sometimes told that until they did so, their teachers' lives would be made difficult and their parents' jobs would be suspended.

The scale and momentum of the rustication movement prompt the question: Why did it come to an end? The short answer is that it died with its champion, Mao Zedong, on September 9, 1976, but there were bigger and more compelling causes. The first was that it was a resounding economic failure, for three reasons. First, the peasants who lived in the areas to which the *zhiqings* were rusticated had no need of their assistance: the extra manpower would not increase yields and merely meant more mouths to feed. Second, there were widespread crop failures because in many instances the land was put to new agricultural uses for which it was unsuited. And third, there was serious mismanagement of the organizations to which the *zhiqings* were sent: embezzlement and other misuses of public funds were not uncommon.

What also heralded the end of rustication was the fact that it was profoundly unpopular with peasants and *zhiqings* alike. We have already seen that for the former the *zhiqings* represented not only help they did not need but an extra liability: for the latter, rustication turned out to be an experience that was the absolute antithesis of what government propaganda and their own expectations had led them to believe. It was typified by backbreaking labor, constant hunger, a monotonous existence and, not infrequently, an abuse of power by those who were placed in charge of them. They had little remedy against persecution and physical cruelty, not to mention instances of sexual harassment and even rape. After Chairman Mao's death, protests, strikes, demonstrations, and petitions began to occur on a scale that would force the government to bring rustication to an end. The policy was officially discontinued in October 1980, and by the end of the decade most of the *zhiqings* had returned to their home cities.

The final, and most absorbing, question is addressed by this book: What was it like to be rusticated? Outside China this is a largely untold story, but a fascinating one. The *zhiqings* who recount their experiences in this book are from the urban areas of Guangdong Province, such as Guangzhou, Shantou, Chaozhou and Meixian, and were rusticated to Hainan Island, which lies off the southernmost point of the Chinese mainland. Rustication began on November 10, 1968, and by 1973 over 110,000 *zhiqings* were living on the island and engaged in the production of rubber, sisal-hemp, palm oil, rice, and tropical fruit. They joined a workforce of veterans or "old hands"—ex-servicemen who had arrived on the island some years before—and the local peasantry. The island is also home to a sizeable ethnic minority, the Li people, who maintained distinct customs and lived in their own separate villages.

The rusticated students were organized like soldiers. In 1954, the Chinese government had set up a semi-military body, the Xinjiang Army Production and Construction Corps, whose purpose was to defend the northwestern border of China and promote economic development and ethnic harmony, and between 1966 and 1970 eleven similar corps were established in other parts of the country. From April 1969, the Guangzhou Army Production and Construction Corps was given the task of strengthening the defence of the southernmost part of China. It absorbed all the state farms on Hainan Island and on the mainland side of the Qiongzhou Strait, along with the South China

Institute of Tropical Crops.

The corps was divided into ten divisions consisting of 148 regiments which were staffed by almost 3,000 officers. It was headed by a corps commander and a commissar from the Guangzhou Army, and this system of command was replicated at all levels: the division, the regiment and the company. In the regiment, the commander worked with a commissar; in the company, a captain worked alongside a political instructor. Within every company, the *zhiqings* were organized into squads, each with its own leader, and all were described as regimental soldiers and issued army uniforms. Some were assigned to the militia, an armed body that each regiment maintained in order to help guard the borderlands.

In theory, the *zhiqings* worked an eight-hour day, six days a week: in practice, volunteer work and inescapable political study sessions, regularly organized by the company or regiment, crammed the after-hours. Every now and then, the whole company or regiment would camp in the jungle for months on end in order to clear land or build terraces for rubber plantations. These were the "major joint campaigns," originally a military term that describes several forces combining in order to storm a stronghold. In October 1974, the Guangzhou Army Corps was dissolved owing to low productivity and poor management, and the state farms were returned to the local authorities. By 1976 all the other army corps of this kind had been disbanded.

Most of the narrators in this book were rusticated to Daling State Farm, located in Baisha Li Autonomous County in western Hainan Island, but between 1969 and 1974, when the farm was under military control, it was renamed No. 13 Regiment of No 4. Division of the Guangzhou Army Production and Construction Corps. As well as clearing the jungle for the planting of rubber and other tropical crops, the unskilled *zhiqings* were required to become instantly self-sufficient, building their own quarters and battling against hunger, heat, pests, and threats of drought. However, unlike those of their peers who were assigned to the villages and communes, they had a guaranteed wage and rationed food ('the iron rice bowl').

Every *zhiqing* was entitled to annual home leave of just twelve days, but so long and tortuous was the journey back to mainland Guang-dong, and so poor the system of transport, that a further nine days were allowed for travel, making twenty-one days in all. Nevertheless, leave was not always granted by those in charge of the *zhiqings*, and even when it was, a lack of money might prevent them from taking it more than once every two or three years. For most, rustication lasted for a period of six to ten years but for some, very much longer. Their final return home took place when they were in their late twenties or early thirties and could, in its own way, be as difficult as rustication had been. In a sluggish economy and for the most part without qualifica-tions, they could hope for no better employment than menial work in factories or the service industries. Born at about the same time as the People's Republic itself, they mirrored its vicissitudes in the history of their lives. With some justice, they have been described as China's lost generation.

Yet despite the grinding hardship of rustication, their stories are not just one long complaint. They tell us how the *zhiqings* were often able to turn hardship to advantage, finding marginal consolations and amusements, cultural diversions, opportunities to play the system, to study, laugh or fall in love. Most important, hardship enabled them to discover within themselves strengths and abilities that they had not known they possessed. Their stories show how oppression can bring out the best as well as the worst in people—not only cruelty, threats, and vindictiveness but dignity, kindness, and generosity. They reveal the resilience of the Chinese people under the severest conditions and, more broadly, the indomitable nature of the human spirit.

Maps

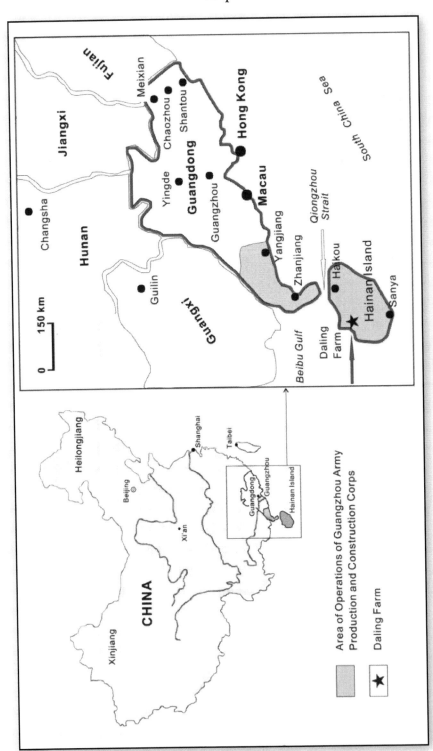

Map 1: Guangdong Province before 1989

Maps

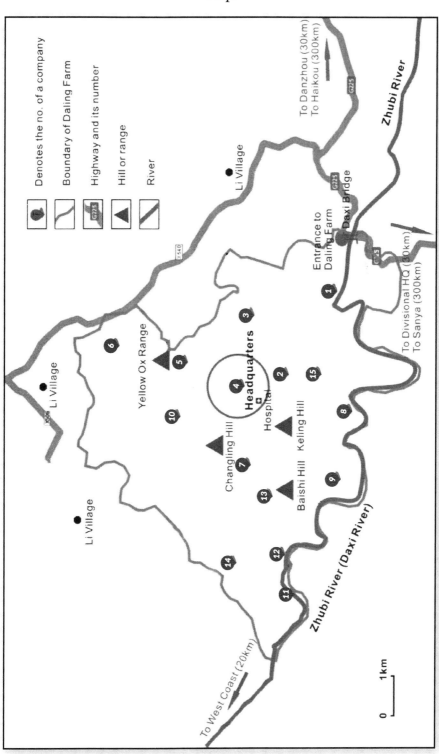

Map 2: Daling State Farm (known between 1969 and 1974 as No. 13 Regiment, No. 4 Division of the Guangzhou Army Corps)

MAO'S LOST CHILDREN

STORIES OF THE RUSTICATED YOUTH OF
CHINA'S CULTURAL REVOLUTION

Leaving Home

"SEE YOU ON THE BATTLEFIELD!"

Huang Ronger

Zhiqing—"educated youth"—is a term loaded with connotations of struggling, bewilderment, pain, and loss. It was the source of strength for a whole generation and embodied their aspirations. For me, it was imbued with idealism.

In November 1968, the third year of the Cultural Revolution, I boarded a Red Guard ship which would carry hundreds of *zhiqings* to Hainan Island. On the pier were those who came to see off their friends or relatives. Some were waving with tears in their eyes, some were calling out the names of those who had already boarded.

In the tearful crowd were my younger sister and brother. My sister would soon be rusticated to Yangshan County. A radical, she was a member of the volunteers in her school who were determined to improve conditions in the remote northern countryside of Guangdong Province by working and living with the peasants. Also in her school was another group of volunteers, among them six girls who were heading up to Heilongjiang Province, China's great northern wilderness. They felt that there should be blooms even on its snowy peaks—that they should penetrate the harshest area of the country. These volunteers were mostly senior students: I admired them for their fierce determination to transform the poorest regions of the country.

I had hoped that my father would also be there to see me off. Before the Cultural Revolution he had been deputy director of the Guangdong Provincial Propaganda Department and deputy chief editor of the official provincial paper, the *Nanfang Daily*. Later, he had been purged and was being held in solitary confinement for prosecution. When I went to say goodbye to my mother, I stopped short of visiting him. To my mind, he was a wholehearted and hard-working revolutionary who was dedicated to the improvement of the lives of ordinary people. When I was in the seventh grade, he gathered all his older children together and recounted his experiences as a member of the Anti-Japanese Guerrilla Contingent: he didn't want us to be spoiled like many others whose parents held high office. Instead, he wanted us to learn from the workers, peasants and ordinary folk, and to dedicate ourselves to the cause of turning the whole world into one single, vast, communist state. Because of his heavy workload, he had never taken me to the cinema, and we had only been to the park together once or twice, so this family meeting was most memorable to me.

In his state of confinement, my father must have craved some comfort from his family. Yet I repressed the urge to see him. I didn't want to implicate my mother, who was by then confined to the suburb of Sanyuanli, where cadres of various newspaper groups assembled for "study sessions." Despite what had happened to her and my father, she asked me calmly to work hard on the farm and not to worry about family affairs. I knew for sure that if I accepted the offer of a permit to visit my father, my mother, also a former member of the Anti-Japanese Guerrilla Contingent, would be condemned for not having made a clean break from my father, who had "taken the capitalist road." With both our parents in high office, our family used to belong to the "special class" which enjoyed many privileges but which during the Cultural Revolution was also among the first to be purged. While members of the special class were either being prosecuted or sent to study sessions, their children were being denounced as within 'the five black categories', a generic and pejorative name for ex-landlords, rich farmers, counterrevolutionaries, bad elements and rightists, and relegated to the lowest level of society. Our spacious house with a garden was taken over and occupied by strangers, and we were forced to cram into a tiny room with only makeshift wooden partitions to separate us from our neighbors.

I was lost in my thoughts when someone on board shouted at the top of his voice: "See you on the battlefield!' This was followed by a resounding chant of slogans from the crowd. I was bemused: we were about to plant rubber on Hainan Island, so where was the battlefield? Growing up contemporaneously with the People's Republic of China, we were filled with a strong missionary purpose: to turn the republic into a rich and prosperous country. Our idols of the day were Lei Feng, Wang Jie, Ouyang Hai—those People's Liberation Army soldiers who in their early twenties had lost their lives in the course of saving the lives of others. Our destiny was to liberate the whole world. Was this the sense in which "See you on the battlefield" had been uttered? Or, in the manic chanting of slogans, was there a hint of madness, the release of certain repressed feelings?

I didn't have the answer. All I knew was that I wanted to be re-educated to become the most popular person among the workers and peasants, the elite of the time. And that was how naïve and overwrought I was when embarking on my life as a *zhiqing*.

FOLLOW CHAIRMAN MAO CLOSELY

Fang Jinqi

16 December 1968

Dear Qi,

Our great leader Chairman Mao has said: "We call on all intellectuals to go and interact with the masses, go to the factories, go to the countryside." "The countryside is a vast expanse where one can flourish." In the sunshine and under Maoism, you have all been taking the road to integrate with the workers and peasants. This is excellent. Chairman

Mao has pointed out a revolutionary path for you to follow. I hope you will follow Chairman Mao closely and make yourself an heir of the proletarian revolutionary cause.

Hong left home yesterday morning to board a ship to Torch Farm in Haikang County in Zhanjiang. He is yet to turn sixteen and is eligible to remain and continue his schooling. But his school is seriously lagging behind: until the end of last month, many of those who should have been rusticated had yet to sign up. As a result, those who could stay at school were implicated, and everybody was urged to sign up for rustication. Hong thought that since it would be his turn to be rusticated next year, he might as well sign up now. Hong wrote to Ming about his intention. Ming wrote back and said that at his meeting with the revolutionary committee at his farm, he was told that since the farm has been recruiting, all applicants were welcome as long as they went through the proper process. Following this confirmation, Hong talked to the *zhiqing* allocation office in our neighborhood and the workers' propaganda troop at his school, went through the correct process, and three days later, all was set and he left on his own for the farm.

Have Ming and Cheng been in touch with you? They have written home frequently and said that all is well on their farms: the hills are beautiful, the water clear, and trees line the paths. The main crops there are citronella, sisal-hemp, and some paddy rice. The work is light, they are happy there, and the farm workers are friendly. There are newspapers and radio, and they can study for two hours each day. There is a sufficient supply of food, peanut oil, duck eggs and salted fish. The farm canteen is well run. The main road is literally just outside their dormitory, the transport is convenient, and they can use their bicycles for shopping. They also said that their production squad at Torch Farm was a superior one, several hundred meters from the headquarters. There is a reservoir nearby with clear and shallow water: they go there for swimming at noon or at night.

They received their first month's salary on the first of the month, and after the deduction for food, they have 6.35 *yuan* left for themselves. The salary is 20 *yuan*. What about you?

The weather in Haikang stays warm even in winter. Guangzhou

stayed warm until yesterday. Today, though, I have had to put on layers of jumpers after the arrival of a northerly wind.

Yan had been sent to work for one month as a packer in a pharmaceuticals factory. On the thirteenth, she was drafted to work on Baiyun Farm. A letter arrived from her today: her job there is to collect seeds from the water spinach. She said she missed home terribly and dreamed about her brothers and sisters all the time.

Your dad and myself have been keeping well. No need to worry. Your dad went for a series of Party consolidation sessions last month in the Marching Forward Commune, formerly the Peace Commune. He worked in the fields in the morning and participated in the Party's consolidation and construction sessions in the afternoon and at night. He came back on the ninth.

Cousin Qing in Luo Village got married on the twenty-fifth of last month. I didn't attend the wedding but sent Hong along on our behalf with some gifts. After staying there for a few days, Hong got straight back to work on his application for rustication to Haikang. It was good that your dad had by then returned from his study sessions. Otherwise I wouldn't have had a clue how to handle the situation at home.

The primary schools in Guangzhou are yet to send their staff to the countryside for thought-reform through physical labor, but some middle schools have already started the process. Your dad is staying behind to look after the school premises and day-to-day operation. He is busy all the time and has to shoulder some teaching as well!

The Chairman Mao anthology and quotations which you asked Jiading to bring home for your younger sister have all been safely received. She has noted down your address. You must have received her letter to you by now?

You must write often to your younger brothers and provide political guidance to them. You should encourage and help each other in thought-reform. Hong is seven months short of sixteen, he is young and ignorant: I am concerned about him. I feel sad since he left. My only consolation is that he is rusticated on the same farm as his two elder brothers, Ming and Cheng. I don't know how he is getting on at the farm, he hasn't written yet.

Their address is: No 1 Team, Torch Farm, Haikang County, Zhanjiang Special Zone.

Let's bless Chairman Mao! May he live forever!

Your mother

RUSTICATION CRUSHED MY DREAMS
Chen Hongbo

The "Up to the Mountains, Down to the Countryside" campaign which took place during the Cultural Revolution was a life-changing event for millions of educated young people. It crushed my dream of becoming a master chef.

Brought up in a family of cooks, I had often heard anecdotes from my father, who was himself a chef, of how the exquisite Cantonese cuisine was a credit to the nation. My family's love of food rubbed off on me: I grew up loving the art of Cantonese cooking. During the economic downturn of the late 1950s and early 1960s, my parents—despite the famine—brought home from the restaurant they worked in such scraps as frog skins and fish bones to keep us from starving. That really left a deep impression on me. The profession of cooking appealed to me: not only could I become a credit to my country but stay clear of hunger. In a large and financially stretched family which spanned three generations, I was the eldest of five children and wanted to earn my keep as soon as possible to help make ends meet and live up to my parents' high expectations of me. After finishing the eighth grade, I applied to study Chinese cooking at a local vocational school.

I was determined to study hard to become a renowned master chef. There were two aspects of our training: classroom-based studies and industrial placement, and every month we would spend a solid two weeks on each. During the placement, we joined a regular shift in a restaurant which began at two in the morning and involved all kinds of arduous and dirty work. After finishing my shift at noon, I would take a break, and then go on to work in another big restaurant. I wanted to seize every chance to gain experience and qualify as quickly as possible. When the Cultural Revolution broke out after just one year of the program, the schools were closed for "revolutionary" purposes. To continue my training, and also to avoid getting involved in the violence and lootings that were spreading across the country, I joined a few classmates in signing up for an internship at the renowned Guangzhou Restaurant and New Asia Restaurant. Aged only seventeen or eighteen, I seemed to have endless energy, and though the work was unpaid I put in long hours and hard work. After a lengthy and intermittent apprenticeship, I had mastered all the essential techniques of Chinese cooking.

Time flies. Soon it was 1968 and we had graduated. Just as I was basking proudly in my success and ready to fulfill my dream, there came the fanatical nationwide campaign of "Up to the Mountains, Down to the Countryside." Out of the blue, our school announced that vocational graduates were not immune from rustication. We were shocked: some cursed, some wept. I was dumbstruck. Then I fell ill with tonsillitis and ran a temperature. To get a permanent cure, I went to hospital to have my tonsils removed. While I was there, it was announced at a school assembly that forty percent of the graduates were to stay on in Guangzhou to wait for an assigned post: the rest, including myself, would be dispatched to the countryside. To this day I have no idea why I was picked while others escaped. When I asked the school authorities, they simply ignored me. On hearing the news, my parents and grandmother were speechless. My grandmother and mother wept all day long. They, too, were unable to understand why I was obliged to be rusticated.

There was no escaping the turmoil of the rustication campaign. Every now and then, we would hear that so-and-so in the neighborhood had been sent to a country village or state farm. My school wanted to make me into a role model for the campaign: teachers took turns to belabor me with exhortations, and a senior teacher was even sent to deliver a pep talk to my family. We asked them time and again why I had been singled out for rustication, but they simply dodged the question by quoting Chairman Mao's highest instruction: "The countryside is a vast expanse where one can flourish." They tried to tempt me by saying that the state farm would provide us with work uniforms. When that failed, they threatened us by suggesting that if I didn't submit to rustication, there would be serious consequences. And indeed in my neighborhood, the revolutionary committee had already joined forces with the employers by suspending the jobs of those whose children had not yet agreed to be rusticated. Since private enterprise was not permitted during that era, any family who lost their jobs would lose their livelihood. In the face of such pressures, I was worried that I might bring unforeseen trouble and hardship to my family. My relatives and neighbors pointed out that a wise man does not fight against impossible odds, and suggested that I should sign up for the sake of my own future. After some delay, and while the nationwide campaign grew ever more fervid, I eventually gave in. As our ancestors have it, a good man will try to start his career in whatever circumstances he finds himself. I also reasoned that since so many of my peers had already joined the state farm, my family might indeed be exposed if I attempted any further resistance. Along with a few fellow students, I signed up for Daling Farm on Hainan Island.

Before my departure, my elderly grandmother bought me an old leather suitcase, and my mother gave me a few *yuan*—a lot of money for my family to come up with—to be kept for any unforeseen circumstances. My mother also gave me a bottle of water so that on my arrival in Hainan I could mix it with the local water in order to avoid an upset stomach, an ancient piece of folk wisdom. When she instructed me to take care of myself, I was unable to speak.

It was my father who saw me off at the pier. After boarding the Red Guard ship—already packed with thousands of rusticated youngsters—I looked down from the jammed deck at my father in the crowd, and wept. I was inconsolable. It was the end of December 1968, on a windy, wintry day. The ship was overloaded and didn't have enough cabins for its passengers, and the gangways along the deck were filled with *zhiqings* like myself who had to take shelter wherever they could find it and sleep on straw mats. There was canvas hanging along the ship to help break the bitter wind, but it was of little use. I wrapped myself in padded clothing and a blanket but I was chilled to the marrow and couldn't sleep. I was also kept awake by a feeling of extreme loss and humiliation. I asked both myself and Heaven why this had happened to me. Why, after I had mastered a useful skill, was I then denied the chance to become a chef and realize my dream? Escorting us was Mr. Lin, the head of studies at our school. We exchanged few words. A month before, his daughter had been rusticated to Nanyang Farm on the island, and he was still nursing a broken heart. Once he had seen us settled in at the farm, he called on her with two packs of rationed sanitary paper for use during her periods.

On arriving at the farm, I was assigned to No. 2 Company to work as a cook. Owing to the extreme shortage of supplies, we would count ourselves lucky when any sort of green vegetables was available. Most days, we chewed and swallowed plain rice with pickled Chinese radishes and, during the wet season, with just salt. Meat was available only on rare festive occasions. Despite the lack of materials to hone my cooking skills, I didn't want them to become rusty. With two books on Cantonese cooking that my father had procured for me, I would attempt to sharpen my skills whenever possible. I wanted to be ready for that chance of becoming a chef whenever it popped up. A few years later, employment quotas were set out for *zhiqings* back in their home cities. For unknown reasons, I and my fellow students were passed over. In 1975 the Guangzhou administration of service industries visited our farm to recruit staff. Here's my chance, I thought! I treated the recruitment manager to sweet potato congee, chatted him up and asked him to give us jobs in the catering industry. After he finished up the congee, however, he bluntly told us that there were no such quotas.

And that was the end of my dream of becoming a master chef.

Arrival

ENDLESS HILLS AND PATCHES OF WEEDS
Weng Ruiwen

I remember that it was on 27 March 1970. After several days of exhausting travel, we thirty-six *zhiqings* from Meixian finally arrived at our destination: No. 11 Company, No. 13 Regiment of No. 4 Division, Guangzhou Army Production and Construction Corps. It was late afternoon. The big Liberation truck stopped in the grounds of the company. It was deadly quiet—around us was nothing but endless hills and patches of weeds. A wooden watchtower stood askew and on its own. Bits of straw on it were waving in the air.

Surrounding the bare ground were several rows of thatched huts, and under the eave of one of them was an ox. Unconcerned by our arrival, the ox continued to eat the grass. Soon, a lean old man with a deep tan rushed out of one of the low-ceilinged huts to welcome us. Shirtless, all he had on was a pair of loose floral underpants. Until then, we lusty *zhiqings* were still singing at the tops of our voices the revolutionary songs which were laced with Chairman Mao's quotations. We froze in astonishment. After a long, long while, somebody cried out: "I want to go home!" Like a burning fuse, the whole group took up the chant of: "I want to go home! I want to go home!" and our voices rang loud and clear in the silent hills around us. We refused to get off the truck. The town official who was put in charge of us was dumbfounded: all he could do was murmur: 'Go home? Go Home? How? It's thousands of *li*[1] away, across the sea. How?"

How, indeed! Exhausted and hungry, we eventually quieted down, though some were still sobbing. Nobody got off the truck.

When the sun withdrew its last rays in the west and brought many people back from work, the peaceful hills at last showed some signs of life. From the distance came the sound of a vehicle's horn and soon an olive-colored jeep pulled up in front of us. Out stepped a middle-aged man in army uniform.

"Report to the Regimental Commander!" somebody shouted. The unexpected appearance of the Regimental Commander reassured us naïve newcomers. In those days, military men were held in very high esteem. He walked toward us and said in a kindly voice: "Comrades, you must all be tired. Aren't you hungry yet? Quick, get off and have some supper." Just a few gentle words, and our hearts melted. Perhaps it was our high respect for a senior army officer or perhaps we were genuinely hungry. Moreover, we were desperate to relieve ourselves. We rushed to get off, and some of the more anguished ones threw their sacks onto the ground and climbed down from the front of the truck. One caught and tore his trousers on a hook on the truck. He dashed into a thatched hut to get changed. In the dim light, he couldn't see well and when he caught sight of a short plump woman in dark clothes, he asked: "Granny, would you kindly step out so that I can change my trousers?" "Granny" went out and met another sweet and naïve teenage *zhiqing*, who asked: "Granny, where is the latrine, please?"

That night we moved into the new thatched huts built with fresh grasses. The mud walls were still wet, but the mud floor was quite solid, and our beds were laid on crutch-like wooden supports inserted into the floor. Since we were a newly established company, nothing in our premises was built with bricks or tiles. It was like living with a primitive tribe: dusty on sunny days, it was slippery in rainy spells, and people falling over were a common sight. We settled in quickly and worked alongside the old hands and the *zhiqings* who had arrived before us. We fought against the forces of nature and dedicated our youth to

---

1. 1 li = 1/2 kilometre = 1/3 mile.

the development of the rubber plantation.

As time went by, we came to realize that the woman whom we called "granny" was an "old worker" from Shangdong Province. She was then only twenty-eight years old, so we decided to call her "plump auntie" instead. In a tropical climate and having to endure harsh conditions for years, the old hands like her all looked dark and lean. Although most of them were around thirty years old, they looked to us teenagers like people in their fifties or sixties and we routinely called them "old workers." The sight of the prematurely ageing "granny" cast a chill on us as if she were showing us what we would shortly become. Oh, hell! The thought of us rapidly coming to resemble her made the cry "I want to go home!" reverberate in our minds.

Forty years later, we too have reached our twilight years and have become "granny" or "grandpa." But what happened to that particular "granny"? I wish her peace and happiness.

WHEN WATER WAS AS PRECIOUS AS OIL
Xiao Peihong

For those raised in a sub-tropical climate, taking a shower is just a daily routine. My first shower in Daling was quite a challenge.

During the first nine months of 1970, the western region of Hainan Island was hit by a severe drought. It was extremely hot and water became as precious as oil. That summer we left our hometown in the fertile Chaoshan plain to become rusticated on Hainan. On 26 July, a Liberation truck dispatched by the regiment picked us up at Xiuying Pier in Haikou City and transported us to No. 13 Regiment. Everywhere it went in the hills, the truck stirred up a cloud of dust: as we were in an open trailer we had to brush ourselves off frequently in order not to become caked in it. When we made it to No. 5 Company after a bumpy ride of seven hours, we, as well as our luggage, were all coated in a thick layer of dust. After a warm welcome from the company officials, we were ushered into our dormitory in a large thatched hut.

Once settled, we craved a shower to cleanse ourselves of stinking sweat and dust. But water was scarce and hard to access: there were just two wells for a troop of more than a hundred people. The well by the cookhouse had a slightly higher level of water, but this was reserved for drinking and rinsing rice and vegetables. To take a shower, everyone was very much left to their own devices. As newcomers, we hadn't the faintest idea where to find water. We turned to Lao[2] Lu, the person who had been put in charge of us during the trip. He told us that it was quite a long walk to the water source, and then asked earnestly if we could swim. It sounded splendid to have a dip as well! The few of us who could swim replied in great excitement that we grew up by the Han River, the second largest river in Guangdong Province, and I also threw in a bit of a boast: 'Backstroke, breaststroke, butterfly stroke, dog paddle, you name it, no problem. Please just take us there!' After assuring himself that we were strong swimmers, Lao Lu cheerfully led the way.

After crossing the Yellow Ox Range, we went past a large area of wilderness that had just been burned to prepare for rubber tree planting, and farther down, a rubber tree propagation field. When we arrived at what looked like a bank, Lao Lu told us that we had finally reached the river. We looked round and were stunned! The river had been dry for so long that all that was left were stones that over the years had been worn smooth by the water. In the lower part of the riverbed, there was a pool of waist-high water, stagnant and yellowish, with a dozen or so oxen bathing in it probably because of the daytime heat. The water was thick and foul-smelling. Some long, dark leeches, each marked with two gold stripes, were swimming in the water or sucking blood from the oxen. Once engorged, some of them were as thick as

---

2. *Lao* ('old') and *Xiao* ('young') are Chinese terms of endearment which are prefixed to a surname to indicate a certain degree of intimacy between the addressed and addresser, and the seniority of the relationship that exists between them. Thus "Old" Lu.

our thumbs. It was a scene of horror! They reminded me of vampires. How could anyone bathe here? We looked at each other in speechless despair. We had wished to wash off our dirt and smell and enjoy a dip, too. We were dumbfounded, and started to miss the homes we had just left behind.

Lao Lu seemed rather embarrassed. By way of an apology, he told us in sincere tones that he worked in the logistics squad and it had been a long while since he was here. He had never expected the river to be in such a state. He promised that come the rainy season, the water would rise to the height of three men and we would have a hell of a lot of fun swimming in it.

Utterly disappointed, all we could do was follow Lao Lu back across the propagation field, the wilderness, and the Yellow Ox Range to our dormitories. We then picked up our iron buckets and walked all the way to a new well at the foot of Maliu Hill. The well was almost dry, with only some very shallow water: we had to use a very small bucket to draw water little by little and then pour it into our bigger ones. I can't remember how long it took to get barely enough water for a cursory shower and a quick rinse of our laundry.

Four decades later, the memories are still as vivid as yesterday. The funny thing is that I don't feel half as bad about that particular episode as I did when it happened. Time can indeed change one's perspective.

Politics

I WANT TO JOIN THE PARTY
Wu Xianfang

For most people in China, joining the Communist Youth League (CYL) is normally a simple process: whether you are in school or at work, if you wish to join and you perform well, it is straightforward. But for those with a "politically incorrect" family background, this was far from the case during the Cultural Revolution. Even if they were the cream of society and put extra effort into everything they did, it could still be a dream beyond their reach. For both their contemporaries and the younger generation of today, the restrictions and hurt that were inflicted on them are hard to understand. A marginalized and disadvantaged group, they had to strive hard to prove their social worth.

After two years of rustication in Daling Farm, I submitted my application to join the CYL in 1971. Yet while those who submitted their applications at the same time were soon sworn in, my application, like a rock thrown into the deep sea, disappeared without a trace. After a few more months of waiting, I could not help but ask our political instructor about it. He assured me that since my rustication, I had put in all-round excellent performances: I worked hard, did what I was asked to do, feared no hardship or fatigue, and was politically progressive. However, owing to my "problematic" family background, it was beyond the power of the company to decide on my application and it had therefore been referred to regimental headquarters. He asked me to trust the Party and its procedures, and to wait with patience. Though his feedback came as no surprise, I was saddened. It was five years since the launch of the Cultural Revolution, yet the "theory of family origin," whereby one's social status was strictly defined by one's family background, was deep-rooted, its impact widespread and overpowering. It was rather naïve of me to expect that as long as I put in the effort, I would be treated equally and fairly just like an ordinary person. I forgot that my family background provided a pretext for the continual discrimination against me.

I was born into an intellectual family. From our infancy, my father instructed us children to study hard, and advance both ethically and academically: we must become upright and useful members of society. At the start of the Cultural Revolution, however, he was denounced as "a monster and demon" and sent to a "cow-shed," one of the makeshift detention centres set up across the country by state companies and neighborhood committees. Labels were slapped on him, such as 'counterrevolutionary academic leader," "historical counterrevolutionary" and "one of the dregs and diehards of the Nationalist Party." He performed manual labor during the day, and at night had to write interminable reports on the state of his own mind and thoughts. He was kept in the cow-shed for several years and not allowed to have regular contact with his family.

The day before I left for Hainan Island, I went to bid farewell to my father, who was still being held in the cow-shed of his college. I was obliged to come up with the excuse that I had to deliver him a quilt. When he learned that the next day I would depart for Daling Farm in Baisha County, his eyes turned red and tears welled up behind his spectacles. I thought that his main concern was his daughter's rustication at the tender age of sixteen. Years later I learned that he was fully aware of conditions in Baisha County. Situated in the western part of Hainan Island, it was populated by the Li ethnic minority, who were dirt-poor and illiterate. It was a desolate area with a high incidence of malaria. But we knew none of that: our schools didn't tell us. All my father repeated that day was that I must listen to the Party, work hard and learn from our designated mentors, the poor and lower-middle peasants. Loath to leave, I nodded.

Politics

Soon after my arrival at Hainan Island, my father was transferred to a "cadre school," a remote detention center where intellectuals and white-collar workers underwent manual labor for the purposes of indoctrination and could enjoy a measure of freedom. Every month, he wrote diligently to each of his children, and in every one of his long letters, he would remind us to pay particular attention to our ideological reform, to work hard and to remain humble toward everyone; and he would also set down how he felt and what he had learned through enforced manual labor and political study sessions. Indeed, his letters mirrored the essence of the headline state political commentaries of the day. Despite the wrongs and torments inflicted on him, his letters contained no word of complaint. Instead he encouraged and instructed us unceasingly. That was what his generation of intellectuals was like: with their unconditional faith and allegiance to the Party and the state, they bore every hardship and dedicated themselves wholeheartedly to the future and prosperity of the country. They had made tremendous contributions to the nation, and their hearts were sincere and benign.

Since my rustication at the farm, I followed my father's instructions to the letter. I strove to make political progress and worked prudently and conscientiously: as a result, I became a role model for the regiment. The story of how I raised pigs on the farm had been turned into a play by the regiment's Maoist propaganda troupe. Despite all this, I still suffered political discrimination. Yet I didn't let this blunt my dedication to work and study. I wanted to prove myself through my actions.

Just as I had given up hope of joining the CYL, our political instructor informed me that after special consideration by the political division of the regiment, my application had at last been approved. An official supported me: he insisted that since I had been a model worker I should be treated as a special case, and so at last my dream of becoming a CYL member was realized. Yet somehow I wasn't excited about this: the shadow across my heart was too dark to be dispelled.

Joining the CYL was a mere token: it said nothing about one's morals or abilities. I believed that genuine gold would shine through. That was what I had set out to prove and also what had kept me going during those gray days of China's history.

ONE TEST THAT I PASSED

Chen Sanxing, noted down by Chen Hongbo

I am from Yangjiang. At the party to mark the forty-first anniversary of our rustication to Hainan, an ex-*zhiqing* recalled that I used to buy alcohol and cigarettes in an underhand way. His casual remark reminded me of an experience during my *zhiqing* life.

Jiang Xinian was one of the rubber specialists who had returned to China soon after Liberation in 1949. During the Cultural Revolution he was denounced as a counterrevolutionary and, nearing the age of sixty, demoted to No 2 Company to undergo reform through a program of supervised hard labor. I was rusticated at the age of sixteen. When I arrived at the company, our political instructor informed me that I had been assigned to an important task: to keep a close watch on Jiang's behavior and process of thought-reform and to report him if he acted suspiciously. I was required to share a bunk bed with him, me on the top one, him on the bottom, with three or four others in the same room. Despite his age, he was forced to perform heavy manual labor out in the elements and, in addition, to clean all the company latrines. Under such harsh circumstances, he grew despondent and took to the bottle to forget his woes. After a long day at work, his hands would sometimes be trembling, but the trembling became less violent after a few drops of alcohol. I couldn't find anything "anti-revolutionary" in his conduct: his situation made me feel sympathetic toward him. Jiang must also have picked up on my honesty and willingness to help: he soon asked me to get him some cigarettes, alcohol, or tinned food from the regimental shop. We dared not speak to each other. If he wanted something from the shop, he would find a scrap of paper, scribble a few words on it, and hand it to me when we were on our own. I would glance at it, nod my head, and destroy the paper immediately.

Sometimes he would raise his thumb to indicate that he wanted better brands. After I got the stuff from the regimental shop, I would tuck it out of sight and hand it to him only when no one else was around. This went on for some time without causing any trouble to either of us. He was so grateful that he wanted to make me a gift, the watch—a luxury item then—that he had brought back years ago from abroad. I would not accept it.

One day, after a few drinks taken alone to drown his sorrows, he murmured that while we had always been boasting of how superior our domestic bicycles and radio sets were, the truth was that we were seriously lagging behind other nations. His guard had slipped, either because he was drunk or just so repressed that he was desperate to say what he felt, but the slip was reported to the company officials. The political instructor asked to talk to me: he wanted me to report on Jiang's anti-revolutionary remarks and conduct. He warned me that my response would reflect my own attitude toward the "class struggle," and that if I failed to report what I knew, my future would be compromised. Under such pressure, my conscience was put to a severe test: if the truth were told, Jiang would be condemned for going against Party policy and principles, and this would put his life in danger; if I kept my own counsel, I would be liable to harsh punishment. After a fierce internal struggle, I felt that if I informed on Jiang, the consequences would be even worse and my conscience would suffer. I told the political instructor that I had never heard Jiang talking. After several coercive attempts, the instructor could get nothing from me to hold against Jiang and the case was dropped. Jiang had a lucky escape and I kept a clear conscience.

My fellow ex-*zhiqings* were touched by this story when, at the anniversary of our rustication, I revealed it for the first time. In the years when everything had been turned upside down, it took some guts to stick to one's guns. Many of the ex-*zhiqings* did exactly that, and found truth, kindness, and beauty in those oppressive times. One *zhiqing* teacher, for example, got his students to volunteer to clean the latrines regularly so that after a hard day's work Jiang didn't have to.

I NEARLY PUT AN END TO IT

Ma Guizhen

It was midnight in the early spring of 1976 and the whole troop was sound asleep. I went alone to the pond by our dormitory. A pale full moon lit up the earth. The only sound was the occasional cry from an unknown bird in the jungle, creating an eerie atmosphere around me. I was despondent: I would soon be denounced as an active counterrevolutionary.

It all happened during a major joint campaign. Toiling all day beyond my physical limits, I suffered severe backache. I was desperate for a break and wanted to visit the clinic to ask for sick leave. One morning when I ran into our captain in the grain-drying area, he asked if I had been to the toilet the day before. "Yes, I went twice, I had an upset stomach . . ." I was lying in order to get some sick leave.

How could I have imagined that a spontaneous ad hoc white lie would have got me into such a dire predicament? That morning, a slogan: "Down with Chairman Mao", was found in the women's latrine. It was a serious incident, and as soon as it was reported to regimental headquarters, a task force was dispatched to conduct a thorough investigation. Every suspect was interviewed, and in order to take a clear photograph of the slogan, the task force even removed the tiles of the latrine roof.

I had been to the women's latrine twice that day and thus became the main suspect. I was questioned and had to defend my innocence. Over the ten days that the ordeal lasted, the harsh tone and stern looks of those in the task force were utterly chilling. I lived in fear every day and could hardly swallow any food. The verdict of attacking the sanctity of Chairman Mao would soon be spelled out, and for that offence I would be convicted as an active counterrevolutionary. When that happened, I would be subjected to public denunciations and a life in prison. Back in March 1970, when I was first rusticated to No. 7 Company, a quiet girl from the Chaoshan area was dragged out for public prosecution during a major political campaign. Up on the stage, and drowned out by our chanting of revolutionary slogans, she just wept and wept without making any attempt to plead her innocence. She was said to have used a newspaper with Mao's picture on it as a chopping board when she cut a sugar cube, which proved, it was alleged, that she possessed an evil spirit and wished to chop Chairman Mao into pieces. She had a lucky escape because soon the allegation was somehow forgotten and dropped. Six years later, it was horrifying to think that I was stepping into her shoes.

The moon was shining on the water, casting my wandering shadow on the pond. I was only twenty-three and full of dreams for the future. I wanted to live, but how could I endure such a severe verdict? In my mind were terrifying scenes in which I was denounced again and again, fists raised and slogans chanted against me. My youth would be cut short, and with it all my dreams and aspirations. The thought of death crept in. I lost my fear of it, and a number of times I nearly stepped into the pool to end my life. Then the image of my frail mother rose up. With my father dying at a young age, my mother had had to bear the hardship of raising three children all by herself, and I still owed her a debt of gratitude. In such circumstances, how could I ever leave the world? I seemed to hear her piercing voice in pain, crying: "Daughter, please don't, don't die . . ." and this brought me to my senses. I came to realize that at that point I was no more than a suspect and that if I chose to die, my innocence might never be proved. I could not allow this to happen. Dawn was breaking, and cockcrow and the noise coming out of the cookhouse roused me. I had to believe in the Party, the organization, and the other *zhiqings* with whom I had spent every day and night since my rustication. I had to have faith that the truth would come out.

The truth did eventually emerge. It was the child of an old hand who had scribbled that offending slogan in the latrine. Due to her tender age, she could not be held responsible for her action. I heaved a sigh of relief. It so happened that pork was on the menu that day. I bought a bottle of liquor and for the first time in my life had a drink. I had never shed tears before, but that day I wept buckets in front of my best friend. With the tears, the horror, sadness, and gloom drained away from my heart. I could tell no one just how glad I was that I hadn't jumped to my death.

THE COUNTERREVOLUTIONARY MYNAH BIRD

Xuan Guangchi, Chen Mingguo, et al.

Hainan Island was once a tropical paradise, its lush jungles harboring a rich and diverse wild life. That was before the Cultural Revolution brought the *zhiqings* in to develop it.

One day in the spring of 1969, as we were setting fire to the jungle in order to open up spaces for rubber plantations, one of the *zhiqings* reached into a hole in a tree and brought out a newborn and as yet featherless mynah bird. He took it back to the dormitory and kept it in a small box. Under our tender care, it grew fast, and soon, fully fledged and with strong wings, it began to fly about. Whatever happened, though, the mynah bird would only hover within our premises and never ventured out to explore its birthplace, the jungle. According to some of the old hands, this was because, having spent its life only with us, it had acquired a smell different from those of its own kind, and this might render it vulnerable to attack back in the jungle. And so the mynah bird accompanied us everywhere: when we were laboring in the fields, it would be flying above us; when we had a meeting, it would patrol along the window-sill or door. The mynah bird seemed happy to be around us and made a lot of contented noises. Gradually it even picked up some of our words and phrases.

Our farm was no different from anywhere else in the country. With politics dominating our routine, we had to review our thoughts day and night; publicly perform the "loyalty dance" to Chairman Mao (by moving our hands from our hearts toward the sun in a gesture of gratitude and allegiance); acclaim each of his highest instructions; and take part in endless rounds of political meetings. Before and after each meeting, we also had to sing the usual revolutionary songs like *The East Is Red, Sailing the Seas Depends on the Helmsman*, and many others that either affirmed the "brilliant leadership" of Chairman Mao or were riddled with his quotations. Being around us constantly, the mynah bird learned the songs in no time. As we toiled in the fields, its singing would help us to relax, and when we heard it in our dormitory, it helped us to relieve our longing for our families. Living thousands of miles from home, we all found the mynah bird a great companion.

One day, when we were having our usual meeting in the canteen, the tactless mynah bird repeated our singing of *Be Resolute*, a song laced with Mao's quotations, in a solo performance from the window sill. At that point, the political instructor was making a speech and yet we couldn't help bursting into laughter. The meeting was supposed to be deadly serious, and its tone was thus destroyed. The instructor was livid and demanded that we drive it away. Later on, we were banned from feeding it so as not to be distracted while listening to the highest instructions from Mao. In such repressive circumstances, none of us dared to disobey. A few days later, the mynah bird disappeared.

It was a great and smart friend of ours. To this day, we wonder what became of it.

A BUNDLE OF SEEDLINGS

Deng Xiaodan

I was among the first Guangzhou *zhiqings* to arrive in Daling—in November 1968. In my five years there, I was reassigned three times, staying in different companies for as briefly as three months or as long as two years. My memory of the experience has become hazy over the years. When I was shown a piece written by a fellow Guangzhou *zhiqing* about her life on Hainan, my comment was that not only could I not find anything interesting to write about, but that if I were to put my experience down on paper, its tone would not be anything like as upbeat. My memory of that era and its atmosphere is rather different from hers. After that conversation, I recaptured my five years' experience as if I were watching a film: the first thing that flashed through my mind was an incident I have always felt guilty about. Though it is something that has been buried deep in my heart for nearly forty years, I am filled with remorse whenever I think about it. I am putting this down as a way of making an apology to my victim.

The incident happened while I was in No. 11 Company, on a summer morning in 1971. At the routine assembly before work, the political instructor disclosed in a piercing and agitated voice that a bundle of rubber tree seedlings had been found in the river the day before yesterday. My heart sank when I heard it: when I looked up, I saw a bundle of seedlings tied to some small stones. My brain exploded: wasn't that what I had tried so hard to lose by sinking it in the river the other day? I was terrified. I wondered if I should own up to it. Yet I reasoned that it would be nearly impossible to track down the offender. I decided on impulse to keep quiet, hope for the best and just see how it would turn out.

The atmosphere at the assembly was oppressive: all was silent. Then, out of the blue, somebody yelled: 'It was Wu Leitong!' Like a kettle of boiling water, the assembly was outraged and jumped down his throat. I despised those rabble-rousers, and hoped Wu would stand up to the volley of condemnations. The hostility was so intense that even if I'd had the nerve to own up, I was by now chickening out. At the beginning Wu did defend himself, yet the harder he tried, the more outraged the crowd became. After some attempts to clear his name, he was forced to admit his guilt under the fierce onslaught of public indignation. I can neither remember how the assembly concluded nor how I went about my work that day. My mind is blank about what happened next.

Rusticated from Guangzhou in 1969, Wu was an affable and carefree chap. But now this wholly innocent and easy-going guy had been framed and found it hard to vindicate himself. I remember that when he pleaded guilty to this "heinous crime" he still wore his characteristic expression of unconcern. Was it the device by which an unremarkable individual could protect himself during an insane era? I had no idea what was going through his mind during and after that assembly: what I knew for sure was that he was wiser and more upright than I. We were no more than casual acquaintances, and because of my guilty conscience, I never dared to get close to him. To my relief, and probably because even the officials had come to their senses and realized that it was absurd to make such a big deal over a bundle of abandoned seedlings, the case fizzled out for lack of conclusive evidence. Had it not done so, Wu might have become liable for more condemnations. A few months later, I was reassigned to No. 15 Company.

I would like to make a clean breast of this "heinous crime" of mine and the motivation behind it. That day, our squad was charged with filling gaps in the plantation with seedlings, and each of us was to work in a specific area. My leg was aching due to a running sore and each step triggered an enormous stab of pain. Since a motto of the time was "Never leave the front-line on account of a minor wound," it never crossed my mind to apply for sick leave. When I eventually managed to drag myself to my allocated area, I found that following a recent typhoon, the river had overflowed and that I would be forced to wade through the flood to reach part of the area I covered. I took a look at the rubber tree seedlings on my shoulder pole: each was no bigger than my thumb. I recalled from a rally I had attended when I arrived at the farm that planting seedlings directly in the newly cleared hills had been condemned as "the reactionary practice of the capitalist." And, indeed, this practice had never been popular in developing the rubber plantations. However, despite the condemnation, it was re-introduced to the farm soon afterward. In official reports, the survival rate of such seedlings was seventy percent: in my two years' experience, barely fifty percent survived. It was ineffective labor. With the acute pain in my leg, the doubt and resentment I felt about it was amplified, and it was in this situation that I committed the "heinous crime" that two days later would be ascribed to an innocent person.

No. 15 Company, to which I was reassigned soon afterward, was located in an even harsher environment. Fortunately, an experiment was being conducted there to improve the success rate of the seedlings. Rather than planting a mass of them directly on the hills, we kept them in plastic compost bags with perforations, and it was only when they had grown to the height of a man that they were planted on the hills with their familiar compost intact. The method was more laborious because we could only carry two young trees (weighing at least eighty *jin*[3]) up the hill on each trip. But the survival rate was a lot higher and more than made up for the extra work involved.

Now that I can finally come clean about this incident, I feel a great sense of relief.

STANDING ON THE PING-PONG TABLE
Huang Ronger

In the early 1970s, when I was still working as a clerk at No. 9 Company, our political instructor ordered me to summon a few Guangzhou *zhiqings* to a meeting at ten o'clock that night. He had just returned from a meeting at regimental headquarters. I was baffled, not just by his grave look, but by such mysteries as why he had only asked for the Guangzhou *zhiqings* to attend, why the meeting was at such a late hour, and why he hadn't, as he usually did, shared its agenda with me.

As it happened, a new political campaign had been launched and next day our regiment would join No. 12 Regiment at a rally organized by the division in order to denounce a counterrevolutionary political careerist. Afterward, each company was expected to expose and denounce on the spot the "counterrevolutionaries" among them, irrespective of whether they actually existed. Everybody knew, though it was never made explicit, that there was a "denunciation quota." To

---

3.   1 *jin* = 1/2 kilogram

prepare for this rally and fulfill our quota, whose numbers could vary from time to time, those of us in the troop who were considered to be politically active were obliged to help in identifying those who were to be condemned the following day.

The atmosphere suddenly turned tense. Who, among us, might we denounce as counterrevolutionary? "It has been reported to me that Zhang Juhua has an inclination to escape to Hong Kong. Let's expose and denounce her," the political instructor suggested. Zhang was a Shantou *zhiqing*. Had he only wanted Guangzhou *zhiqings* to attend the late-night meeting in order to minimize the risk of a leak? He then suggested that, for the time being, we should content ourselves with just one target at a time.

Unlike most officials, our political instructor was an intellectual: he was endowed with unusual analytical power and was quite eloquent. Although he was only engaged in light work due to his poor health, we had a high regard for him. The secret meeting of less than half an hour reached an important decision. That night, he also asked that during the rally we "monitor the situation very carefully," which we took as a signal to mean that we should ensure the denunciation didn't get out of control.

The next day, several thousand of us sat on a makeshift platform on a rubber plantation. A Guangzhou *zhiqing* was brought in one of the division wagons. A former student from Guangzhou No. 4 Secondary School, he was the secretary of his company's Communist Youth League. After descending from the wagon, he was escorted to the podium with a piece of cardboard hanging from his neck. On the cardboard, were the words: "Suppress the counterrevolutionary." Among the long list of crimes that were read out by a divisional official, the most striking was the one that he had plotted to seize power from the Party. After the public condemnation, he was escorted out, and we were ordered to ferret out and denounce those counterrevolutionaries within our own troops.

Our political instructor moved us away from the center to a quiet corner. He sat us in a circle and then, as planned the night before, the Shantou *zhiqing* Zhang Juhua was singled out to stand in the middle.

The person who exposed her shouted: "You have always said how wonderful Hong Kong is. Have you ever plotted to run away there? Come clean!" As expected, Zhang denied it. After several rounds of deadlock, the political instructor dismissed her. An awkward silence descended.

Then a commotion erupted among a few Chaoan *zhiqings*: they pointed the finger at their stout squad leader, a Shantou *zhiqing* named Ah Xiong. All under fifteen, they accused him of bullying them into washing his laundry and similar offences. Ah Xiong didn't come across as an ill-natured person: he had, for example, helped his young fellow-townsmen by rectifying their errors at work. Now that he suffered a loss of face, he looked embarrassed: he lowered his head to avoid direct eye contact with us. But his offence didn't fit the bill of this political campaign. We talked the Chaoan *zhiqings* out of any further denunciation.

During another awkward silence in our troop, we could hear outbursts of condemnation from the other troops.

Then my friend Jia, sitting next to me, tugged my shirt and told me that Ah Qun, an old schoolmate a few years my junior, had been denounced by his troops. And indeed, when I turned around in the direction of No. 5 Company, I saw him standing in the middle of his troops. I didn't want to know anything about it and turned back. Ah Qun had always been a conceited guy and, in his eyes, everybody was inferior to him.

Soon, Jia told me that my old schoolmate nicknamed Harman had been singled out in No. 6 Company. Harman and I were in opposing Red Guard factions during the Cultural Revolution. I gloated over his misfortune but couldn't really see on what grounds he could be condemned. I had observed that it was usually three categories of *zhiqing* who tended to be picked on by company officials: those who were work-shy, those who had a "politically incorrect" family background, and those *zhiqings* who were "politically backward." Harman was none of those things.

Thankfully, the gathering of our troop concluded without any great surprises.

Soon after the rally, I was dispatched to work in the regimental campaign office. We learned from our political commissar that most of those who had been exposed and condemned at the rally were not counterrevolutionaries: we were to investigate each case and rehabilitate those who had been mistreated. I must admit that like most of the children of high government officials, I never thought much of our political commissar: when he analyzed political situations for us, all he did was echo a classified official paper. I knew because I was among the privileged few who had access to the paper. But the cautious way he conducted the campaign in our regiment made me change my mind about him.

Soon after I joined the campaign office, Ah Qun told me that he had been framed and that he had been "standing on the ping-pong table"—liable to be the target of constant public condemnations in his company. Soon, Harman too came to see me in secret and disclosed what sort of "crimes" he had been condemned for. As the secretary of the Communist Youth League, he had organized a study group to read the works of Marx and Lenin. This was turned into evidence of what was alleged to be his careerist ambition to take over the Party leadership from the political instructor. Because he worked hard no matter what the weather and was keen to enliven the leisure of the troops, he was also accused of showing off. He was undergoing supervised hard labor and was made to clean all the latrines. When his colleagues were ordered to expose his crimes, all they could pin on him were ridiculous things such as that he never dismantled his mosquito net in the morning—the vice of a capitalist.

I agreed with our political commissar in his analysis of the cases. In my opinion, there were three major reasons for the high number of victims. At the beginning of the rally, the division had ferreted out and condemned a political careerist: hence each company was under pressure to follow suit. Second, and crucially, the number of "counterrevolutionaries" who were uncovered and denounced during a campaign was a measurement of the performance of the company officials. A failure to find any would reflect negatively on them: it would be a sign that they were not politically active or fully committed to the campaign. (With hindsight, it was clear that although the political instructor in my company didn't want to leave a stain on his character by seeming indifferent to the campaign, he also didn't wish to get too many *zhiqings* into trouble.) Third, and also very important, there had always been a latent tension between the *zhiqings* and their officials. Although most *zhiqings* had barely completed their secondary education, they were much better educated than the officials, most of whom were current or former servicemen from the rural areas. This tension was particularly acute between the offspring of high government functionaries and their less literate and articulate officials. Some grassroots officials whose pride had been repeatedly injured might well have adopted the campaign as an easy way to avenge themselves on one or two arrogant *zhiqings*. In fact, I was certain that neither Ah Qun nor Harman were careerists, let alone plotting to take over the Party leadership: they were merely victims of their own imperious demeanor and of the hidden tension between *zhiqings* and grassroots officials.

I remained in the campaign office for a few months to help clear up the cases. To my recollection, all those who were mistreated were eventually rehabilitated, with most being assigned to a different troop in order to avoid direct contact with their malicious accusers. The case of a Shantou *zhiqing* in No. 5 Company was, however, filed for further investigation. He had allegedly used a sharp knife to destroy the portrait of our great leader.

When the ad hoc office was closed, I returned to my old company.

THOSE RIDICULOUS TIMES

Jia Hongji

The early 1970s were marked by a number of high-profile mass political campaigns which involved our army corps as well as everyone else. During one that took place in 1970, I was called up to a task force with the aim of assisting the Party committee at No. 3 Company.

Headed by our regimental chief of staff, the task force was made up of a few farm officials and veterans and three *zhiqings*, including myself.

One member was Lao Wu, a grassroots official from a working class family. Despite having a weather-beaten face which was scored deeply by wrinkles from exposure to the tropical sun, he must only have been in his thirties. Of medium height and rather stout, he was taciturn and looked honest and astute. Since he was the only "redeemable cadre" in the team, I was curious about how he had got stuck with that label. It transpired that he had flouted one of what were then known as "commands from heaven."

During the Cultural Revolution, the farm on Hainan Island, like everywhere else across the country, was turned into a "red sea": Chairman Mao's highest instructions, portrait, and profile dominated all the public spaces, such as walls and bulletin boards. The typical propaganda template dictated that on the left side of a squared framework was, in a round circle, a portrait of Mao either in a People's Liberation Army uniform or in his trademark tunic; and on the right side, Mao's highest instructions. The latter usually occupied three times the space of the portrait.

Lao Wu, an old hand, was a competent squad leader and a good hunter. Before waves of *zhiqings* were dispatched to develop rubber plantations and defend the southernmost part of the country, the island was a vast hunting ground abounding in such wildlife as boars, muntjacs, and pythons. It was said that although wildlife wouldn't actually sneak on to your dining table, as was claimed about northeast China, there was still plenty to hunt. One night, just before he set out on a hunting trip, Lao Wu tested his rifle, as usual, and adjusted the front sight. He quickly spotted a round target in the distance and once he had lined it up in the front sight, pulled the trigger. Bang! As the gunshot sounded, he realized that the perfect "target" was none other than Mao's portrait!

Lao Wu was thrown into prison. It was not until spring 1969, about the time that the Guangzhou Army took control of the state farm, that he was rehabilitated with the label of "redeemable cadre." His time with the task force was, in effect, a period of probation before his likely promotion. And, indeed, a few months after the task force was disbanded, Lao Wu was reinstated as a captain in No. 15 Company.

One day after my return to No. 9 Company, those of us working in the cookhouse were, out of the blue, sent to fetch beef from No. 15 Company. *Beef?* We could hardly believe our ears: it was only during the rare festive seasons that meat was served in our canteen. When I met our supply chief at supper that night, I learned to my dismay that the unexpected "feast" had come at a ruinous cost to Lao Wu!

As in all newly set up companies, conditions in No. 15 Company were primitive. While the *zhiqings* had to build their own thatched huts even on their own time, the living conditions for those veterans who had families were scarcely better. Although the veterans were allowed to expand their living space by adding a small thatched shed as a kitchen and shower room, it was a strictly DIY task in the sense that they also had to gather the building materials from the hills. One day, during lunch break, Lao Wu borrowed an ox-cart to gather and transport some materials. On the way down the hill, however, the ox—which that morning had been hauling firewood for the company cookhouse, and was now pulling building materials under the fierce mid-day sun—sank to the ground, white foam oozing from its mouth. All coaxing failed. Irritated and desperate, Lao Wu fetched a bucketful of water from the cool stream and splashed it onto the ox's head. But the beast never stood up again, and that was why we were treated to the beef. Soon, Lao Wu was removed from his post.

Another memorable event from my stint with the task force at No. 3 Company was one that involved three new Guangzhou *zhiqings*. During the Cultural Revolution, secondary education was curtailed by two to four years, and so the secondary school graduates of 1970 were only about sixteen. Confronted by the harsh realities of rustication, they wrote on the door of their dormitory: "Guangzhou Embassy to Hainan Island."

This idiosyncratic expression of their homesickness and disappointment was perceived in that insane era as a "new occurrence of the class struggle." The reference to a "Guangzhou" embassy was also seen as a suggestion that their hometown was independent of both China and

Hainan; and there was even a suspicion that the youngsters had been egged on by radio stations in hostile countries. Though they escaped charges, they had really got themselves into deep trouble by representing themselves as people who needed to be rescued. Decades later, when I think about them, I wonder if any of these "envoys" to Hainan have indeed been active in international affairs.

Hunger

GREEN DRAGONS CROSSING THE SEA
Li Haiming

Of my ten years as a *zhiqing* on Hainan Island, five were spent as a cook. The cookhouse was a thatched hut of between forty and fifty square meters, with a grass roof and dirt floor. The walls were a mixture of mud and grass: they didn't reach the roof, which allowed drafts to come in from all sides. The only things that were built of concrete were the stoves and the water and rice receptacles. Between us, we four cooks catered for more than a hundred and fifty people in our troop: three meals a day, together with boiled drinking water.

We were obliged to rise in the wee hours to prepare breakfast, and the shift rotated between the four of us. On the morning shift, a cook had to get up at around three thirty in order to be ready to serve breakfast at six, so that the troop could start work in the hills at seven. On my first few morning shifts, I was too restless to fall asleep. The "tick, tick" noise of the alarm clock by my side sounded loud and disturbing. I checked the time every hour, fearful that I would oversleep and cause everybody to be late for work. I woke up one morning at two and dared not return to sleep; I got up to get ready, and waited for about an hour before anyone turned up.

There were some rather frightening experiences, too. One day, as I was about to light the fire in the stove with a kerosene lantern in my hand, I caught sight of some people lying by its side, covered up in old blankets. It was such a shock that it chilled me to my bones. They turned out to be peasants from neighboring Danzhou who had been chopping wood in the hills during the day. By the time they had finished, it was too late to walk back home. The night was cold, so they came to our cookhouse to sleep by the stoves and keep warm. On another occasion, two shining objects reared up in front of me as I was absorbed in cooking. I screamed in horror, thinking I must have seen ghosts or demons. When I came to my senses, I realized that they were the pair of glasses of a squad leader who was dressed in dark blue, the typical color of our clothing. In the pitch darkness, all I could see at first glimpse were his glasses reflecting the kerosene lantern in the cookhouse. That morning he was attending a meeting at the regimental headquarters eight to nine kilometers away, and with no bus service or bicycle available he had to walk. That was why he had turned up so much earlier for his breakfast.

Many *zhiqings* envied me. For them, being a cook was a good job: exempted from toiling with a hoe or a pickaxe out in the elements, the cooks could also take more food. Though a cook might have a lucky escape from the drudgery other *zhiqings* suffered day in day out, I could never bring myself to eat more than my food ration. I had made up my mind that I would work hard to cook for the troop so as to impress those in charge of us. I did so for my own future and also to hang on to the job.

Life on the farm was toilsome: short of oil and food, and at an age when we were growing fast, our individual ration of twenty kilograms of rice per month could barely keep the majority from starving. When I cooked, I would try to keep back about one kilogram of cooked rice from the last meal, mix it with the raw rice for the next meal, and then add the right portion of water so that, when cooked, it was just right and brought out the tender texture of the rice. This way, the yield of cooked rice increased too. My efforts were much appreciated: when I was on duty, everybody could have a larger portion than usual. There were one or two months each year when the only vegetable that would grow in our fields was water spinach. To make it palatable during those dull months, I never chopped the vegetable, but instead cut each one by hand, a time-consuming process. I never stir-fried it, either, but instead blanched it and served it topped with hot oil and salt. During these lean spells, I took care not to blanch the water spinach too early. What I did instead was to prepare everything in advance, such as having the water spinach already rinsed and snipped, the oil hot, the salt measured, and a wok of boiling water ready; and then I would blanch the water spinach only when the troop started to turn up from work. This impeccable timing gave me extra stress but I was immensely satisfied to see people enjoying their hot meals despite the lack of choice. We invented a good name for this dish: "green dragons crossing the sea." In fact, we thought up one for every "good" dish: for delectable winter melon, "even-better-than-lard winter melon," for example. It sounds like a dish of squid and lard, doesn't it? In reality, it was plain winter melon cooked with oil and salt, and there wasn't even a hint of meat in it. That was how we found fun amid hardship and kept our spirits high!

The cookhouse was not far from the Zhubi River, and by the river was a well which was dry except when the river water was high. After water had been drawn from the well, it was poured into a trough that flowed into the receptacles in the cookhouse. When the river level was low, there was little or no water in the well and we would have to take water from the river. Carrying water was an effort: barefoot and with trousers rolled up, we used big iron buckets for this task. Two buckets of water on a shoulder pole weighed more than fifty kilograms, and the path from the river to the cookhouse was between forty and fifty meters. It was a sloping path, and as well as trudging along the sand by the river we sometimes had to tramp into the river for clean water. There were three water receptacles in the cookhouse, each measuring two and a half cubic meters. Apart from what was boiled for drinking water for well over a hundred and fifty people in the troop, the water was for cooking purposes. Cleaning and washing were carried out at the river. Before my rustication, I had never carried water on a shoulder pole. When I first worked as a cook, my shoulders became red and swollen under the heavy weight and were unbearably sore. Wobbling along with buckets of water presented its challenges, such as trying to keep your balance while your feet were being scorched by hot sand in the summer and your body bathed in sweat under the fierce sun. In winter, the water was cold and it was windy by the river: life was tough.

During the various campaigns to open up the hills, trees were felled and vegetation destroyed and degraded, which threatened water conservation. The damage to the environment brought flash floods with every heavy downpour, yet the river would run almost dry within a few days. 'Mountain streams? easy come easy go!' was how it became. As a result, the well was dry for most days of the year, and we had to resort to the river for water. I never grasped the technique of rotating the shoulder pole to distribute the heavy load: I could only carry it on my right side, which eventually gave me a hunchback and uneven shoulders.

To accelerate rubber planting, major joint campaigns were constantly being launched by assembling several troops together to tackle one specific area. Typically lasting about a month, such campaigns involved several companies camping on the hills in crude makeshift huts. We opened up the wilderness, dug holes for trees, and built terraces on the hills. After one area was tackled, we would move on to another: it was a spectacular sight. During these campaigns, a rough thatched hut would be put up near a water source to serve as a cookhouse and a few stones laid on each other to make a stove. With a large iron wok, we cooked, boiled water, and then delivered food and drink to the troops. In mid-afternoon, we would provide snacks of sweet potato soup or congee. Finding our way round the hills wasn't always easy. With food on our shoulders, we sometimes got lost or even stumbled on the zigzag, uneven, and undulating paths. On one occasion, the boiled water tipped over and I had to return to the cookhouse to fetch more.

Life on the farm was tough. Each year there was a month when, owing to the incessant, heavy downpour, there were no vegetables at all. During the wet season, the only dish was pickled Chinese radish, and when it ran out, all a cook could come up with was plain salted rice with oil, prepared by adding oil, salt, and soy sauce to boiling water to make a sauce and then blending it with the rice to flavor it. That would be a quiet time in the cookhouse, but then owing to the non-stop rain, dry firewood was hard to come by and we had to run all over the place to collect sticks and parch them. Pork was obtainable only once or twice a month. The peasants in neighboring Danzhou sold pigs to us surreptitiously: such transactions were "capitalist behavior," so if caught, those involved would be punished. Each time a pig was delivered to us under cover of darkness, we would stay up until midnight to butcher it. There was no such practice as taking time off in lieu of extra hours worked, and we had to report to work the next day as usual.

Every now and then, the farm would improve our poor diet by buying some iced sea fish from a Hainan fishing company. When they were delivered, it would usually be eight or nine o'clock at night. If the weather was warm, as was the case for most of the year, we would have to stay up all night to cook it before it went bad. The most common sea fish was eel, a meter in length and as thick as a bowl. We called it "long fish": it is tender and tasty. One night, regimental headquarters was due to show a North Korean revolutionary film, *The Flower Girl*. In an era when cultural life was impoverished, this was a festive event, and people would walk miles to catch it. It would be one or two in the morning when they returned to their dormitory. Despite the late hour, they would rise for work at the normal time before dawn. It might well be that in our attempt to get supper ready earlier so that no one would miss the film, the fish was not fully cooked, or that due to the warm weather it was already bad when we received it, but on one occasion nearly thirty people fell sick after eating the eels. Some of the victims were doing so poorly that the doctors were summoned from the regimental hospital.

There were about two hundred people in my company, including spouses and children, and we were allocated three tonnes of rice each month for all of us. The rice was delivered from the warehouse by a Liberation truck, and it was the cooks' job to unload it. We carried the rice, packed in linen sacks weighing a hundred kilograms each, on our backs. First we offloaded them from the truck, then carried them through to the cookhouse before emptying them into the rice receptacles. The receptacles were one and a half meters high and several steps up from the floor. One day when I was ascending the steps, the sack tipped over, injuring my waist and legs. After unloading and storing the rice, we would be starving until the next meal: no snacks were available between times.

Probably thanks to the climate and soil, the Hainan cassava was big; it had a high protein content and was delectable. The skin came off easily if you sliced it lengthways and then peeled it to both sides. The first time cassava was available in our company, there was an amusing incident. As we were preparing it, an intellectual who had been demoted to our troop rushed into the cookhouse and warned us that cassava was poisonous. To rid it of the poisonous element, he advised us that it should be sliced, soaked in water for three days, and then thrice boiled in fresh water. To avoid any incidence of food poisoning he offered to supervise this process. When the old hands heard about this, they burst out laughing and explained that Hainan cassava was not at all poisonous and could even be eaten raw. The intellectual would not accept it and called the farm hospital for confirmation. When it confirmed that the old hands were right, he insisted on monitoring those who had eaten the cassava to see if they showed signs of food poisoning.

I helped to slaughter a water buffalo once: it was not an experience for the faint-hearted. The water buffalos the local peasants sold us were old, feeble, and deformed. Slaughtering one took a huge amount of water and was therefore conducted near the river. This was an unnerving process that required several strong men and experienced butchers, and would take up to four hours if things went well. But if the water buffalo put up a fight, it would become even more strenuous—a real test of mind, physical strength, skill, and experience. When it was over and done with, we left the unwanted innards in the river, which would usually be cleared away within no time by the hovering eagles. We took extreme care in disposing of the hide: if it was discovered, we would be taxed by the local authorities. We dropped it into the cesspool to let it dissolve, which, it was believed, would turn it into fertilizer, which when applied to the fields would produce succulent vegetables.

My five-year stint as a cook taught me how to cook with a large iron wok, how to butcher pigs, and many other skills that a city guy would otherwise never have picked up. It was a tough five years with many inexpressible hardships, but it was not without its joys and pleasures.

FORBIDDEN FRUIT

Ma Guizhen

Renowned for its fruit production, No. 7 Company was also known in the regiment as the "fruit company." When a regimental commander was trying to explain at a political assembly the meaning of the phrase "A high reputation is hard to live up to," he observed: "It's like in our army production corps. Everybody assumes that No. 13 Regiment of No. 4 Division specializes in fruit production. In reality, the only company that produces fruit is No. 7 Company; the rest are all in rubber planting. And indeed, even within No 7. Company, there is only one squad that looks after the orchard. This is what is meant by 'A high reputation is hard to live up to.'" Those of us in the fruit squad were thrilled!

The orchard we were tending must have been at least a thousand *mu*[4]—nor were the fruit trees confined to it. Some, like the jackfruit and mango trees, which looked good and whose fruit tasted even better, lined the path to provide shade and were scattered around our dormitory as ornaments. The variety of fruit in our orchard was such that I struggled to remember all their names. In 1970, soon after our rustication to No. 7 Company, we joined the ex-servicemen and old hands in the major joint campaigns to open up the wilderness for rubber and mango cultivation. As part of our day-to-day routine we also participated in the daily study sessions of Chairman Mao's works and the political commentaries from the three main news publications. We were young, simple, and ignorant. We were also extremely conscien-

---

4.   1 *mu* = 1/6 acre.

tious and would not even pick up fallen fruit to eat it. After a hard day's work in the fields, I would help out in the company cookhouse and also take part in various kinds of voluntary work organized by the company. Whenever I heard myself commended by the officials, I would feel elated.

As the fruits were starting to ripen and the orchard filled with their gorgeous scent, we found it ever harder to resist the temptation they presented, especially since they caressed our heads and shoulders whenever we walked past. Although occasionally at lunchtime the company would allocate to the troop some small pieces of fruit such as mango, from time to time a few of us would still pool our meager savings to buy a jackfruit to share. We were at the age when our bodies were growing fast and plenty of nutrition was required to maintain our growth. Combined, the poor diet and the heavy manual labor we performed every day had the effect of making us hungry all the time: we felt constantly like reincarnations of a hungry ghost. The plain truth was that we never had enough to eat, yet to utter that truth would only attract the criticism that we were "unhappy with socialism" and get us into trouble. It was a truth none of us could afford to mention.

We were on our way back from work one day when a sudden gentle breeze swathed us in the heavenly fragrance of ripe jackfruit. Exhausted and hungry, I was enraptured and my steps began to slow down to allow my workmates to pass me. When they were far ahead, I went back to the source of the smell and saw on a tree a fully ripe jackfruit. I knocked at it lightly here and there and could tell that it was soft and dry inside and ready for eating. How I lusted for it and would have plucked it then and there had I not also been feeling ashamed of my own greed. I was reluctant to leave it there but neither could I act on my impulse. So I took several turns up and down the path, touching and smelling it whenever I returned to the tree. I knew I should do the right thing: buy one from the company. Yet my meager salary had long been used up, I hadn't a penny left. As I was being torn by conflicting thoughts, I was again transported by the smell. I could no longer resist: I pulled the fruit from the tree, cut it in half with my sickle, and one by one, picked out the segments of fruit and put them into my mouth.

It not only smelled good, it tasted wonderful. I had never had such delicious fruit: I felt ecstatic.

After I had devoured the whole jackfruit, I rubbed my hands on the grass to get rid of the residue on my fingers. However, the fruit has a distinctive and pleasant smell that lingers in the mouth for a long while: it could easily betray me when I rejoined the troop. Gripped by a sense of guilt, I tried hard to keep a distance from my workmates. I skipped lunch, for after devouring the whole fruit I was in any case too full to eat, and for the rest of the day I guarded my little secret and took steps to avoid company.

That was the first time I stole a fruit from my "fruit company." Though it wasn't worth much, it was company property. Like a little kid who has stolen candy at home and dreads being caught and criticized by his parents, I remained apprehensive for the next few days. Four decades later, I can still remember how nervous and scared my theft had made me.

A DISH OF CONGEE AND SOLE
Zhang Huixin

For the young generation of today, it's hard to imagine how tough life was on the farm and how lean times were when we were rusticated. Although there was a small shop in the company and a basic variety store at the regimental headquarters, all we could afford were the barest essentials such as salt, cooking oil, soy sauce, vinegar, matches, and lamp oil. The range of candy and flour treats was not only narrow but far beyond our pockets. Our monthly salary was only about twenty *yuan*, so how could we afford such luxuries? Fortunately, the local peasants would sometimes come in to sell their cheap produce, such as sesame, glutinous rice, sugar cubes, and duck eggs. It was because of their supplies that every now and then we could afford to improve our diet.

For example, for seven *jiao*,[5] we could get a mugful of sesame seeds, and on these occasions we would ask an old hand for the use of their kitchen and stir-fry it. Emptying it into a jar with a wide neck, we would mix it with sugar. Then whenever we fancied a snack, we would have a spoonful of it to ease our hunger pangs. It smelled and tasted great and in my opinion was far more piquant than the sesame cakes of today. At times, we would add a cup of glutinous rice to a pot of water and boil it to make sweet congee, and just before it was served add a duck egg. It was the tastiest of any evening snack.

One day, we came by some green beans, and remembering how green bean congee was prepared at home, we cooked a delicious pot of it. It was a Sunday afternoon. We went to an old hand's kitchen and boiled glutinous rice and green beans in a large cooking pot of water. When it was done, we added sugar and then carried it carefully back to our dormitory. Since it was too hot to eat, we removed the lid and the whole room filled with its gorgeous smell.

Then, all of a sudden, we saw a shoe fall into the pot. It belonged to someone who was sleeping on an upper bunk! In those days, we slept on bunks, and there were five bunks in each room for ten *zhiqings* to share. In a panic, someone snatched the shoe out of the scaldingly hot pot of congee.

"Is it still eatable? It's so dirty now."

"Oh no, we can't!"

"It's such a pity to throw it away."

"It would be such a waste!"

. . .

After a brief debate, we carried the pot back to the old hand's kitchen and brought it to a boil again to disinfect the congee. When it was served, we took care not to stir the mixture at the bottom to avoid any debris from the shoe. Fortunately, nobody suffered food poisoning!

---

5. 1 *yuan* = 10 jiao = 100 *fen*.

BLACK MARKET

Kong Dexiang

To relieve the shortage of food, our company, like many others, raised pigs. But because of the scarcity of feed, it usually took a long time before a pig was big enough to slaughter. To improve the poor diet of the troop, the company would sometimes send people to nearby Danxian to procure slaughtered pigs. Well, either because of my big build and sheer animal strength or my nimble mind (especially where food is concerned—now please don't laugh at me!), I was always the one whom our captain dispatched on such errands to accompany the vegetable squad leader, Chen. In those days, trade was strictly a state monopoly: as well as fulfilling the state quota, the peasants had to turn over their surplus to the state as part of their duty to contribute to the public good. When we purchased pigs from the peasants, we were in a gray area because we were appropriating a surplus that was owed to the state—a desperate measure that every company resorted to in those days. Every time Chen and I were sent on such an errand, those who saw us would be thrilled and exclaim: "Great! We will have an extra dish! Wonderful! Pork will be served!'

The peasant whom we usually dealt with was a village chief, a friend of Chen, who shared his surname. It was said that his ancestor was a servant of the great poet and statesman of the Song dynasty, Su Dongpo, when he was banished to the remote Danxian. At his home there were still a few scrolls of calligraphy and paintings that were hundreds of years old: he felt proud of being a descendant of Su's servant. Despite growing up in an isolated rural area, he seemed different from the average peasant, for one thing he was literate. Once I got to know him, I called him "Danxian Chen." I told him he was the best educated in the village, and he readily accepted the compliment. He was helpful and meticulous: we trusted him implicitly.

We were once sent to purchase pigs on the eve of the Spring Festival. It was an unusually warm night for that time of year, and as was our habit, we set off in the early evening to avoid drawing attention to ourselves. We went straight to the village chief's home and asked for two slaughtered pigs. He told us that on this occasion the village had yet to fulfill its state quota for surplus pigs: every now and then, an inspection team would be dispatched at night to conduct a spot search. But he told us not to worry and that we would certainly get what we were after. After asking his wife to boil us some sweet potatoes, he went off on business. About half an hour later, while we were eating the sweet potatoes, a youngster charged in without knocking at the door and told Chen's wife, "An inspection team has just turned up. The chief has asked me to hide the two farm guests." We followed him promptly into the woods by the village. From afar, we could see torches flashing and there was a lot of shouting and other noises in the village. How unfortunate, I lamented, to have come when the inspection team was making its rounds! After about half an hour, the noises died away and the youngster came to escort us to Chen's home. We continued to eat the boiled sweet potatoes. We waited patiently: soon it would be half past midnight. When we had arrived, Chen told us that a few days before, some members of another company had been caught red-handed by the inspection team, and their money had been confiscated. I grew anxious. Then all of a sudden, the youngster rushed in, and without a word, grabbed our hands and pulled us out of Chen's house. It turned out that the inspection team had made a surprise return and had demanded to speak to the village chief. This time, we were taken to the woods on a hill outside the village. And from there, we could see the flashing torches on the way to the village chief's home. I reckoned that since the village had not fulfilled the state quota for surplus pigs, the inspection team must be returning to resolve the issue with the chief. By this time, the vegetable squad leader and myself were bathed in cold sweat: we shivered in the cool breezes. After a little while and to our great relief, 'Danxian Chen' appeared right in front of us and announced: "Great! I have finally seen off the inspection team; moreover the slaughtered pigs are ready. Please go and weigh them now." I remarked how resourceful he was and then followed him to the homes of two peasants who raised pigs. As usual, the pigs had been divided into four equal portions and tied tightly to two shoulder poles made from freshly felled tree branches. As agreed, the two peasants carried the pigs to the border of Daling Farm, and only then did we hand over the agreed payment in cash. We thanked "Danxian Chen" profusely and then with the poles on our shoulders and flashlights in hand, we struggled as quickly as we could toward our company. Fearful of being caught by the inspection team, we were entirely oblivious to the burden on our shoulders. When we eventually made it back to our company, dawn was breaking and the sight of us caused great jubilation. Overjoyed, everybody tried to give us a hand to carry the pigs into the cookhouse.

That day, the sale of alcohol in the company corner shop tripled.

FISHY BUSINESS
Li Huguang

No. 11 Company in Daling Farm was set up along the lower reaches of the Zhubi River. Before the jungles were destroyed, the water level was quite high. From the late 1960s, trees were felled, the wilderness opened up, and hills set fire to in order to make way for a rubber plantation. During the deforestation, the water level gradually dropped. Soon, you could abandon your boat and simply wade through the river with your trousers rolled up. The clearance of vegetation had devastating environmental repercussions! Every typhoon was followed by a flash flood six or seven meters in depth and muddy, raging rapids. Just a few days after the downpour, however, the water would have ebbed away, leaving shallow pools in the riverbed. To conserve water, the locals built a dam downstream out of sand and mud. It worked, and soon the water level started to rise. The clear and fuller river was not only the main source of drinking and cooking water for several troops along the river, but every evening we also bathed and washed our laundry in it.

During a quiet lunch break one day, there was a loud explosion. Soon, some *zhiqings* who had been washing their laundry by the river rushed in and explained that some locals had thrown explosives into the river and there were many dead fish floating on the water. None of these *zhiqings* could swim; they urged us to go and gather the fish. The mention of fish prompted us to race to the river: it was understood that whatever we caught we could keep. It was noon on a mid-summer day; under the fierce sun, it was hot by the bank and the sand burned our feet. But we didn't care: we just patrolled the bank and as soon as we saw a fish would dive into the water. Sometimes several of us went after the same fish and it was a case of whoever was the best swimmer could claim the prize. Most of the time, it was the Guangzhou *zhiqings* who got there first because they were better long distance swimmers. When we reached the bank that day, most of the fish had already been taken by the locals, leaving few for us. The river was very clear and the sunlight very strong. I took a deep breath, dived three meters down to the riverbed and began searching. When I could no longer hold my breath, I would surface, take a deep breath, and dive back in again. Eventually, I caught sight of a shining white object and when I swam close to it, I found that it was indeed a dead fish. About thirty centimeters long, with its stomach blown wide open, it had sunk to the riverbed. I was thrilled and surfaced with my fingers hooked in its mouth. When there were no more dead fish to be found, we returned to our dormitories with our trophies.

It was such a long time since we had had flesh on our menu that the fish was delicious and we absolutely relished it. After that, whenever we heard the sound of an explosion from the river, we would drop everything—even while working—and race to the water to claim our prizes. We soon learned that if there was an explosion on the Zhubi River, a rare delicacy was at hand.

Gradually we learned that most of the dead fish wouldn't float to the surface till the next day. In wintry days, the dead fish were still okay—

in summer, however, being soaked in the water all night, they just didn't keep well. If the locals were exploding fish in winter, we would go to the river the next day. No matter how chilly the water was, we would strip and jump into the river to harvest them and improve our diet.

After a while, the number of fish in the river declined drastically, and soon they disappeared altogether. When we heard the sound of an explosion, we wouldn't even bother to go and check. The practice devastated the local eco-system and was banned by the regiment. But the rule didn't apply to the locals, especially not to the Li, who were left alone and not really under anybody's control. When they exploded fish, we went to claim a share of their catch—a sure recipe for arguments. As the number of fish diminished, they would guard more jealously what they deemed to be theirs and theirs alone. There were two kinds of locals: the peasants from Danzhou, and the Li. If it was the former, we didn't have to worry too much; but if it was the Li, we had to be cautious. One day a Meixian *zhiqing* got hold of a dead fish after an explosion and was seen by a Li man, who asked him to drop it, but he refused. The Li man ran after him and even threatened him with a machete. Though the *zhiqing* escaped, we knew for sure that claiming a share of the exploded fish from the Li was no laughing matter.

One year a big typhoon was forecast: all farms were on the alert for imminent damage to their properties. The floodgates of the dam in the upstream Zhubi River were lifted to avoid flooding. As a consequence, many fish were swept downstream to where we were. It was a Sunday, and on our one day off we were all minding our own business. Suddenly somebody yelled that there was a wealth of fish floating in the river: the locals must have poured poison into the water. Exhilarated, we rushed toward the river and when we arrived, we were stupefied: we had never seen such a massive amount of fish floating on the water! We jumped into the river in great excitement. The fish, however, were merely stunned and when we reached them, they recovered instantly and darted away. We changed our tactic by using both hands to catch them by the "neck," the area slightly beneath their gills, then inserting our index or middle finger into the mouth to grasp it before we returned to the bank. The female *zhiqings* or those who couldn't swim would then strike the fishes' heads hard on the ground before putting them into a bucket. That day the boisterous crowd along the bank was in a jubilant mood. Since the fish must have been held back behind the dam for a long time, they were big—one *zhiqing* caught a fish weighing over seven kilograms. We had never seen such an enormous fresh-water fish.

Most of us had caught some fish that day, and in the spirit of sticking together through thick and thin, we shared our trophies with the rest of the troop. With the smell of fish everywhere, it was festive. Rhyming the word for a fishy smell with "hope" in Cantonese, we chanted: "Where there's a fishy smell, there's hope": what we hoped for was that the fish smell would boost our chances of returning home and reuniting with our families. When, in high spirits, we were preparing the fish, our assistant nurse came to warn us not to touch them because of the risk of food poisoning. But we knew for certain that the locals would only apply harmless substances to the water so that the fish remained safe for consumption. Besides, who had the luxury of throwing away such a delicious and available meal? We gutted the insides before cooking the fish with its head. We fried the leftovers with the meager oil that we had saved for future consumption. We were fortunate: on that occasion nobody in the troop suffered from food poisoning. Some *zhiqings* came up with a piece of doggerel: "Without fish, in poor shape, with fish, in good shape."

And indeed that was a time when we had to toil day in and day out without getting enough food to keep pace with the growth of our young bodies. To keep our hunger pangs at bay became one of our main aims, and whenever we came by some food, we felt happy. Whether or not the food that was put on our table was toxic was a question we could not afford to ask. Our priority was simply to be able to eat.

FORAGING

Mei Fuming, Chen Hongbo

As our ancestors have it: "Those living on a mountain live off the mountain, those living near the water live off the water": one must make use of one's local resources. Daling Farm is situated in the western region of Hainan, with its many companies located either along a river or at the edge of the jungle. In the lean years, when our daily staple was only pickled Chinese radishes, oil and salt, or, on good days, water spinach to go with plain rice, we harnessed the wisdom of our ancestors to our survival instinct.

The Zhubi River, known as Daxi River on Daling Farm, was normally tranquil, clear, and inviting. Every day after work, we *zhiqings* in No. 8 Company would go there for a dip to ease away our fatigue and wash our grimy bodies in the late evening glow. Before the jungles were cleared, there would be scores of fish in the water for us to play with. It was great fun. Every now and then, the Li living nearby would cast a net to catch them and sell them cheaply to us. But this irregular supply could never quell our craving for food. One of the *zhiqings*, nicknamed Elder Brother Yong, grew up in western Guangzhou. Before rustication, he used to catch fish, shrimp, and frogs to sell in a makeshift local market. When schooling was suspended at the start of the Cultural Revolution, he was packed off to his ancestral home in a rural area, where he would follow his uncles and cousins to the river to drop fishhooks at night and return the next morning to gather the catch.

One summer, after a series of typhoons, both the rubber plantation and our vegetable field were devastated. For a long time, we lived off plain rice with pickled Chinese radishes, water spinach, or at times just soy sauce. One day, Elder Brother Yong recounted his experience in the ancestral village and asked why we didn't simply follow suit in order to improve our diet. We jumped at the idea only to find that we had neither the line nor the hooks for the task. To our sheer amazement, one of the Shantou *zhiqings* who grew up by the sea had, on the advice of her fishing family, packed fishing tackle in her sack when she was rusticated in 1968. When she showed us, Elder Brother Yong realized that it was for casting a long net by the sea and wouldn't work for fishing at a short distance. Following his advice, we cut the fishing line into a dozen or so short lines. We then tied one end to a fishhook and the other to a bamboo stick about twenty centimeters long. As for bait, we searched high and low around the farm, and for a while we were stuck and couldn't find anything suitable. Eventually, along a deserted hill path near a small reservoir, we came across some marshland overgrown with grass and in it, some tiny fish. We kept them in a bucket of water. When we went to the river for an evening dip, we followed Elder Brother Yong's instruction to set the bamboo sticks near where the fish tend to gather—places which were shaded or dense with water grasses. To optimize the chance of luring them, the bamboo sticks were arranged in such a way as to let the bait float in the water so that it flashed conspicuously under the moonlight. Come next morning, we would go and check every hook, hoping for a catch. There were good days and there were bad days: the fish caught in this way were incredibly fresh and delicious, and to this day, we can still remember the thrill of tasting our first catch. We tried all sorts of live things as bait, such as worms, fireflies, and even leeches. Through practice we found that baby frogs which were the size of a thumb, and which we caught in the rubber tree propagation field, made the best bait.

When we first arrived at No. 8 Company, we were surrounded by virgin jungle, and amid the thick and overgrown bushes there abounded such wildlife as muntjacs, masked civets, and wild boars. After hunting, the Li would come and sell us some of their trophies. With our meager salaries and, I should add, as typical Cantonese, we would drive a hard bargain. In one deal, I remember that we managed to get down by five *jiao* the asking price of ten *yuan* for a huge mountain turtle that must have weighed over twenty-five kilograms. Such a rare delicacy normally costs a small fortune! And of course we were so hungry that a squad of twenty *zhiqings* devoured it in just one meal.

After we opened up the wilderness, it was common practice to set fire to the hills and, as a consequence, many forms of wildlife lost their natural habitat. One evening after a major joint campaign which involved No. 11 Company, I was leading my troops back to our dormitories. At the border between our company and No. 9 Company, our gaze fell upon a large lizard. With black skin and a long body, it was crawling on the ground with its head up and its tongue sticking out. Once it saw us, it darted away. We were consumed by hunger after a long day on the joint campaign and also a long spell without any meat. Thrilled by the prospect of a good dish, we sprang into action to try to catch it. It was very alert but it didn't survive our numerous pickaxes. We wrapped it in a sack and carried it back to our cookhouse with our pickaxes. That night we had a feast. Of course that was by no means our first experience of it, nor was its meat tasty. But in such famished times taste wasn't particularly high on our agenda.

BLOODY BUT UNBOWED

Zhu Jianqiang

About four decades ago, when I was rusticated to Hainan, I worked for a time as a regimental cook. The Chinese say that "The cleverest housewife cannot cook a meal without rice": as a cook, my toughest challenge was the scarcity of any produce. During drought or wet spells, when the fields failed to yield any vegetables, the only dish I could put on the dining tables was pickled Chinese radishes; and when they ran out, then for every single meal there was just soy sauce to go with the plain rice until weather conditions improved.

Every time we came back to our farm on Hainan Island from a home visit, we would bring some food with us. Not that our families in the cities had a better life, but our parents would always scrabble around to give us something that we could fall back on in Hainan. The commonest foods we brought back in our sacks were sugar, Chinese sausage, and a jar of salted black beans cooked in lard. Whatever our families could afford would go back with us to Hainan.

Water chestnut is believed to have cooling properties and is perfect for fighting the heat of a tropical climate such as that of Hainan Island. Using sugar and some water chestnut powder brought back by myself and some other *zhiqings*, we made boiled sweets. One day, just as we were about to dig into them, someone yelled: 'Hey, how come there's so much sesame in them?' When we looked, what we saw was not sesame at all but armies of ants. What could we do? The ingredients had come from so far away and with so much effort.

"Turn the lights off and eat them!" somebody muttered. What a great idea! And so we devoured the tasty sweets in the dark. After all, ants were good for our health, or so we would have liked to believe.

Before working in the regimental canteen, I worked for a spell in a company canteen. The cookhouse was a thatched shed, and every day before sunrise I would take a kerosene lamp there to prepare breakfast for the troop. Water was drawn from a well, and then carried through to the cookhouse and stored in receptacles. The happiest time was when pork was on the menu: good news travels fast and the whole troop would be in a festive mood for the entire day.

The regimental canteen was in much better condition than any of those in the companies. Its cookhouse was tiled, and water was drawn from a tap. Because Daling Farm was state-owned, and between 1969 and 1974 army-run, the supply of rice, at least, was guaranteed. But anything else such as vegetables, meat, and poultry depended on how resourceful the supply chief was and how well he fared on procurement trips. Sometimes, for example, the supply chief had to cycle more than twenty kilometres to the beach to buy some fish, and sometimes to the Li villages for meat and poultry. At times when he was lucky, he might even come across the Li right after one of their hunting trips and bring back a wild boar or a deer.

One day our supply chief observed that it was a long time since we'd had pork, and he wanted to do something about it. In the quest to put pork on the table, I went to a Li village with him that evening. It was a moonless night and it took us about half an hour to walk there. When we arrived, there was already a newly butchered pig on a long table: the supply chief must already have made a deal.

After a quick check to see if we were being watched, the supply chief handed over the agreed sum of money in cash. All was quiet in the village. I quickly heaved the pig over my shoulder and ran as fast as I could back to regimental headquarters. It was illegal to butcher a pig without a permit from the state: if we were caught by the tax bureau, our meat would be confiscated and its cost would not be refunded to us.

The pig must have weighed over fifty kilograms, and it took me a good half hour to hump it back down the rough track. It was not until I reached the cookhouse that I realized I was drenched in blood from head to toe. My appearance reminded me of those popular Chinese literary descriptions of how a bandit would escape in pitch darkness after a brutal and bloody attack. The mental image put a wry smile on my face.

Learn from the Workers!

LEARNING FROM THE WORKERS

Lin Yuhua

Fine weather, New Year's Day, 1974

Today, a Guangdong provincial delegation paid a visit to our regiment. I was invited to attend the discussion forum as my company's representative. Their visit shows the care and support of the Party toward us *zhiqings*: it reassures me that it is absolutely necessary and right for the nation's educated youth to participate in the "Up to the Mountains, Down to the Countryside" campaign. While I was reflecting on the journey I have been through since my rustication began more than three years ago, it became evident that every step I have taken was guided by Party principles, and supported and helped by the farm workers and my comrades. It is through them that I have grown from an ignorant teenage girl into a member of the Communist Youth League, and been transformed into a primary school teacher. I must not become complacent: I must work even harder and set myself a higher benchmark. At the forum, a few episodes returned to my mind, and I shared with the participants some of the lessons I had learned from the workers during my development.

In 1972, I was reassigned to a company to plant rubber trees. The daily quota for each person was twenty. Lacking experience and know-how, I lagged behind my team. By noon, I felt scorched by the sun and anxious about my slow progress: I was desperate to get it all done and return to the dormitory. With a blatant disregard for quality, I rushed the job. As a farm worker walked by, he saw the rubber trees I had just planted and asked to speak to me. He patiently explained and demonstrated to me how to plant a rubber tree in such a way as to give it a head start. He taught me that we must think of every action we take as an act of revolution! If we care only about quantity rather than quality, we will have to rectify situations later on, resulting in a tremendous waste of time and effort. And what a loss to the revolutionary cause that would bring! His terse remarks were a heavy blow to me. I felt embarrassed and ashamed of myself. Indeed, even though the task we are engaged in is humdrum, it is linked to the global revolutionary cause! Rubber is a crucial component in the construction of socialism: the farm workers toil assiduously, day in and day out, to develop rubber plantations for the nation. They have set us an excellent example! Once I realized this, I managed to endure the fierce sun and started to plant rubber trees one by one with great care and enthusiasm. When I finished that day, I was the last one left on the plantation.

Since my political values haven't been fully reformed, they influence my conduct. When I was working in the field one day, I was stung by a wasp. It was painful and I walked quickly toward the dormitory. When I was walking past the grain-drying area, there was a lot of sesame on the ground. All of a sudden, a shower came and many of my workmates rushed to collect it. I paused and wondered if I should help, but I was more concerned with the pain on my swollen finger. Just as I was about to run on to the dormitory, I saw a farm worker dashing out from his room to join the crowd. He was in poor shape and had been confined indoors for several days, yet he too was helping out. When I saw him, I felt ashamed of my self-preoccupation; I turned back to the grain-drying ground and helped to rescue the sesame.

Chairman Mao has commented: "The cleanest people are still the workers and peasants. Although their hands are deeply tanned, and there might be manure on their feet, they are still cleaner than the capitalists and the petty bourgeois intellectuals." At an assembly one night, there was a pile of manure right at the point where my queue started. I stayed clear of it, with a handkerchief covering my nose. The queue looked awkward due to my not standing where I should have. A farm worker spotted it: he came with a spade and removed the manure. He uttered not a single syllable, but I felt a sharp slap across the cheeks. I felt awful. It was a good slap! It hit deep inside my soul! It made me realize that in comparison with the workers, we educated youth are superficial! We badly lag behind them! In the course of our re-education, the only approach is to learn modestly from the workers, to integrate with them and go through the mill so that our thoughts and values are reformed. Only in this way can we become the heirs of the proletarian revolutionary cause.

Although these incidents are in the past, I will never forget them. They are imprinted on my mind, teaching me what I need to do in order to achieve my re-education. Now that I have been reassigned to work as a teacher, an educator, I must bear in mind what Chairman Mao has instructed us: "Those working in the education sector, the educators, must subject themselves to re-education . . . in the course of the great social transformation, that is their priority." I now realize that to become a good teacher, one must first become a good pupil. There are many things that can never be picked up from a book. I must learn from the working class, the workers and peasants! I must learn from my pupils in school, stay faithful to the Party's educational task, and devote myself to the revolutionary cause!

THE EGGS IN THE CRADLES
Lu Sui

In my eight-year life as a *zhiqing* in No. 7 Company, I was assigned to many jobs, the most memorable being a stint working in the nursery.

The nursery was housed in two rooms in a thatched hut which had been our dormitory when we arrived. After we built and moved into the tiled buildings, the hut was turned into a nursery. Bare and basic, it admitted drafts from every direction. And like a typical thatched hut on Hainan at the time, its roof was made with grass, its wall with a mixture of yellow mud and grass, and its floor with mud. Joined by a connecting door, the classrooms were primitive: there were two tables, several wooden cots, and two rows of cradles in one room, and simply a row of wooden beds in the other. On the beds were straw mats and ragged blankets. That was all the equipment the nursery had.

In our care were more than twenty children, ranging from two-month-old babies to pre-school toddlers. They were kept in two groups: a playgroup for those below three and a group for those above. Four of us staffed the nursery: two local workers and two *zhiqing*s. One of the workers doubled as a cook, the other worker and my fellow *zhiqing* were responsible for the playgroup, and I looked after the older group. Although we had different areas of responsibility, we worked together and helped each other out.

Conditions in the nursery were primitive, and we had to work hard to keep up with the demands that were made on us. The children were clad in rags, usually made from the worn-out cast-offs of the adults; some were barefoot all year round because their families could not afford a single pair of shoes for them. The diet was poor: breakfast was plain salted congee. Thick fine congee with Chinese yam was a delicacy only the marginally better-off families could afford for their newborn babies. There was no milk powder, let alone fresh milk, and owing to malnutrition, the children all looked green and thin. Toys, educational tools, picture books, and drawing pencils were unheard of.

We started early in the morning so that the workers could drop their children off before they went to work at seven o'clock. Usually, the children in the playgroup arrived first while those in my class would have their breakfast at home. Once the playgroup infants started to turn up, we would feed them: with two of us looking after the new-born babies, the other two would look after the slightly older ones. With more babies than we could attend to, we would put three in a group on the bed, then with three bowls in one hand, we would use the other hand to hold a spoon and feed them in turn. After they were fed, we sat them on the potties. To make sure they didn't fall off, we would use a piece of old cloth to tie them loosely to the bed. Once they were settled on the potties, we would then move on to feed another group of three children until all had been fed and put on the potties. It was only then that we could start to do other things.

Weather permitting, I would take the children of my class out into the open air, play games with them, and teach them to sing. When it rained, they would be confined to the classroom, where there was nothing to entertain them but a row of bare beds. The children under my care were older and could be rather mischievous and even naughty: since there was nothing to engage them with, it was quite a challenge to keep them from feeling bored and starting to fool around or getting into a fight. I had to make up stories or invent some indoor games for them.

The children were usually collected for lunch at home and then returned to the nursery for the rest of the day. After their return, we would wash the younger ones and then put them in their cradles for a nap. One day, a miracle occurred: as one of us was uncovering a cradle, her gaze fell upon an egg. Where could it have come from? Was a fairy tale being enacted before our eyes? It turned out that while we were taking our lunch break back in our dormitory, a hen had flown in through the window or half-open door, and having chanced on the soft and warm hollow of a cradle, had laid an egg there. At that time, we were all dirt poor and the *zhiqings* usually ate nothing but plain rice with some pickles or soy sauce. But whenever we found another egg in a cradle, we never thought of sharing it among ourselves. Instead, we would add it to the congee for the children: they needed it more than we did.

After the older children were given a quick shower, we would take their laundry to the river to wash. We had no soap or detergent. All we could do was beat the laundry on the rocks repeatedly—just as the female soldiers did in well-known revolutionary films. When the children woke up in the late afternoon, it was again time to feed the younger ones with plain congee while the older ones would be allowed to play in front of the hut. Our job would not be finished until all the children were collected by their families. That was the daily routine in the nursery. I soon grew to love the children under my care.

I was only twenty when I started in the nursery, and I was the last one to join the team of four. Inexperienced and with no training in child-care, I picked up skills from my colleagues. The two workers, reticent but hardworking, didn't just pass on their experience to me with great patience; they treated me like their own child. Despite the harsh conditions they endured, they would never forget to invite me to eat with them whenever they could put something tasty on the table. Before I left the farm, one of them sewed me a big sack for my personal belongings, and invited me to a farewell meal with her family.

I learned and gained a lot during my time at the nursery. I was deeply grateful for the love, care, and help of my colleagues. After my return to the city, I was faced with all sorts of challenges, including those presented by fame and money. But throughout my life I have been able to keep a grateful heart, thanks in no small measure to the formative experiences of my *zhiqing* life.

Becoming Iron Girls

WEEDS GREW UNDER OUR BEDS

Wu Xianfang

It was more than four decades ago. As time goes by, the memories are sometimes blurred, sometimes vivid. When they are blurred, I cannot even recall those involved or the specific event; when they are vivid, it seems as though they happened only yesterday.

November 1968. When the Liberation trucks overloaded with Guangzhou *zhiqings* arrived at our destination, the captain led us to a row of new thatched huts and told us that they were built especially for us by the old hands on the farm. None of us had ever seen such huts: they looked so exotic, and in great curiosity we rushed over to the female section. It was in fact just a big hall: the walls, framed by tree trunks and bamboos and made with mud-coated straw, had not yet dried out; the floor, too, was wet and smelt of fresh mud. Inside were rows of beds to be occupied by twenty of us teenage ex-schoolgirls. We sensed that our collective life was about to start in earnest. Giggling, we took a good look around at the hall. Some wondered if the low-ceilinged roof would leak when it rained; some observed that since the beds were merely resting on what looked like wooden crutches, they might collapse once we climbed on to them; some pointed out that there were weeds growing under the beds . . . After much giggling and excitement, we eventually settled down to this new chapter in our lives.

Though the thatched hut was rough, it was indeed warm in winter and cool in summer, and we soon got used to it. Living like a large family, we shared everything, even if it was just a bottle of lard or a small roll of Chinese sausage; we shared our joys and looked after each other, come rain or shine; we worked together to meet tough challenges. Despite all its unexpected demands, life was harmonious.

One night, just as we were getting ready for bed, there was a sudden scream. When we dashed to its source, we found one of our roommates, pale and frightened, yelling: 'Snake! Snake!' Her hand was trembling as she pointed to a wooden beam. As our eyes followed her finger, we saw vaguely, in the dim light of the oil lamps, something that looked like an iron hook. When a torch was shone on it, we were all terrified: holding its head up toward us was a bamboo leaf green snake. The girl was hanging up a mosquito net when she nearly touched the snake on the beam. We quickly picked up things we could reach to attack it, but to no avail: eventually, though, it was frightened away by our noise. From then on, every time we hung up our mosquito nets, we would be on high alert. Who knew when some other snakes or centipedes might decide to drop by?

The renowned No. 7 Company specialized in growing tropical fruit. Responding to the national call to develop rubber plantations rapidly, the regiment also ordered us to plant rubber trees. With a large group of new *zhiqings* joining the troop, the company was injected with new blood and soon we became the main force in opening up the wilderness for rubber plantations. A few years after our arrival, the plantation outgrew the orchard. The land was mostly hilly, and on the hills was virgin jungle, full of the sweet, fresh scent of plants and the strong aroma of medicinal herbs. Our arrival sent monkeys and little squirrels into hiding, and frightened pheasants flying up into the sky, their beautiful wings making tapping sounds as they spread. This was the landscape that we were ordered to open up for rubber plantation.

The several dozen *zhiqings* were divided among the existing squads, and an old hand was placed in charge of each. Besides the squad leader, there were several other old hands who were mainly from the rural areas of Zhanjiang, many of them ex-servicemen or with families. Our squad leader was an ex-serviceman. Our tools included scythes, sickles, axes, hoes, and spades. We learned from the old hands how to open up the wilderness. First, we had to chop down bushes, young trees and creepers with scythes, then clear the ground, then cut down the big trees with axes or crosscut saws. When the trees were dry and the weather allowed, we set the hills alight. Then holes would be dug and terraces built to prepare for rubber tree planting.

Opening up the wilderness sounded easy to us. It came as a surprise to discover that it involved so many procedures, all of them requiring backbreaking labor. The challenge was tough, and for us sixteen- or seventeen- year-olds who had been brought up in urban areas, even cruel. Somehow, though, we got through it.

The weather on Hainan Island was as fickle as the face of a newborn baby: it could change at any moment. A clear sunny day could suddenly become overcast and then drench us with a heavy downpour. When the downpour stopped, the sunshine returned. In the fierce heat, we could hardly tell the rain from the sweat on our bodies. Days and days of opening up the wilderness covered our soft hands in blood-filled blisters that soon built up into thick calluses. Small wonder that the hands which not long before had been used for holding pens could now wield axes and chop down trees. We set off for work at dawn and returned at dusk; we went up to the hills with dew on our feet and came down in starry nights. Over ten hours' manual labour each day consumed us physically: it was a good thing that we were young, with an apparently endless supply of energy. The strenuous labor we performed in such harsh conditions built our bodies; it also equipped us with many manual skills; and it strengthened our resolve, something which was to benefit us later in life.

Chopping down trees to clear a wilderness might sound straight-forward, but it is in fact a skilled labor that demands not just strength but experience. To fell a tree on a slope, one must first chop the side of the trunk that faces the higher part of the slope. When one has cut two-thirds of the way through the trunk, one can then give the other side a few blows until the tree collapses of its own weight toward the lower part of the slope.

One day, after clearing the saplings and bushes left from previous work, we were tasked with chopping down all the big trees left on a steep hill. We worked in groups, my group occupying the middle area. Suddenly there was a shout: "Run, run!" and before I could even react I heard the rending of wood and the rustle of violently shaking foliage: a huge tree was falling toward us. I froze. An old hand pulled me down the hill, shouting "Run, quick!" We hadn't moved far before it hit the ground. As I looked back, I found to my horror that I was standing in the fork of the tree: had I been but a step behind, I would have been knocked down and buried alive under its enormous trunk. It was not just the trunk that was huge: it also had a sprawling crown of branches and dense foliage. It grew on an extremely steep slope and by the time two boys had cut two-thirds of the way into the trunk on the upper side, the remainder could no longer support its weight and suddenly snapped. The two boys hadn't taken into account the various factors that could lead to the fall of the tree. Furthermore, the groups had not been working far enough apart from each other. It could have been a major disaster.

I bid farewell to the farm in the second half of 1975. To my certain knowledge, what many *zhiqings* achieved after their return home had much to do with the mental and physical toughening they had experienced during their years of rustication.

DIGGING WELL

Fang Jinqi

Without a river near No. 3 Company in Daling, we had to rely on three wells for our water. Including spouses and children, there were about three hundred members in our company. The cookhouse was responsible not only for cooking three meals a day for all of them, but providing boiled drinking water. Drawing water was an essential part of the daily routine. Every day nearly a hundred buckets of water were raised and poured into a trough that led to receptacles in the cookhouse. It was not a job for the frail.

In 1970, there was a severe drought and the water level in all three wells dropped fast. To protect the potable water for the troop, a well was reserved for the cookhouse. After work and supper, the well seventy to eighty meters away from the cookhouse would be continuously surrounded by those who were drawing water or washing clothes. When the water level dropped below what could be drawn up by a bucket, a man or boy would be sent down to draw the water manually. After he filled the bucket, he would shout and the one waiting at the top of the well would pull the bucket up.

The dire shortage never triggered any argument: we just accepted it and queued patiently for our turns to draw the water. If we were in the queue when it was time for supper, for example, we would ask a youngster to hold our place or leave a bucket to stand in for us. When it was impossible to fill half a bucket even manually, a hole was made by pushing aside the stones and sand in the well so that water would flow into it, making it easier to fill the bucket. We called this "pushing water": the water gathered in this way was usually thick with sand and mud and had to be distilled for half a day before it could be used.

To ease the crisis, some would avoid the peak hours and draw water only at noon or midnight, when it was quieter, and some would walk all the way to the vegetable field or the school to draw water from the wells over there. The school was about two to three hundred meters away, and after taking a shower and washing our laundry, we would usually carry two buckets of water back to the dormitory.

After some research, it was decided that by the end of that year another well would be essential. Besides the technicians, the labor of digging was assigned to us, the youth special task force. Since the working area was so tight, we were divided into four groups and worked in shifts. With seven to eight in a group, each of us had a different job: digging or transporting or disposing of the mud. As we got deeper and deeper, it became harder to dig and more strenuous to cart the mud away. When pickaxes were not strong enough for the job, we switched to mattocks. We also had to lift the mud up to ground level, bucket by bucket. As we reached a depth of five meters, we began to see water seeping through the stones. We quickened our efforts and worked through the night until we reached the static water level. Clearing the bottom and laying bricks were then left to the technicians to complete.

From the start of digging to the completion of the well took us about a month. When it became functional, it relieved the water crisis. As we dug it, we *zhiqings* became more united. Some of the overseas Chinese students who were attached to our regiment produced a song-and-dance entertainment based on our experiences and called it "The Iron Girls Digging Well." It was put on as a regimental show.

Toward the end of the digging, we had a happy surprise. When we went to work one rainy afternoon, two of the female *zhiqings* climbed out in a state of terror. They said they had seen something long down there and suspected it might be a snake. I thought that in such muddy water it was more likely to be a fish than a snake and ventured down to investigate. The water was nearly one *chi*[6] deep and when I waded through it, I could feel something slippery around my feet. It felt like an eel. Since the well was small, it didn't take long for me to catch it. It was indeed an eel, nearly two *chi* long and weighing about a quarter of a kilo. After we finished our shift, we took it to our squad leader's home and cooked it with congee. It was fresh and very tasty.

THE TRIALS OF CUTTING RUBBER

Huang Siqin

When I first arrived at Hainan Island as a *zhiqing*, the farm was under military management. Of the dozen or so companies in the regiment, the conditions of mine, No. 2 Company, with its tiled-roof dormitory, were probably among the best. In front of it was a large field on which

---

6. I *chi* = I/3 m.

were planted many fruit trees: mango, jackfruit, papaya, and so on. Every year when they blossomed, we would be immersed in a heavenly scent. There were many pretty *zhiqings* in our troop; one of them was even featured in a documentary film about the orchard in our regiment. Every evening after work, we girls would sit under the mango trees to relax, inundated by the lovely scent, and also to admire the pretty women as they walked briskly to the canteen for supper. It was a way to help us unwind, to forget our fatigue and the loneliness of living so far away from our homes and families.

I worked as a rubber cutter. At around three thirty in the morning, we would get up, have some congee while we were still dazed and sleepy, put on the cutter's headgear with a light, pick up a bucket and walk along the winding hill path to work in the rubber plantation. Cutting rubber before sunrise yields better results: the rubber runs more smoothly and the quality is better. After sunrise, the opening in the rubber plant dries up quickly, reducing the yield. Each cutter was required to cut about three hundred trees across one and a half acres within the two and a half hours before dawn. In order to meet the quota, there was not a moment to spare. The lights on our headgear looked like fireflies dancing in the darkness; in the tranquil hills, all we could hear were our own soft footsteps as we trod on the dry leaves. There was a pattern and rhythm in the way we moved along the lines of trees: after finishing one tree, we took a few steps to the next, pulled the rubber strings, rubbed the rubber cup, shook our wrists, and slashed a few times on the tree—then the white rubber came out from where the blade of our machetes had cut. We moved along the terrace and our steps were almost as choreographed as those of disco dancers. Inevitably, the rubber spilled and dripped onto our gradually stiffening clothes: when there was a breeze, we all smelled pungently of rubber and sweat.

As I was absorbed in my job one morning, I felt a sudden stabbing sensation on my finger, and the pain shot up into my armpit. When I looked up, I saw a scorpion on the cup. It must have stung me when I touched the cup. It was pitch dark and, consumed by pain and panic, I cried loudly and helplessly. An old hand working nearby heard me and ran to my rescue. He quickly put my red and swollen finger into a bottle of ammonia. Within no time, the pain eased dramatically. I learned that it was quite common to be stung by a scorpion when cutting rubber, and that ammonia is extremely helpful in easing the pain.

As rubber cutters, we also came across many black-headed red centipedes racing over our feet, and at times snakes, too, slithered past. In fact, the rubber plantation was host to all sorts of poisonous pests—scorpions, snakes, crickets, centipedes, bees, mosquitoes . . . you name it. We were absolutely terrified when we started, but after a while we got used to them and would no longer panic or scream when we encountered them. After cutting rubber from around four-thirty in the morning till ten, we would carry the heavy bucket of rubber back to the company. Working in such a harsh environment under such tough conditions certainly tempered us at a young age. And in the first ten years of our return to the city, we would still hear in our dreams the alarm clock that had been set to wake us up in the wee hours for another day of rubber cutting.

In 1996, we ex-*zhiqings* were invited back to Daling Farm to mark its forty-second anniversary. When I returned to the dormitory we called home, the place that for all these years had been haunting me in my dreams, everything looked faintly familiar. It was where we had spent our most innocent years, where we had encountered the most memorable experiences of our lives. I was relieved to find that both the living and working conditions had hugely changed for the better.

ALL THE YOUNG LADIES HAVE FAINTED
Yang Heping

In 1970 I was a sixteen-year-old secondary school student in Meixian and was exempt from being sent down to the countryside. My father had laid out a plan for me: after my graduation from the junior secondary school, I was to join the army. But our great leader instructed us that "The countryside is a vast expanse where one can flourish." Posters carrying this observation, which was interpreted as a command for people to go to the countryside, were on every corner: I could think of nothing but to answer the call of Chairman Mao. Without consulting my parents, I took our household registration booklet to the neighborhood committee and signed up secretly for rustication on Hainan Island. On 24 March, wearing a green military uniform and with a large red paper flower on my chest and a military bag on my shoulder, I followed a serviceman and embarked upon the long journey to the Guangzhou Army Production and Construction Corps on Hainan.

Soon after I arrived, a major joint campaign to open up the wilderness was launched. Camping in the hills, we set off before dawn with our sickles to open up the virgin jungle, felling young trees and hacking down bushes and creepers. At dusk, we returned to our camp with firewood for the cookhouse on our backs and singing a popular song about the life of a soldier: "As the red sun sets in the western mountains, we soldiers are returning to camp after target practice . . ."

Two or three months into the major joint campaign, the political instructor informed me that I had been reassigned to work at the regimental headquarters. I was dumbfounded, and would become an immediate object of envy among the *zhiqings* because the move would free me from daily physical labor in the open air.

The day I was to due to leave for my new post, the only vehicle in the company, an ox-cart, was dispatched to take me with my single piece of luggage to my new post. Along the winding and rough path to the foot of the hill were several rubber plantations cultivated by various companies of the regiment.

The regimental headquarters was housed in two one-story tiled houses which were said to have been occupied by Russian experts in the 1950s during their visits to help develop the local rubber plantations. The building at the eastern end housed the political division, the command office, the archive room, the duty room and a meeting room; the one at the western end housed the production division, the logistics office, a studio and telephone operation room, and a laboratory. Between the two buildings was a small piece of bare ground in the middle of which was area where assemblies were held and films screened. Behind the headquarters was a rubber plantation.

The telephone operators were members of the guard and messenger squad, managed by the command office. Apart from the operators, the squad was made up of the tall and bulky members of the regimental basketball team.

Arriving on the same day was another Yang. Since we were younger than most of the other *zhiqings* and *Yang* sounds like the Chinese word for a lamb, we were nicknamed the "two little lambs" of the regiment. We two little lambs worked in shifts to operate the telephone system day and night.

Conditions on the farm were really harsh. There were only two types of vehicle in the regiment: trucks for the transport squad, and a Beijing jeep in which the regimental commander and the political commissar made their inspections of the companies or traveled to meetings at the headquarters of the division or army corps. In each company, there was just one bicycle for the supply chief to use to make his frequent visits to the regimental headquarters or to procure fish, meat, and poultry from nearby villages and towns to improve the diet of the troops. All phone calls, internal or external, were connected by us. Telephones were at the heart of the regiment's daily operation. We were young, however, and didn't grasp the importance of our job: we were merely following instructions from a higher authority.

The switchboard consisted of thirty lines with twenty pairs of circuit cords. A code was allocated to each of the fifteen companies of the regiment as well as its construction squad, transport squad, animal husbandry squad, hospital, rubber factory, and school. With the help of a veteran worker and a *zhiqing* named Xiao Chen, we soon mastered all the codes. The most efficient way to communicate with the outside world was through the switchboard.

There was a cabled telephone in each company. The office where the phone was kept was some distance away from the nearest dormitory: when the phone rang, it was uncertain whether anyone would hear it and pick up. Whoever answered was responsible for getting the wanted person to the phone or taking a message. If the handset was not replaced properly, the phone wouldn't work and the company would be virtually isolated from the outside world.

The operation of the rotary dial switchboard was entirely manual. When we were on the night shift, what we feared most was a visit from Lao Hou from the production division. His job was to keep track of production and, my God, was he meticulous! With his frequent requests— "Xiao Yang, please get me Companies 1 to 15"— whoever was on duty would be obliged to make frantic efforts to contact all fifteen companies for him, with a request that its clerk or captain report the day's or month's production figures. It was nearly impossible to get an immediate connection with each company, and whenever we managed to get hold of anyone, we would turn to Lao Hou and yell: "We've got Company No. X on the line, please talk." At the end of each month, when daily and end-of-month figures had to be verified and double-checked, was particularly hectic. Not all the calls could be connected smoothly, and when situations got a bit frenzied, people on the other end of the line would respond with a classic quote from that much-watched film, *Lenin in 1918*: "Oh dear! All the young ladies have fainted."

One day in January 1974, with the army officers in the command office going in and out frequently, the atmosphere in the headquarters all of a sudden became extremely tense. A communication staff officer walked into our operations room and announced that, from then on, no work calls or private calls were allowed, and that we were to pick up the front-line reports from the division every fifteen minutes. After the announcement, he sat down and stayed with us. We later learned that the well-known Battle of the Paracel Islands[7] had begun. The army corps was charged both with opening up the wasteland and guarding the border zones. The war reports told us that to the north was the revisionist Soviet Union; to the east, Japan; to the southeast, the American imperialists and Vietnam. We were also reminded constantly that "Our enemies will never stop scheming to destroy us," giving us

---

7. A naval engagement which took place in January 1974 between China and South Vietnam near the Paracel Islands in the South China Sea, and which resulted in victory for China.

the impression that the Third World War was about to break out. Most of the *zhiqings* had their knapsacks packed and were ready to head to the battlefields as soon as the call came. Hainan Island is at the southernmost end of the country, so when fighting broke out in the Paracel Islands it became the front line.

Another unforgettable episode was the Great Tangshan Earthquakes, which claimed some two hundred and sixty thousand lives in July 1976. Following the disaster, more earthquakes were predicted and Hainan was put on the highest alert. During those days, everybody who lived in the tiled houses slept outdoors, and some would simply make a tent with a rope and a piece of plastic and suspend it between two rubber trees as their bedroom. We reported to work in a tent set up outside the operations room.

Located in the hills, the regiment, like the whole island, had a poor transport system. Those who wanted to visit the outside world would first have to come to regimental headquarters and then walk for an hour to the bus stop at Daxi Bridge to wait for a long-haul bus that stopped en route at Haikou City and other destinations. On their return from home leave, they would have to get off the bus at Daxi Bridge and walk for twenty minutes with their luggage to the nearest company, No. 1 Company, in order to call for help with their luggage on the rest of the journey. I was most energetic and efficient whenever I received requests to transfer calls from such people: with a heavy load on their backs, they deserved all the help they could get. I would keep dialling the rotary dial switchboard until the phone was picked up at the other end and the request for help passed on.

Broadcasting and telephones in the regiment shared the same cable, and on the switchboard there were separate lines for internal and external calls. To ensure that both lines were in good order, we two little lambs would be guarding the internal lines while the veteran worker and *zhiqing* Xiao Chen would maintain the external ones by making regular checks along the cable and, when necessary, cutting away with sickles the weeds or twigs that were entangled in it. To reflect the top priority of our lives, which was to sever any connections between ourselves and our class enemies, we named this maintenance work "cutting the line." Hainan Island is frequented by typhoons, and during the typhoon season they had to brave stormy weather to maintain the line. Sometimes, instead of taking a break after a night shift, we would follow them on their rescue efforts during the day.

The switchboard provided the only connection between the regiment and the outside world. No. 7 Company specialized in fruit production, and among the tropical fruits it produced were ivory mango, sunset mango, egg mango, avocado, and jackfruit. The Pearl River Studio even made a documentary film about it. During one mango season, I was asked to dial the division, then ask the division to dial for Haikou City, and then get a connection to Beijing: it was the first time I heard on the line "Haikou speaking," "Beijing speaking." Eventually I was able to hand the phone to the regimental commander. It transpired that all this effort was simply because No. 7 Company wished to send the fruit to Chairman Mao in Beijing. For a very long time, I remained exhilarated by the part I played in all this.

There was a famous oil painting, called "I Am a Seabird," produced during the Cultural Revolution by Pan Jiajun of the Guangzhou Army. It shows a female telephone operator salvaging telephone lines during a storm. It appealed to me as if it were an actual depiction of us at work.

DUTY BEFORE STARDOM

Lin Yuhua

In August 1971, after a stint in the Maoist propaganda troupe which had been touring the regiment, I was reassigned to work in No. 7 Company. Located at the foot of Changling Hill, it was previously known as the Changling Company until the Guangzhou Army Production and Construction Corps took control and turned the entire Daling Farm into No. 13 Regiment, No 4. Division.

One of the first things I realized was how great a variety of fruit it was producing. The company had propagated many species of tropical fruit such as mango and avocado, and every time I saw the beauty of the orchard, I wanted to have a photograph taken there! I dreamed of putting on my quasi-army uniform, of posing like a dashing soldier, and sending the photograph to my parents back home.

When I first learned about the opportunity to be rusticated on Hainan Island, my parents didn't want me to sign up. But I had heard that all the farms were under military control and that every *zhiqing* would be given a People's Liberation Army uniform and become a regimental soldier. Wasn't that a great honor? I pestered my parents and finally got my way. In summer 1972, my parents inquired in their letters if, after my two years' rustication on Hainan, I could at least send them a photograph of myself.

In a remote mountain village back in the early 1970s, it was no small feat to get a photograph taken. Among the two hundred or so *zhiqings* from my home region of Meixian, none, as far as I could tell, had a camera. Moreover, the regiment was without a single photo studio. To have a photograph taken, you had to go several hours by bus to the studio in the town of Nada in neighbouring Danxian, or the one in our own Baisha County. One day, I went with my best friend to have a photograph taken in the studio in Nada. With our army uniforms on, we posed for the camera as proud and dignified regimental soldiers. Since color photography was not yet available there, we asked the studio to apply green to our uniforms. When my parents saw their daughter in army uniform they were highly delighted.

In July 1972, some big news ran through the regiment: the Pearl River Studio was coming to No. 7 Company to shoot a documentary called *Great Fruits on Treasure Island*. At a time when it was such a luxury just to get one's photograph taken, it was incredible that someone was going to make a film about our orchard. It sounded like the most amazing thing ever. Everybody was excited and went about getting ready for the occasion: tidying up the locations, spring cleaning up the orchard, transporting mangoes, planting mango trees, and so on. To present the best possible image of the orchard, we even picked mangoes from trees which were outside the location and sewed them onto those within the frame of the camera. On the day of the shoot, I got up extremely early. After brushing my teeth and washing my face, I plaited my thick hair, unplaited it and plaited it again until I was fully happy with it. I put on a light purple shirt under my beloved army uniform. Since the only mirror I had was too small, I walked to the pool nearby and examined my reflection in the water to check if the colors of my shirt and uniform matched. I wanted to look my best for the camera. Who knows, I might be spotted by the director and featured in the film!

It was a fine and beautiful day, and everybody looked radiant. On the instructions of the producer, some shots were taken to show us picking, selecting, and transporting the mangoes. Then the director shouted for me to come to his side. He showed me how he wanted me to stand while picking the mangoes: the posture for a frontal shot, a profile shot, one with a basket in one hand while picking the mango with the other, and so on. I followed his instructions eagerly and earnestly and repeated the same actions and postures many times in front of the camera. The shooting took about two hours, and the frontal shot alone took more than half an hour. I was exhilarated: I felt like a star.

Several months later, *Great Fruits on Treasure Island* was released. It was March 1973 when it was shown in Meixian, and the premiere coincided with the date on which I was due to return to Hainan from my home visit. What should I do? If I could stay for just one more day at home, I could catch the film. But that would delay my return to Hainan. After some fierce debates with myself, I decided that I had to abide by the regiment's rule: I gave up the opportunity to attend the film's premiere in my hometown. After my return to Hainan, my mother wrote to tell me that our orchard looked splendid! She also revealed that there were many shots of me in the film. Though my mother always lived frugally, she paid to watch the film seven times and told everybody she met who could be bothered to listen to her, "My daughter Yuhua is in the film!" In the decades that followed, I never saw the film, which remained a great regret for me.

In 1996, more than forty ex-*zhiqing*s from Meixian paid a visit to

Daling Farm for its forty-second anniversary. A friend told me afterward: "What a pity you couldn't make it to the anniversary. In the exhibition room, there was a blow-up of you taken from the film *Great Fruits on Treasure Island!*" After so many years, it was indeed time for me to pay a visit to Daling. In March 2002, Sanya City hosted the world t'ai chi tournament. I signed up as an amateur practitioner of t'ai chi, and once again set foot on Hainan Island.

The date that the tournament finished coincided with the thirty-second anniversary of my rustication to Hainan. I rented a van and asked to be driven straight to Daling Farm from Sanya City. After a ride of more than three hours, I arrived at the farm just before noon. I was treated by the farm officials to a great meal. After lunch, the farm manager arranged for a jeep to show me round. I asked if I could perhaps be taken to the exhibition room first, but it so happened that the person in charge was on a business trip and nobody else had the keys! I was slightly disappointed, but once I caught sight of the familiar and beautiful orchard, I was elated and took as many photographs as I could. When I was talking to the old workers, I asked if they remembered me. "Of course," they said fondly, "You are the Meixian girl, the beautiful young woman in the *Great Fruits on Treasure Island!*" We all laughed heartily. I was grateful for that film: it helped me to be remembered not just by the old workers and ex-*zhiqings*, but in Daling itself.

In the nearly forty years since the film was made, what has served to fix the experience in my mind is a photograph taken by our political instructor. It's a shot of me picking mangoes, and right next to me is the Pearl River Studio cinematographer training the camera on me. Whenever I see this photograph, it transports me back to a time long ago.

I recently got a surprise which more than made up for all the regrets of forty years. Thanks to the efforts of some ex-*zhiqings*, Pearl River Studio offered us a free copy of the film! For the first time in four decades, I am able to look with my own eyes at the image of my youthful self.

Finding the Path

HOW I LEARNED TO LOVE PIGS
Wu Xianfang

I left school at sixteen and, together with my schoolmates, went to the Daling Farm to become a *zhiqing*. Starting in the production squad, I opened up the wilderness for the planting of rubber trees. After two years of such toil, I was transferred to the logistics squad, a surprise move considering that I was already a model worker. But my new job was regarded as the lowest and dirtiest of all the jobs on the farm. I was to raise pigs.

The change of environment couldn't have been more drastic: at the production squad, I'd had the companionship of the old hands and my fellow *zhiqings*, and no matter how hard it got, we chatted at work and remained cheerful throughout the day. On the pig farm, my only companion was one old hand, and a herd of lazy pigs that wanted nothing else but to eat and sleep all day. At first, it was hard. Secretly, I blamed the captain. I wondered why on earth it fell to me, among so many *zhiqings*, to raise pigs. At that age I could endure hardship and toil but not solitude and loneliness.

After a while, I found that pigs are in fact rather like humans. Whenever I entered the sty, they would shake their heads and wag their tails while scurrying around me, grunting. Their friendly nature made me increasingly fond of them. At the end of each month, when a pig had to be picked and slaughtered to improve the poor diet of the troop, I would be upset: after all, I had raised it from a piglet.

Located at the foot of a hill and about two kilometres away from the company, the old pig farm was right next to a field used for growing vegetables for the troop. On the hilltop opposite was a tiled-roof building, the company's primary school. Simple and crude, the farm was a row of five or six sties with low ceilings, each holding seven or eight pigs. Nearby was a stream, the only source of water for the farm and the vegetable field. Every morning, I would walk with the old hand to the company cookhouse, collect two big buckets of swill, carry them back to the pig farm, and empty them into a large iron wok for the preparation of feed. Although there were only a few dozen pigs, it took some effort to raise and look after them properly.

Before I joined, there was just one keeper on the pig farm. We *zhiqings* tended to call these farm workers "old workers," though in reality, they were young or at most middle-aged. This "old worker," my boss, was a woman in her thirties who was married with four children. A life of manual labor in the open air had aged her prematurely. She was short, probably just one and a half meters tall, and her wide face was marked by wrinkles and her hands by calluses. Naturally quiet and reticent, she was inclined to set an example by her actions and to teach me through her body language. An expert and an old hand at raising pigs, she was efficient, neat, conscientious, and attentive to details. After work, she looked after me like a mother. The diet in the company was poor, and at an age when we *zhiqings* were growing fast, we badly needed nourishment. Yet food was scarce, and with our low pay, life was tough. Despite the hardship and with a big family to support, my boss would invite several of us to her home for a special treat whenever she cooked dishes like chicken, pork, or anything that in those days was hard to come by. Kindhearted, simple, hardworking and meticulous, she looked as insignificant as gravel on the ground. To me, she was honest and admirable. A good teacher and helpful friend, she was also my role model. She passed on all her techniques and experience, but more significantly, I discovered in her a simple grace and goodness, an assiduity and dedication to work. She was not only my boss, but, at a crucial stage of my life, my mentor.

Finding the Path

We adhered to the traditional method of pig-feeding, chopping up sweet potato leaves, sweet potato, cassava and rice bran, adding them to the swill and cooking them until they turned to mash. Pigs have a large appetite: the wok measured two meters in diameter, and a full wok of feed would only provide one meal. Keeping up with what they needed for their daily three meals required several trips to the vegetable field for the sweet potato, cassava, and green shoots. After several years on the pig farm, my shoulders grew strong and I could easily walk briskly while carrying a load of fifty kilograms on a shoulder pole. As the stock of pigs grew and the demand for food became much greater, we were allocated an ox-cart to help transport the feed. One day, as I was about to descend a slope on the cart, a sudden explosion from the hills startled the ox and it galloped wildly down the slope. I tried to restrain it, but the normally placid beast went berserk on the rough track, putting our lives in imminent danger. All I could do was hold tight to the halter, and it was not until we reached a flatter track that it began to slow down. It was a lucky escape.

My first home leave came after more than two years toiling on the farm. With my father still in the "cadre school" to undergo enforced manual labor and "study sessions" and my elder brother also rusticated, only my paternal grandmother, my mother, and my younger sister remained at home in Guangzhou. After a few days with my family, I paid a visit to my brother, who was rusticated to nearby Wanqingsha in Panyu. Rich in fish and rice, Wanqingsha was a land of rivers and streams, and boats were its main means of transport.

The farm there was different from those I was familiar with on Hainan Island, and I found everything novel and fascinating. Thanks to my occupation, I was particularly interested in the local breed of pigs kept by the peasants. Small and fat, their round buttocks and stomachs almost reaching the ground, they had short hair and black and white spots on their bodies. The breed on my farm was big and white. From conversations with the locals, I learned that their breed has some good and distinctive genes. Although their build is not large, they are heavy, with tender and delicious meat, and, besides, they do not have the strange odor of the big white pigs of Hainan. Furthermore, unlike the big white pigs, they are hardy and acclimatize well. It struck me that if we could cross the two breeds, we might create a fine hybrid. I visited all the local peasants and eventually found some newborns. Plump, well proportioned and healthy, they looked adorable. I chose a black and white male: with black spots amid the white hair, it was cute. When I explained my intention, the keepers, with great generosity and enthusiasm, offered it to me free of charge. They even taught me how to feed it. After my return home to Guangzhou, I fed it with milk powder, a luxury we could barely afford for ourselves. I even asked my mother to try her best to buy milk powder for me to take back to the farm.

The pig was an instant favorite at the farm. Because it was so tiny, I kept it in my dormitory. After my milk powder ran out, I went to the regimental shop to buy condensed milk for it until it learned to eat rice and fodder. I am not sure why—perhaps it was the way I kept it or perhaps it was pampered—but it didn't acclimatize and soon died. My plan for crossbreeding was aborted.

When I first started as a keeper, I thought raising pigs was easy: all that was needed was to keep the sty clean and feed them. This wasn't true at all: it took a lot of knowledge and experience to do the job well. There was a turning point in my attitude toward the matter. After lunch one day, I found that something was not quite right at the farm: it was deadly quiet. I sprinted to the nearest sty and was frightened by what I saw. The pigs had all collapsed, covered in their own vomit. I checked the whole farm and found the same scene everywhere. When I consulted my boss, she said that the cause could well be cassava poisoning. With composure, she told me that water spinach and wild amaranth were the cure. I ran to the vegetable field and collected two big bucketsful, rinsed and chopped them, then squeezed out their juice. We then fed it to the pigs, one by one, with a sharp-pointed bamboo. It took the two of us a whole afternoon before we were done and the pig-sties cleaned. After a while, some of them started to stand up and walk to the trough for water. My boss commented that this meant they were on the mend, and it was only then that I could calm down and relax a bit.

Finding the Path

I learned from the incident that in order to do my job well, I must learn how to treat sickly pigs. I decided to devote myself to it and started by learning from my boss how to identify the common medicinal plants. I also accompanied our assistant nurse in collecting medicinal plants from the hills, learning about their healing properties and uses. I asked my mother to send me books on Chinese medicinal herbs, veterinary science and pharmacology, which I devoured at night. I also learned by practice, and I picked things up fast. I was later sent to study veterinary science in the regimental headquarters and on other farms, and after several years of study and practice, I gradually picked up the skills of treating pigs, such as vaccination, the collection of medicinal plants, castration, artificial insemination, selective breeding, and the delivery of piglets—and I became a vet. Vaccinating a pig should not be conducted as gently as treating a human, but instead must be done in a swift manner with the needle injected firmly and accurately into the back of the ear. My interest in veterinary medicine, though prompted by the sheer necessity of my job, was rooted in a childhood ambition to become a doctor. The Cultural Revolution disrupted my formal education, but strangely enough, it also became the making of me and turned me into a vet on the farm.

The pig farm eventually became too small for the increasing stock and a new one was built. There was a stream at the foot of the hill near the troop headquarters. The water was clear, and on the far bank was a flat piece of land. This was where the new pig farm was constructed.

One morning, we carried the swill to the bank in rain. After two days of thunderous downpour, the tranquil and clear stream turned strange: a swift current was formed upstream, and the flood spread across several dozen meters, at least twice its usual width. When we waded through it with the swill, the water was waist-deep. My boss observed that if the wet weather continued, it would soon become impossible to carry the swill across to the farm, and the pigs would starve. We decided then and there to carry over as much swill as possible while we could still wade through the swollen flood. We returned to the vegetable field and carried loads of sweet potato, cassava, and rich bran across the river to the pig farm. For most of the day we were so thoroughly wet that the unwholesome effect of feculent water on female hygiene never crossed my mind. Nor did it once occur to us that the rising water level posed an imminent danger.

By the time we had stocked up a good supply of food and got the pigs fed and the pig-sties cleaned, it was already dusk. When we were ready to make our way back to the company on the far bank, the water had already risen considerably. As we lifted the buckets and waded hand-in-hand to the middle of the river, the water was chest-deep. There the current was swift, with big rocks underfoot and whirlpools forming beneath the surface. Just as I felt that I could not stand firmly on the riverbed and struggled to stay upright, I slipped, lost my balance, and was swept along by the rapids. I tried to swim ashore but was unable to catch hold of the weeds growing along the edge until I was washed tens of meters downstream. Exhausted by the time I dragged myself on to the bank, I collapsed, shivering with cold.

In May 1991 when I was visiting Guangzhou Cultural Park for the *Photographic Exhibition of Guangdong Zhiqings on Hainan—An Historical Witness of Ordinary Life*, I spotted an old photograph of a *zhiqing* grave. The caption said that after a record flash flood, the likes of which had not been seen for several decades, the pig farm on low-lying land had been swamped and the young *zhiqings* who were working there had been drowned in the flood.

The picture reminded me acutely of my similar experience. I felt immensely sad for the loss of their lives and realized once again what a narrow escape I had had.

FINDING THE PATH

Chen Guanli

In the journey of life, some people we meet make a profound difference to the route we take: they might be a friend, a relative, a mere acquaintance or a colleague. Their impact can be so great that it affects our thoughts, perceptions, ideology and values; and it can also be so intangible as to shape us at a subconscious level.

During the political upheavals of the 1960s, I was deprived of parental love and guidance in my childhood even before my schooling was brought to an abrupt end by the Cultural Revolution. Despondent, I could, however, resemble many of my contemporaries in giving a politically correct answer if asked what my aspiration was: to sign up for the "Up to the Mountains, Down to the Countryside" campaign and become a member of the "elite" group, the workers and peasants. The unspoken truth was that my father, a teacher, had been denounced as a rightist in 1957 and thrown into a political prison. During the Cultural Revolution, my mother, who was also a teacher, was implicated in his "crime" and detained by her school. Deprived of any source of income, I could fend for myself only by signing up for rustication. Before I turned sixteen, my mother had urged me: "Whatever happens, son, stay alive."

Life as a *zhiqing* on Hainan Island gave me a fresh start. Soon, however, during the endless major joint campaigns to open up the wilderness, we were forced into heavy manual labor. But the backbreaking physical challenge wasn't the hardest part. In the spring of 1970, a new political drive was launched across the country to prosecute and eliminate the "active counterrevolutionaries," many of them intellectuals who just by wanting to make their voices heard found themselves, fatally, on the "wrong" side. As a *zhiqing* whose family members were denounced as counterrevolutionaries, I was coerced into making incessant confessions about their "problems" and my own. I was forced to inform and conform. The letters from my mother kept bringing me nothing but devastating news: "your father has died in prison"; "your elder brother has passed away in prison, please stop writing to him"; "your sisters have also been implicated and have passed away . . ." Every single letter from my mother filled me with apprehension: when I opened it, my hands would be shaking. While the other *zhiqings* eagerly awaited the letters from home for the news and comfort that their dear ones sent, mine brought overwhelming sadness. The last thing I wanted to hear from anyone was "You have mail." And every time there was a visit from a regimental official who would help to bring over the letters, I would be consumed by fear. I prayed that there would be no letter for me. Those were the darkest hours of my life.

The exact time escapes me, but at some point our company began to build tiled houses as dormitories, and I was assigned to work in the squad that made bricks and tiles. Our squad leader was middle-aged, an old hand from Lianjiang called Liu Qiqun. When young and without his deep tan or mustache, he must have been a handsome man: we all called him by his nickname, "Elder Brother Si." Once I got to know him, I found him easygoing and always ready to give us a helping hand. He was like family to us. And unlike many of the veterans, he was literate and highly articulate. With a good sense of humor, he helped us to forget for a short while the toil and hardship we were enduring. He seemed to know how to lift our spirits. On top of that, he knew by heart many traditional Chinese classics such as *The Romance of the Three Kingdoms* and *The Water Margin*, and he was a consummate storyteller. Every time he finished a story, he would quip, "Please don't forget that this is all feudal, capitalist, and revisionist stuff. You should criticize it and get your brains disinfected." Sometimes, when we were really tired at work and wanted to take a break, we would beg him for a story, and if he didn't comply, we would warn him that we were going to report him for spreading feudalism, capitalism, and revisionism. That usually did the trick and he would give in, though not without first calling us a gang of infernal rascals.

One year, some of the cassavas and sweet potatoes that we had planted in the woods were devoured by wild boars. I was assigned to join Elder Brother Si to patrol the fields and keep the boars at bay. We were on duty from eight at night until dawn the next day. Our job was simple: every now and then, we walked through the woods, struck cymbals, set off some fireworks, and yelled a little so that the racket would scare the boars off. We also deterred them by lighting fires around the fields. We built a shed at the east end and another at the west as our shelters, and occasionally we would get together for a chat. During one of these, he suddenly observed: "You seem to have a lot on your mind." I confirmed that that was indeed the case. He looked concerned but said nothing. He seemed like someone I could trust so I said: "Now that we're on our own, I don't mind telling you the truth. But please keep this absolutely to yourself." He nodded his head, and I began to confide to him the details of what had happened for well over a decade to my family during the various political campaigns. Finally, I revealed that before I was rusticated, I had regularly endured canings and beatings because of my family. Now that I was forced to make constant confessions about my family and myself, I was no longer sure that I would be able to get through it all. He was silent for a long while. Then he said: "I really don't know what to say. You don't deserve this. Whatever happens, your mother is still alive and you must stay alive, too. There is bound to be a way for everyone. Trust me."

From then on, he was even more considerate to me and kept an eye on me at work. He also kept his word not to reveal my secret.

I have taken his advice to heart, advice which I believe has subconsciously helped me to go through hell and back. In the three decades since I left Daling, I have lost touch with him. His voice, smiles and other facial expressions, however, have stayed as vivid as ever in my mind. I remain grateful to the person who helped me to get through it all.

May heaven bless him!

MY INSPIRATION

Hou Jingjie, noted down by Liang Yongkang

Rustication was a life-changing event. Among my peers, some had set out for Hainan Island with revolutionary fervor, some only grudgingly. At the age of just fifteen, I signed up owing to an instinct for survival.

My father died of a cerebral haemorrhage when I turned nine. Four years later, it also struck my mother, paralyzing her and leaving her incapable of taking care of herself: our family lost its only source of income. With the pocket money I got from my father before he passed away, I bought several dozen children's picture books and became a street vendor, displaying my wares on the ground. By 1965, I had over a hundred books and drew a rather handsome income of eight *jiao* per day. However, soon after the Cultural Revolution broke out in 1966, such books were denounced as "feudal, capitalist and revisionist" and I was deprived of the sole means of supporting my family. At the age of thirteen, after my primary schooling, I therefore became a casual unskilled laborer. Later, I followed my eldest brother and became a porter, vying with the grown-ups for whatever heavy work came our way in that sleepy town of ours. After more than ten hours of back-breaking lifting and shifting each day, I could buy food with the several *jiao* of wages I had earned and even contribute to keeping the family afloat.

We were living at the bottom of society, yet I was easy about it: I couldn't see any other way for an unqualified teenager to get on the social ladder. I also became aware of the importance of hard work.

When the frenzied "Up to the Mountains, Down to the Country-side" campaign swept Meixian, I learned that the Guangzhou Army Production and Construction Corps offered a salary and rationed food. I signed up without hesitation. Yes, I had heard that life on the island was harsh and that the work was punishing, but to me it seemed so much better than fending for myself in my home town as a child laborer.

In No. 9 Company, I suddenly found myself living under the same thatched roof as many *zhiqings* from the big cities, an unusual experience that gave me warmth and relieved the loneliness I had felt as a child laborer back home. At only fifteen, I was well looked after not only by my fellow *zhiqings* who were older, but by the veterans. I got on particularly well with our squad leader, Jia Hongji. A former student of the elite Guangya Secondary School in Guangzhou, he was from an intellectual family and had been rusticated for two years before my arrival. Despite his privileged upbringing, he was upright, humble, always ready to help, and extremely hard-working. He was a living Lei Feng, our role model, and indeed, in today's terminology, the "idol" of our troops. His exceptional work ethic made a natural bond between us. Our great leader, Chairman Mao, had called on us "to become noble-minded and pure, men of moral integrity and above vulgar interests, men who are of value to the people." With that as our benchmark, we helped each other to live through the tough challenges of Hainan Island. For someone like me, who had lost my parents in my formative years and was barely educated, the exposure to the educated youth of the major cities, and in particular my friendship with Jia, turned out to be the best thing that could have happened. And indeed, years later, when I set up my own business, I would recall what I had learned from him—the plain truth that "there is no gain without pain." It remains the motto of my life.

Together with another *zhiqing* from Guangzhou and two female *zhiqings* from Chaozhou, Jia and I were assigned to grow vegetables for the whole troop. Though none of us had relevant experience, we were undeterred. Following the advice of the old hands, we developed three plots along the Daxi River. On the plot right next to the river, we planted green-leaf vegetables that demand intensive care; next to it were gourds and beans, and farther away were those slower growing vegetables that keep well, such as Chinese cabbage. With hard work, we learned that as long as we knew the soil conditions and planted accordingly, we could almost meet the daily demands of our canteen.

Unbeknown to us, we were fighting on many fronts, and in those lean years and harsh conditions, physical labor was not the only demand that was made of us. In one year, for example, we found that after a typhoon had battered us, the rudimentary embankment we had built had been damaged by floods from the upper stream, ruining the vegetable field and most of our crop. To get vegetables back on the table, we swiftly repaired the embankment. Our initiative and hard work paid off. Indeed, we had such success with our vegetable field that we were able to share our experience with other vegetable squads in the regiment. We took pride in our work and our hard won reputation.

Whenever possible we made pickles with the extra yields. During the wet season, when nothing grew in the field, pickles were our staple, and those with a larger stock of them would have to help out the troops who were less prepared. One year we found that although a good amount of juicy and crunchy stock had been preserved in the good old-fashioned clay jars, we were being served with drier ones which had been stored in the new and hastily made cement pots. Perplexed, we confronted our supply chief. To our surprise, he revealed conspiratorially that since the juicy pickles were heavier, they could fetch four more *fen* per kilo. We were thus deprived of the superior pickles when our taste buds needed them most!

One year, to make the supply less monotonous, we decided to grow tomatoes. When we asked around, however, we found that none of the vegetable squads in the regiment were growing them. Why? Because the local kids would have picked and eaten them long before they were ripe! As a precaution, we gathered the kids together and told them that if they helped to guard our crop, they could have as much of the first harvest as they wanted! We also made the most unruly boy, the son of our deputy captain, the chief of the "police force." Guess what? Our strategy worked!

Later on, when for health reasons our political instructor was moved to the regimental school, I was also moved there to grow vegetables for the teachers and pupils. There must have been several hundred of them, and the demand for three meals a day posed a new challenge to me. Armed with my experience from the company vegetable squad, I laid out a plan to make effective use of each plot, set about improving the soil conditions, and put in more work than ever. Soon, however, I became aware of an unexpected threat. Although the local Li were inexperienced in tending their fields, they liked the taste of our vegetables and took to pilfering them. They would also let their livestock stray into our field. While a film was being shown at regimental headquarters, for instance, some of them would disappear from the open-air cinema and sneak into the field to help themselves to our crops. Together with the school authorities, I enlisted the village chiefs in a campaign against such practices. In addition, we would also guard the field during the movie nights to stop the pilfering. It was, however, important to maintain good relations with the Li: we had to remain gentle in our approach and sometimes just look the other way.

Finding the Path

Our ancestors say "Those who defeat others are competitive, but those who conquer themselves stand strong." My job to supply the school canteen taught me one important lesson. The school's latrine was a valuable source of manure. Between the vegetable field and the latrine was the school playground, which in the evening was always teeming with energetic students. When we made a detour through the school with the manure on our shoulders, some boys would grimace and call us "stinky," which resulted in much laughter at our expense. It was demeaning, and I became despondent for a while. But when I asked myself what made the vegetables tasty and put a smile on everybody's face, I recovered my self-esteem. And I even took pride in being nicknamed the "huge manure bucket" because of the size of the bucket I carried at least twice a day. I defeated my inner enemy and gained respect through my dedication.

I became a role model in the regiment. In those days, the award came in the form of an enamel mug, and I must have been given at least seven or eight of them over the years. By a popular vote of the school, my salary was also raised by one point, an honour conferred on only three percent of the troops.

I considered my rusticated years uneventful. Huang Ronger has reminded me of an incident in which I pulled him out of a well we were digging just seconds before an explosion. I can see the risk I ran. But life was dirt cheap, and at that critical moment I certainly didn't take mine too seriously. Indeed, I soon forgot about the incident, but Huang remembers it vividly.[8]

I stayed on the farm for nine years, during which time I began as a teenager who had signed up to be rusticated for a livelihood and ended as a young adult with a strong work ethic. I had never dreamed that I would achieve anything significant: all I did was throw myself into my everyday duties. Honors and reward came as a consequence, but they were never a goal. In retrospect, I see that the experience helped to shape my character. I learned from those nine years that as long as you make a proper effort, it will be recognised no matter how humble your

8.   See Huang's piece *My Lucky Escapes*, p. 287.

roots or your role. In the several decades of running my own business, that ethic has shaped me. I remain grateful to my fellow *zhiqings* for what they taught me during that time. They are a perennial source of inspiration.

JOURNEY OF A BAREFOOT DOCTOR
Wang Guangzhen

December 10, 1968: that was the day I was rusticated to Daling in Baisha County, Hainan Island. The company I was assigned to, Changling Company, managed an all-season orchard with fruits such as mango, jackfruit, orange, avocado, longan and rambutan: of the ninety-three varieties of mango produced internationally, twenty-three of them were being grown in our orchard.

Five months into my *zhiqing* life, our political instructor informed me that I had been selected by the regiment to attend a three-month medical training program at Baisha County People's Hospital: on its completion, I would return to serve the troops. In the catchphrase of the day, he urged me to "treat this training opportunity as a political task."

To be honest, I wasn't enthused and would have been delighted if I had been assigned to teach. As I understood it, our re-education as *zhiqings* was to last for no more than three to five years, after which we would be sent home. To become a barefoot doctor implied that I would be "rooted" on the farm for the rest of my life! However, since it was a "political task" and also a decision which came from regimental headquarters, my immediate response was: "I must try my very best to do it." That promise has kept me in the medical profession ever since.

Learning-by-practice
Six *zhiqings* from other companies joined me for the basic training program.

We started by working in the wards: taking temperatures, feeling pulses, measuring breath and taking blood pressure, followed by learning to inject in both muscles and veins. For the diagnosis of diseases, we learned from actual cases about symptoms and examinations, diagnosis, and determining treatment. Two weeks later, we were tasked with keeping a record of the four main functions of the body of in-patients, and whether there were any symptoms of inflammation: reddening, swelling, high temperature, pains, or organ malfunction.

My most memorable experience was of the operating theater. For the sake of the patients, protocol had to be strictly adhered to in order to keep all the instruments sterile and the theater staff scrupulously disinfected. In following the protocol we were rather clumsy at first. As interns, the first operation we took part in was an appendectomy. A forty-five minute procedure, it involved administering anaesthesia, marking the excision point, disinfection, incision, reconnection, excision, reduction, ligation, suturing, and applying a sterile bandage. Despite the surgical masks that we wore, the odor of blood was so pungent and lingering that after the operation we were unable to eat.

Conditions in the operating theater were extremely poor: under the broiling, unshaded lamps was the operating table, and next to it a feeble electric floor fan. In the warm summer, medical staff were obliged, as usual, to put on full surgical attire—cap, mask and gloves, with eyes being the only part that was uncovered. In such conditions, the surgeons would perspire profusely and have to rely on the nurses to wipe away their sweat. Sometimes operations followed one after the other, and they would have to count on the nurses to feed them with buns and water to keep their energy levels up. Over the years the strain took its toll on them—our training surgeon, for example, developed gastric disease. He never gave us any homework: instead he shared with us his experiences as a medical student. He told us that before their first operation, he and his fellow interns would compete to see who could make the longest ligation. The story inspired us to find some thread so that we could practice our ligation skills. Before injecting the patients, we would use water to practice on ourselves how to insert the needle, release the medicine into the body, and remove the needle.

Soon we were allowed to work as surgical assistants. My task was to open up the excision to allow the surgeon a good view of the infected tissue or organ, reconnect some minor blood tissues, resect the diseased tissues or organ, then ligate and apply a sterile bandage. The main purpose of my involvement was to help speed up the procedure: I strictly followed the surgeon's instructions.

Starting from scratch, with no medical training whatsoever, we were all most grateful to the doctors and nurses for the friendship, tolerance, and love they gave us. It was through them that we picked up the basics of medicine. They inspired us with their professional dedication.

Blood was in extremely short supply, and we usually had to call on servicemen, officials, and paramedics for donations. One day, after we had performed an appendectomy and repaired a hernia, an emergency patient was rushed into the hospital. He had fallen from an ox-cart overloaded with sugar cane and its wooden wheels had run over his stomach: his life was in imminent danger. After immediate tests, one of us, He Ning, was found to match his blood type. She donated 200cc of blood and was "paid" in kind with a glass of fresh milk. It was not until the training program was over and we had all returned to our companies that we learned from her close friends that she had been in poor health, and that after the donation she had fallen ill. Two hundred cc of blood may not sound like much today, but those were lean years, when the best dish on our canteen tables was lettuce. During the Cultural Revolution nearly everybody suffered from malnutrition.

The three-month training program at Baisha Country People's Hospital didn't turn us into qualified doctors. By seeing how our efforts contributed to the well-being of the public, we had, however, grown to love the profession.

Chinese herbal medicines

The hills in Daling were overgrown with medicinal herbs. Led by a barefoot doctor, an experienced practitioner of traditional Chinese medicine, we trekked the jungles and valleys to search for, gather, and process many materials and applied them to the patients—with satisfactory results.

Some of these medicinal expeditions were rather dangerous, and could even be life-threatening. One effective painkiller is the "price-less," a vine-like plant whose stem tuber, the medicinal part, looks like an over-large sweet potato and which can weigh more than five kilos. It grows only on precipices. The doctor who was our mentor and guide was a graduate of a normal school in Haikou City, and had volunteered to settle in the mountainous Miao ethnic minority areas to help develop education. He had put down roots there by marrying and starting a family with a Miao woman. After more than ten years, it was said that many of the local cadres were his former students: his words were highly prized.

Using sickles to hack our way through the jungle, we trekked for nearly two hours before we caught sight of some stem tubers of the "priceless" on a precipice. In the sunshine, their oval leaves looked intensely green. Their spectacular appearance was vividly captured hundreds of years ago by a renowned Qing dynasty painter, Zheng Banqiao, in his poem about rocks and bamboo: "Clinging to the green cliff, you root deep into rugged precipices / tempered by rough conditions, you brave the winds of every season." We were overjoyed by our discovery. From then on, we were mostly treading on sharp and jagged rocks that threatened to penetrate our worn-out shoes. The track was so treacherous that we could easily have slipped off the precipice. When we reached a "priceless," we first made sure we were on firm ground before we reached out to pull its vine and the stem tubers. Sometimes we had to suspend ourselves in mid-air by tying our wrist with one end of a rope and fixing the other end to the foot of a tree, like creating a special-effects shot for a film. When we eventually returned to our base with baskets of "priceless," we encountered a rather unorthodox method of catching fish that was employed by the local fishermen. They first cast a net across the downstream part of a river and then stirred the upstream water with sticks and suchlike to drive the fish down into the net. That day, the boisterous activity and the fishermen's delight with their harvest were the best reward for our aching bodies.

I received much support and encouragement from my fellow *zhiqings* in furthering my study of traditional Chinese medicine. Some shared with me their own experience of the prevention and treatment of the discomforts and ailments commonly suffered in the jungle. A former classmate of mine even invented a transmitter-like appliance which used electrotherapy to help relieve the occupational aches and pains of the farm workers. It is a shame that the appliance didn't survive—it would have merited a place in a *zhiqing* museum.

A long journey

Upon my return to my company, I worked as a trainee of Lao Deng, a senior assistant nurse. A veteran, he had worked in the company for more than ten years and had gathered a fair amount of experience.

During one of the major joint campaigns, the wife of our captain fell sick and suffered seizures during which she screamed madly and then became paralyzed. Inexperienced and at my wits' end, I could only ask several stout *zhiqings* to help me carry her all the way down to the dormitory at the foot of the hill. Lao Deng applied acupuncture immediately and she made a quick recovery. This triggered gossip that she had faked her illness in order to avoid the extreme hard labor which typified a major joint campaign. Some even took her "abnormal" behavior as a new form of class struggle. Judging by the pain she seemed to suffer at the onset of the seizure, I didn't think that she had faked it, but neither could I make sense of what was happening. During the regular sessions in which we were expected to "recall the sorrows of the past and savor the joys of the present," our captain had recounted his life as a beggar during the bad old days. He also encouraged us to sample the extremely poor diet that the Red Army and the lower classes had endured before the Liberation of 1949. Our captain had had his fill of sufferings in that vicious society, yet now it was being suggested that his wife had degenerated into a "capitalist." I was certain that it wasn't true.

With these skeptical thoughts, I consulted my cousin in Guangxi who was a qualified doctor. She wrote back and revealed that what the captain's wife had suffered was an hysteria triggered by certain circumstances or stimulants. During a seizure, the patient would scream violently and then claim that some part of her body was in pain. The best treatment for it is a form of suggestive therapy that the patient can readily accept. Before treatment, the doctor must establish a relationship of trust by talking to the patient in a persuasive yet authoritative manner: the administration of a sedative also helps. Following this correspondence, my cousin sent me many medical books to widen my perspective and strengthen my medical knowledge.

Becoming a barefoot doctor

I didn't become an assistant nurse (the same as a barefoot doctor if one worked in a regimental hospital) and work on my own until I was reassigned to the newly established No. 13 Company at the foot of the Baishi Hills. By then, it was nearly a year since my medical training had begun. The clinic there was poorly equipped, and soon after my arrival, I got a carpenter to make a Chinese medicine cabinet which was large enough to hold more than a hundred herbs. Every day after work, my fellow *zhiqings* would bring in the common medicinal materials they had gathered during the day. Gradually I built up a good stock. I did it both by collecting and processing the raw materials from the hills and by digging up a piece of land by the river to grow some herbs myself. Every morning, we would boil a large wok of herbal tea and pour it into the military water bottles so that the *zhiqings* could drink it at work. Since it was made from fresh ingredients, the smell was heavenly. To prevent and treat common ailments early, we got everybody involved in a mass campaign to raise the awareness of hygiene, health and well-being in the company. Apart from acute diseases such as malaria, fever, and stomachache, which were treated with Western medicines and techniques, most of the common illnesses were treated with acupuncture, moxibustion, or Chinese medicine. Our efforts paid off, and by my third year in charge, the clinic was awarded a red flag by the division for its role in raising the company's standards of hygiene and public health.

As my responsibilities increased and the pressure of work built up, I became more attached to Baishi Hill. After work, I would trek the hills and play with the wild animals such as monkeys and muntjacs. Monkeys are not just funny but highly intelligent. Whenever a sentinel monkey spotted a rifle, it would signal to the rest and they would vanish into the hills without trace. But if you were only carrying a shoulder pole, they would stay put in their favorite haunt, the big banyan tree, no matter how close you got. Sometimes they would even tease you by brushing you with branches from the top of the tree. At the foot of one hill there was a clear pool. In the evening, some of the muntjacs would come by and drink from it. As if they hated being overlooked, they would utter a clear and melodious bell-like sound which echoed through the hills. The landscape of the tropical jungle valley is exhilaratingly beautiful. I just adored it. If it were not for my father's insistence on adhering to family tradition, I would have named my son Shanqing ("green hill") and my daughter Shuixiu ("clear water"). In vain, I had to leave these beautiful names where they belong: with the hills that I love wholeheartedly.

In the twenty or so years since the *zhiqing* chapter of my life ended, I have visited the Baishi Hills six times. Though the circumstances are completely different, the scenery remains just as serene and beautiful. I always revel in its lush green foliage and the intoxicating scents of betel nut blossoms carried on the breeze. It has become my second home.

AN OLD CODGER AND SOME YOUNG PEARLS

Chen Yanhua, Dong Zhennan, Zheng Xiuhua, Deng Jingxi

Formerly known as the Nada Propagation Center of the South China Institute of Tropical Crops, Daling State Farm had since 1954 been conducting experiments to produce high and stable yields of rubber and to propagate species that would resist viruses and typhoons. From the beginning of our rustication in November 1968, we educated young people were naturally drawn to the project, and in our own company alone, No. 2 Company, there was a popular team called "the rubber propagation experimental group."

The team's first task was to breed two types of bacteria, one to be used as an antibiotic fertilizer, and the other as a rubber hormone to stimulate growth. Since this required an environment which was free of other bacteria, we first had to build a thatched laboratory out of grasses and mud, about twenty square meters in size. We then built a bacteria-free chamber by using needles and thread to sew together pieces of plastic film. For benches, containers, frames and supports, we turned to the carpenters in our company. With the addition of scales, tubes, beakers, flasks and a big wok for disinfection, our crude and simple lab was assembled—no small feat given our poor resources and, not least, the fact that those who built it could do so only in their free time.

The disinfectants that were available at that time were rather harmful: prolonged exposure to their foul and lingering smells could result in damage to the liver and lungs, not to mention their immediate impact on eyes, head, and respiratory tract. Yet there were no precautions: we seldom had the luxury of waiting until the heating agents had evaporated before we could enter the bacteria-free chamber. This was mainly because no one in the team was exempt from toiling in the plantations or on any of the major joint campaigns. In other words, our involvement in the project was in addition to our run-of-the-mill jobs as farm workers. Not that any of us ever uttered the slightest complaint. You see, one of the pet phrases of our formative years was: "Tough or not, look back to the twenty-five thousand *li* of the Long March: tired or not, remember what our revolutionary forbears have been through."

One person was an exemplar to us budding rubber specialists: "Hu Laotou," or "Hu the Old Codger," an honest and simple scientist demoted to our team from the South China Institute of Tropical Crops. Cheerful and with a strong Hubei accent, he was comical in appearance. After slaving away in the plantations alongside us youngsters, he would pass on to us his encyclopedic knowledge of rubber. Rubber was crucial to national defense, especially at a time when an embargo had been imposed on China. Not a natural habitat for rubber, Hainan Island is the one place in China that comes closest to it. Rubber trees had been grown from seeds or seedlings which had been brought back by overseas Chinese, but which were now becoming exhausted and providing an ever decreasing yield. To cut our heavy reliance on imports, we needed to propagate species which would resist viruses and give high and stable yields. However, discovering whether a newly propagated species was any good took three consecutive crops and a minimum of twenty years—a long period of continuous trials and tests without guaranteed results. It was no secret that those who were involved in propagating a new species might never live to know whether their labor of love had succeeded. Despite the frustrations and daunting challenges ahead, Hu the Old Codger seemed optimistic about China's future in rubber development, something that was most encouraging and inspiring to us youngsters. From him, we learned that stamina was essential in a project of such scale and strategic importance. And soon, on instructions from headquarters, we also got involved in propagating new species under the guidance of Hu the Old Codger and some other old hands.

As well as working on propagation and experiments with bacteria, vaccines and new species, we collected first-hand data for pest control on behalf of regimental headquarters and the South China Institute of Tropical Crops. Adjusting the theories we were given to various localities, we also devised practical ways of preventing pests and containing their spread. This sometimes required us to spray lime sulphur on trees which had been infected by a powdery mildew. We had to perform the process at night, using a mechanical device which we carried on our backs and which weighed several dozen kilos. We lacked any protective masks or clothing, and after spraying the woodlands we would be covered in white powder and begin to resemble Santa Claus. The crude device made deafening noises, and since we had no earplugs they would still be reverberating in our heads long after the night shift had ended. These, together with the lingering smell of lime sulphur on our bodies, would keep us tense and wakeful for a good few hours, exhausted though we were.

Although Hainan Island has a tropical climate, there are wintry spells when just before sunrise the temperature hovers between two and five degrees Celsius. Seedlings and young plants are then vulnerable to frostbite, and temperatures in the propagation centers had to be closely monitored. Once the temperature dropped below five degrees, we set fire to the slightly dampened firewood and straw which were scattered around the vulnerable areas and thus raised some air-warming smoke. Despite this precaution, there were times when we needed to "rinse the stems" before dawn in order to prevent the seedlings from being damaged by melting frost as the sun rose. To do this, we would brave the chilly weather by collecting buckets of water from the river, carrying them on shoulder poles to those places where the air was stagnant from high condensation, and wetting the lower part of the stems of the young plants. A full bucket of water could only rinse seven to eight plants, and it therefore took at least two hours for the troops to treat all those that were at risk. During such emergencies, we barely had time to put on our shoes before dashing out with buckets and poles, and those who did would have to remove them before wading to the middle of the bitingly cold river to collect water. Our efforts were not always successful. The most disheartening failure was the trial of what we nicknamed "Pearl", a new species of rubber developed by the Chinese Academy of Sciences. In an unusually cold winter in the 1970s, we were woken up in the wee hours by Hu the Old Codger to rinse the stems of our precious young Pearls. Despite our best efforts and frostbitten toes, none of them survived.

Notwithstanding the hardship, crude equipment, and the extra workload that it involved, and thanks greatly to our unsung mentor, Hu the Old Codger, we persevered with our projects. Our stories were covered by the *Regimental Soldier's Paper*, and we were even invited to tour No. 4 Division to report on how we were trying to develop new species of rubber. Not all our *zhiqing* friends could understand our enthusiasm and dedication, but it was a significant episode of our youthful days, and we remain immensely proud of the effort we put in.

Dog Tired

SLEEPWALKING

Huang Jian

When I was in primary school, old revolutionaries were regularly invited to tell us their life stories. Some of them recalled that when the Red Army was relocating or on the run, they were in such a hurry or such danger that they couldn't afford to take the shortest break: at times during the Long March they were so tired that they would be sleepwalking. As a little boy, I often wondered how anyone—so worn out that his eyes were closed—could still move his legs? Never did I anticipate that this would one day happen to me.

In the second half of 1972, the whole nation was engaged in another fervent campaign: "In Industry, Learn from Daqing; in Agriculture, Learn from Dazhai." In other words, "Work away in pursuit of self-sufficiency." Since we belonged to a production and construction corps, our regiment was called on to learn from Dazhai, a mountain village in the north that had turned its barren soil into productive land by (so myth had it) relying entirely on its own manpower and hard work. Many new companies were set up to hasten the development of rubber planting in our regiment, with most of the new recruits still living in a primitive thatched hut. To improve their living conditions, the army called on us to learn from Dazhai by "toiling on the hillside fields by day and working on the dormitory construction site by night."

No. 8 Company was one of the new companies: there was only

one tiled building, which housed company headquarters. Nearly two hundred *zhiqings* were squeezed into a few crude thatched sheds. During the campaign to learn from Dazhai, the company held an assembly to announce that in order to relieve the pressure on accommodation, we were to build within three days and three nights a big tiled building measuring two hundred square meters. Since we had little training and only the most basic tools, this was an incredibly bold idea, and yet in that insane age it received fervent support from the whole troop, and even regimental headquarters backed it by assigning the transport company to help move building materials.

Those were three unforgettable days and nights, an experience of a lifetime. While the men worked as builders, the women shouldered the rest: mixing sand, moving bricks, passing on the materials, and so on. In theory, the troops worked in three shifts to keep the construction going day and night: in practice, many worked round the clock—fuelled wholly by an impetuous passion. When the building took shape, we were exhilarated by the miracle we had wrought with our own hands for the Guangzhou Army Production and Construction Corps.

When the captain announced in the wee hours of the third night that the building was complete, the troop was engulfed in a mood of celebration. When our euphoria waned, however, many were so exhausted that they fell asleep in soiled and sweaty clothes without even the energy to take a shower.

I couldn't sleep that night. It was a Sunday. I had to go to Bangxi to get some food. Because of the harsh living conditions, every Sunday, our only day off, some *zhiqings* would go to a rural diner in Bangxi to grab all of its uncooked loaves or buns. Sometimes a single *zhiqing* would grab over a hundred of them on behalf of more than a dozen or so *zhiqings* in the troop. That day, it was my job to buy food for both my friends and myself in order to make up for the meagreness of our dull canteen meals. Timing was crucial: if I turned up late, there might not be enough left for us. It was a weird time: however great the demand, the only diner in town couldn't care less whether there was enough for its customers, and it would never increase its stock!

After that night's celebration, the few of us who had this errand—

some from Meixian, some from Guangzhou—jumped straight into the river to rid ourselves of the dirt, sweat, and fatigue of the past seventy-two hours before setting off for Bangxi. It was pitch dark on the rough ox-cart track: with just one torch among us, we trod carefully. The walk would normally take an hour.

For the first half of the journey, we were vigilant due to the rough condition of the track. Exhaustion had yet to catch up with us. Then, the track improved greatly and with the crack of dawn it became a bit more visible. For some reason, my eyes began to feel sore and leaden, and no matter how hard I stretched my eyelids I just couldn't keep my eyes open. Our chatter died away; our footsteps mingled with the noise of insects in the otherwise hushed hills. Soon, even the insects went silent, too.

Then all of a sudden, there was a noise: I fell to the ground. I woke up: I must have been sleeping for a while. My friends had a good laugh at me as we resumed our trip in silence. Soon, I slipped out of consciousness. Another fall: I woke up and continued walking. After this had happened I don't know how many times, we were suddenly hit by a chorus of barking: we were entering a Li village, and the sky was much brighter. Dogs in the Li villages were notoriously fierce: the sound of them woke me up. We hurried on toward Bangxi.

Being the first customers in the diner that morning, we cleaned out its stock of loaves, buns, deep-fried doughnuts and pancakes, and we loaded them into our bags. Delighted, we did some shopping for everybody in Bangxi and then set off on our way back. Bangxi was only a small town: to walk round it would take no more than ten minutes. There was nothing to keep us hanging around.

On our way back, I tried hard to tell from the footprints on the track where I had fallen down. From the Li village to where I had started to fall down was at least three kilometres, which meant that I had sleep-walked for almost that distance. When I handed over my purchases to my friends, I told them what had happened, but none of them laughed with me. Was it because they too had had such a weird experience?

MAKING SUGAR

Li Huguang

One of the features of our *zhiqing* experience was the scarcity of all produce and resources. To help relieve the shortage, each company, as well as striving continuously to improve its main products, had to become nearly self-sufficient by raising pigs, growing its own vegetables, and cultivating such cash crops as peanuts, cassava, sweet potato, and sugar cane for the troop. To a large extent, the policy helped to improve the quality of our lives.

Our sugar cane field measured five *mu*. At the end of 1978, the sugar cane grew so well that a good harvest was anticipated. To turn the cane into sugar, we contacted a neighboring village for help. In addition to their press and boiler, they could provide two specialists to give technical advice and assistance. The village workshop was a little way downstream on the river that ran through our camp. Our boat could take more than five hundred kilos of sugar cane on each trip: it all seemed rather convenient. When everything was in order, all the troops were involved in harvesting and loading the sugar cane on to the boat, ready for it to be transported downstream and stored by the workshop.

At first, everything went smoothly. Before the last batch of sugar cane was loaded, the boat had already reached its capacity. But since there wasn't much left, we loaded it on anyway to save another round trip. There were five of us to man the boat.

It was a wet day, overcast and cool. Since we were traveling downstream and the boat was overloaded, some water spilled over the decks during the journey. When the boat reached a bend, it was exposed to rough wind and waves, allowing more water to rush in. As we rowed, the boat bobbed up and down, letting yet more water in. In the end, we had to row the boat into a cove protected by water bamboo.

As the wind freshened, it began to drizzle. Though wrapped in raincoats, we shivered with the cold and our lips turned blue. It was getting dark, and we could get into big trouble if we failed to unload the sugar cane on to the bank by the workshop. However, although the boat was no longer bobbing, water continued to seep in whenever the waves hit it. We were worried: if we didn't find a remedy, the boat would soon sink!

There was no way for us to get outside help. After I had calmly assessed our situation, a solution dawned on me and I asked the team to follow my instructions. Standing at the head of the boat to push aside the water bamboo, two *zhiqings* on each side of the boat would pull the water bamboos backward which should then propel the boat forward. This way, the boat would remain stable and no more water would seep in. It worked, and though we moved slowly, we eventually made it to our destination.

By then, our captain and the troop had been anxiously waiting for us on the bank for some time. Our ex-serviceman captain was a Hakka, and ever since he was put in command of our company, he had got rid of many of the leftist policies and regulations. He had even managed to persuade me to join the Communist Youth League at the age of twenty-four, and later promoted me to squad leader. After leaving us instructions, he put me in charge of sugar production under the supervision of the two local specialists. Leaving a few *zhiqings* behind, he departed with the rest of the troop by boat. From then on, we would work non-stop for five consecutive days and nights until the job was completed.

The sugar cane juice press in the workshop was powered by a diesel engine. Larger than those commonly used in the herbal teahouses of Guangzhou, it could take three or four stalks of sugar cane at a time. The boiler was rectangular, with a row of six or seven woks each measuring sixty centimeters in diameter. After the cane juice was poured into the woks, a fire was lit to bring it up to the boil and reduce the water content. When it became gur, a quantity of pulverized lime was added to solidify it and then the gur was poured into the molds. When it cooled down, it formed blocks of sugar. During pressing, it was crucial to maintain the right temperature: if the temperature was too high, the cane juice would burn; if it was too low, it wouldn't turn into gur. The process was quite exacting and technical. Each block of sugar measured thirty centimeters long, four centimeters thick, and six or seven centimeters wide.

The work was shared out among us: some were responsible for collecting and transporting firewood in an ox-cart, some for tending the fire, some for feeding the sugar cane into the press, some for removing the residue, some for pouring the cane juice into the woks, some for cooking food for the whole team. Since all the jobs were closely interconnected, none of us could afford to stop and the whole team had to work without cease. There was no time for sleep, and we had to make do with just a nap here and there whenever we spotted a moment in the production process that we were not needed. We didn't feel hungry but were seriously deprived of sleep.

Every other day, our captain visited us with a supply of sweet potato wine and meat. And so for five consecutive days and nights, we didn't even stop to wash up, brush our teeth, or take a shower. We were lucky that the weather was cool and it didn't rain. Otherwise it is hard to imagine how we would have coped.

When all was done, we loaded and shipped the blocks of sugar back to the company. We were given two days off, and after a proper shower, I fell into a deep sleep.

Some of the sugar blocks were put aside for the future, and on special occasions used for sugar soup in the company canteen, but most of the produce was allocated equally to every member of the troop. With three or four sugar blocks each, a block weighing five or six kilos, everybody was happy. It was a real treat for us.

Making the Best of It

MY ZHIQING LIFE

Ren Jie

Applied to a particular generation at a particular time, the term *"zhiqing"* carries multiple meanings. Although my rustication occurred forty years ago, the ideas, insights, motivation, and indeed bewilderment that grew out of it have influenced my life ever since.

When I boarded the Red Guard No. 8 ship at Taigu Pier in Guangzhou on 8 November 1968, I, like so many of my peers, was imbued with the ambition to search for the "revolutionary truth." After a calm start along the Pearl River, the voyage quickly turned rough when we entered the South China Sea. Then the ship turned westward toward Hainan Island, the scene of my fateful rustication.

I had fond childhood memories of Hainan Island. My first visit there had been in 1954. To consolidate the defense system and develop the local economy, the state had just appointed Fang Fang, then the Party secretary of Guangdong Province, as director general of Hainan Construction. Many capable people were dispatched there to assist in the project, and my father was appointed a supply chief of its logistics department. I remember going with my father in his jeep around the island to its various military harbors and outposts, coming across numerous tanks, guns, and warships. The experience inspired me to become a "hero" one day, to be engaged in something grand and impressive. To this day, I have photographs of myself as a child, dressed up as a dashing naval officer.

The return trip, however, was unlike anything I had anticipated.

A dossier during the Cultural Revolution had found that my father had many "unresolved historical problems" (a finding which years later, in 1974, proved to be baseless). That verdict gave me and many in similar situations the bitter taste of being condemned as the children of "landlords, rich peasants, counterrevolutionaries, rightists, traitors, moles, and capitalist-roaders." I could not understand how people like my father could come to be denounced as "evil". At the age of only sixteen, having said goodbye to his well-off family in Southeast Asia, my father had joined the army and during the Anti-Japanese War was made a captain charged with catching spies. So it was incomprehensible that my father and I should now be regarded as enemies of the new China that he and his revolutionary companions had helped to establish. When my father taught me the song "Seagull," he told me that this seagull, like the one described by the Russian writer Maxim Gorky, never broke its wings during storms. Instead it kept its head up against the wind.

On Hainan Island, the first challenge was the extreme poverty that extended to every aspect of our lives. From the day we arrived at No. 5 Company on Daling Farm, we stayed in a thatched hut. Located at the foot of the Yellow Ox Range, the hut consisted of a framework of tree trunks which was filled with a mixture of straw and mud and roofed with grass woven from bamboos. The beds were made by driving wooden supports into the dirt floor and topping them with a wooden board and a straw mat. Our only "private property" was the clothing we wore and the bed-sheet we slept on. The door was made of bamboo and had no lock. Our dormitory was a long hall, and the only partition between the areas for boys and girls was a mud wall which was no higher than we were. At bedtime, if those on one side of this partition were too noisy, the other side would protest fiercely, and this triggered even louder arguments and much noise from both sides. But we were just a group of teenagers whose one ambition was to build the nation and devote ourselves selflessly to its mission. Our consuming idealism helped us to endure and even ignore the harsh and impoverished conditions around us.

In the second half of 1969, the Guangzhou Army Construction and Production Corps was established, and Daling State Farm, like other farms on Hainan and Zhanjiang [see map], was transformed into a military regiment. For us *zhiqings*, being under military supervision brought even tougher challenges: 1970 became "a year of raging fire," with major joint campaigns, a term borrowed directly from the major military campaigns of the 1940s, following one after another. In May of that year, we camped by the Zhubi River, and in order to break the embargo on rubber which had been imposed on us by hostile foreign countries, threw ourselves into the campaigns of opening up the wilderness for rubber plantations.

It was noon when we arrived at the Zhubi River. To ensure that we had a place to sleep, the boys were tasked with going up to the hills to fell trees for beams while the girls cut grasses for the roof. Using wooden supports driven into the ground, we made a wide bed, with one end for the boys, the other for the girls. On the first few nights, the girls hung a plastic sheet between us, but at the end of each day everyone was so exhausted from work that this ritual was soon dropped. Nothing happened, though, because we were still too young and naïve to give much thought to courtship or romance.

As fast-growing teenagers, we were desperately hungry after toiling all day. To keep the pangs at bay, I tried everything—walking to the river to drink from it, boiling arrowroot powder to make snacks, and so on. During the time we were setting fire to the hills, our deputy captain caught a python that had been trapped in the fire and cooked some pieces for us. There was a group of mango trees on the far bank of the river. I happened to swim there one day and found to my happy surprise many mangoes that had fallen to the ground. After giving myself a good feast, I brought many back to the camp and shared them with my fellow troop members. From then on, the far bank became our favorite spot.

Despite the harsh conditions, we remained in high spirits. Our role model was a person who had not only learned all of Chairman Mao's works by heart but worked hard on the plantation. We all looked up to him.

We were young and optimistic. We looked forward to changing our fate. Some of us were involved in writing, composing, and performing a suite of songs, *I Love My Army Corps.* Others wrote poems and published them on the bulletin boards. I still remember all the lyrics of all the songs in *I Love My Army Corps*. On a recent business trip to Taiwan, I was asked to give a performance at a reception, and had no difficulty in remembering the words and music to one of the songs, "Walk in the cloud, step on the dew. I look up at Venus and march forward. Picking stars for my bucket, I welcome the splendid sunrise." The song was not just an expression of the spiritual state of the *zhiqing* life, it was my personal hymn to a world full of unpredictable changes and challenges.

The regiment resumed its state farm status in late 1974, with the *zhiqings* returning to their roles as ordinary farm workers. During that time, I was transferred from rubber planting to a rubber cutting squad. Initially I thought it would be a nice change from toiling under the scorching sun in temperatures as high as forty degrees Celsius. What happened in fact was that we had to get up at three thirty in the morning and finish cutting two hundred and eighty trees before sunrise. Rubber collection was at eight thirty, and the produce had to be delivered to the collection station by ten. This tight schedule meant that we had no more than four hours' sleep a night, and all we ate before rushing to work was a bowl of congee. It was still pitch dark while we were walking to the plantation. I was so exhausted one day that I dozed off at work.

While many argue that their lives as *zhiqings* were a total waste of time, I believe that had I not been tempered by the experiences of those days, I would never have managed to resist the many distractions of life and focus on what mattered most: to read, and to run a successful business. In a way, it was my background as a *zhiqing* that helped me build my business empire.

MAKING THE BEST OF IT
Zheng Xiuhua

I was rusticated to Hainan Island when the whole nation was swept up in the fervor of the "Up to the Mountains, Down to the Countryside" campaign. When I arrived in October 1969 at Daling Farm, then known as the No. 13 Regiment of No. 4 Division of the Guangzhou Army Production and Construction Corps, I was just sixteen years old. Like many of my contemporaries, I was imbued with the grand ambition to dedicate myself wholeheartedly to the corner of the country that most needed us.

Together with other new *zhiqings* from Yangjiang, I was sent straight to a series of study sessions convened at No. 6 Company. Unprepared for the wretched state of our thatched dormitory, we wept all night. One of us even called out hopelessly for her mother. Having never left home, we had been thrilled by the prospect of our first journey and our encounter with the outside world. We bought diaries to note down the memorable moments on the long and winding journey to Hainan, the exact time when we arrived at Zhanjiang City and Haikou City, and so on. And now that we found ourselves in a strange and desolate place, far away from our families and the comforts of home, our excitement suddenly evaporated.

I woke up early the next morning, and when I opened my eyes saw something dark on my mosquito net. When I sat up to take a closer look, I could not help but scream and jump out of bed: on the net was a centipede of twenty to thirty centimeters long! Back home, centipedes were tiny, but owing to the island's high humidity and the many damp, shaded corners in the thatched hut, they grew here to a huge size. The locals were quite used to them: to us teenage girls, they were monsters. From then on, I would check my bedding inside and out before going to bed and, even then, I would sometimes wake up in the middle of the night in a panic.

After study sessions which were spread over more than twenty days, I was assigned to No. 2 Company to work in the production squad. Located in the tropics, the island is subject to fierce sun, so after a few days of toiling in the fields, our soft skin reddened and peeled. Although we were performing heavy manual labor day in and day out, our diet was so poor that all we sometimes ate was salt and soy sauce in a bowl of plain rice. For those of us who had grown up in urban areas, life had never been so tough.

Being hundreds of miles away and constantly feeling famished, we missed our homes even more. To relieve the shortage of food, our families would scrape something together for us. Since my hometown, Yangjiang, is renowned for its salted black beans, they were usually what came in the parcels from home. Occasionally, there were treats such as salted fish, sugar, and deep-fried lard. Having some deep-fried lard to eat with the salted plain rice was a real treat for every *zhiqing*. Its wonderful taste has lingered in my mind for years.

I shared a room with two other *zhiqings*: Yang from Guangzhou City and Li from Hunan Province. Yang used to provide "century eggs" – preserved duck eggs with beautiful patterns—and Li provided bean curd, and we would share whatever we had. In those lean years, our families at home didn't have much to eat either. When I gave a small portion of salted black beans to a Guangzhou *zhiqing*, I learned years later that he thought they were too precious for himself, so he kept them in a small bottle and on a home visit gave them to his mother.

With barely any food to eat with the plain rice, we were forced to improvise and become resourceful. One day, as we were walking to the rubber plantation, we found some pepper shoots in the forest wind-break. We picked the shoots and blanched them with salt: they were tasty. After the heavy downpours of spring, a myriad of mushrooms would suddenly appear in the damp woods, and we would pick and cook them for food. The old hands warned us that we should pick only the sharp-ended ones because those with round ends were poisonous. We were lucky to have such local knowledge.

One day, I went to a Li village with two other *zhiqings* from Yangjiang and we spotted many jackfruits on the trees. Before we left for Hainan, we had been warned that if we so much as looked at the Li men when they walked by, they would kill us with the machetes that they carried on their waists. When we first arrived on the island, I didn't dare even to glance at them and neither did my friends. Gradually the truth dawned: it was a myth. Indeed, when I smiled at them, they smiled back at me. I realized that the ethnic minority was not necessarily the "uncivilized tribe" that public perception had it. On this occasion, when we came across the first Li man in the village, we greeted him and even offered him a cigarette. He was friendly to us. We inquired if the jackfruits were for sale. He asked us to be his guests and pick whichever we fancied on the tree for just one *jiao* each! We were thrilled by such an incredible bargain and picked a few to take back to our dormitory. Since they were not yet ripe, we wrapped them in our clothing and kept them in the kitchen of one of the old hands. Our lust for them was such that we went and checked at least three times a day to see if they had ripened.

Though life was tough, we managed to stay upbeat, mostly just by teasing each other. One day, as we were sharpening our machetes after work, Dong and Fu came up to me and asked: "Hey, why were you carrying manure at two o' clock last night?" "I wasn't." "But we both saw you. Are you suffering from somnambulism?" They looked serious and concerned; my heart sank. I turned to my friend Chen and asked: "Is this true?" Amazed by my foolish look, she said, "Absolutely!" Although I pretended that I didn't believe a word of it, I was worried. A few days later, Dong told me again that he saw me carrying manure at two o'clock the previous night. I denied it, but Fu said: "You must be suffering from somnambulism. Ask Auntie Zhang, she saw you too!" Auntie Zhang, an old hand, was an honest soul, so if she had confirmed it, it must have been true. I became seriously worried about my state of health. It was said that a somnambulist wouldn't know what he was doing even if he was committing a brutal murder with a machete. How horrifying if I turned out that way! And what if I jumped into a reservoir at midnight? The thought of it terrified me. When I returned to the dormitory that evening, I asked around and all my roommates confirmed that they had never seen me sleepwalking. I went to ask Chen again, and when she saw how apprehensive I had become, she told me they were just teasing me. I couldn't believe her and the next day, went to double check with Auntie Zhang. She told me she had never caught me sleepwalking, either. It was not until then that I could calm down and realize that I had indeed been made a fool of by those two rascals.

Finding joy amid the hardship was one of our specialities. It was our good fortune that there was never a shortage of talent among the troops: someone could always be found who could sing, or play the erhu or some other musical instrument. One of the *zhiqings* from Yingde, I remember, had a fine, sonorous voice. I always liked to be around when she sang and I let her voice carry me a long way from my immediate environment. According to some of the *zhiqings* who were responsible for raising the company's pigs, even the pigs were thrilled by her singing.

Though decades have passed since my rustication, I can still remember some episodes of my *zhiqing* life as vividly as if they had happened yesterday. Despite the harsh conditions, I have many fond memories. After we returned to our homes years later, the bond between us ex-*zhiqings* never waned, but instead grew stronger. For me, my fellow *zhiqings* are like brothers and sisters.

BATHING IN THE OPEN

Hu Zhimin

We were rusticated in November 1968 during the feverish climax of the "Up to the Mountains, Down to the Countryside" campaign. When we bade farewell to our hometowns and joined the army of "soldiers" to fight on the "battlefield" of the mysterious Hainan Island, we were all infatuated with lofty ideals. Never had we been prepared for the destitute conditions at our destination, the wilderness of Baisha County, which we had to open up and where we needed to build the facilities to ensure our barest survival.

Soon after my arrival, I was moved from the established No. 2 Company to the brand new No. 8 Company. Apart from the captain, we so-called "regimental soldiers" were teenage *zhiqings* drawn from many places. We started everything from scratch, such as building that biggest essential, our dormitories. After locating a relatively flat area in the hills, we cleared it, constructed the framework of a thatched hut from tree-trunks, and built the walls with straw mixed with mud. Finally, we knotted bamboo strips with grass in order to make a roof. With the exception of the brown dirt floor, everything indoors—beds, desks, stools—was made with branches or bamboo. In the hills, water was scarce and our only well was reserved for cooking and drinking. To transport water from the well to our cookhouse, we broke numerous bamboos in two and built a trough by connecting these bamboo tubes together. The trough was several dozen meters long. As to bathing and washing, we were obliged to go to the river more than two hundred metres down the track.

Being mere teenagers, a big row broke out between us as to who could occupy the upstream area for bathing and washing. The boys maintained that since we were unclean, we only deserved the down-stream area, but we were having none of this nonsense and wouldn't let them get the upper hand. In the end, it was the captain who made the decision: the girls would have the advantage of bathing upstream, and that was that. While we cheered with joy, the boys turned their backs in frustration.

Our "changing room" on the bank was a makeshift thatched cabin no taller than us, and our "bathtub" was the clear river. The first time we took our bath, we were all so shy and modest that none of us removed her underwear. We would first swim for a little while, then go up to the bank to apply some soap, and then return to the river for a good rinse, all with our underwear on. Gradually, though, some of the more audacious girls stripped naked before jumping into the river, frolicked with each other, and even dared the other girls to follow suit. Eventually, we were able to overcome our sense of modesty and propriety and bathe in the nude.

In the circumstances this was no small feat: thanks to several years of indoctrination during the Cultural Revolution, the word "nude" equated to "obscene," "lewd," and even "depraved." As a group of naïve teenagers, who would have imagined we could become so "wild" and devoted to simple pleasures when society as a whole was governed by extreme puritanism? And yet bathing in the clear river turned out to be one of the happiest experiences of our *zhiqing* lives. Every evening, as the sun cast its glittering, alluring light on the water, we would breathe in the balmy evening breeze, strip off our clothes, which were so heavily soiled by a hard day's toil, and bask in the soothing water. In fact, once we overcame our initial shyness, we learned to look at each other with innocent eyes, and even teased each other about our figures. We shared harmless jokes and had great laughs together. The water, cool and soft, gently lapped over every inch of our naked skin, caressed our tired bodies, calmed our stressed out minds, removed our fatigue, and lifted our doubts and unhappiness.

One day, a girl suddenly screamed in utter fear: on the far bank, among the trees and bushes, she had spotted a man moving about. Instinctively, we grabbed towels or items of clothing from the bank, and those with nothing to cover themselves with ducked into the water or turned their backs on the man and put their hands over their breasts. Some of us yelled in an attempt to drive him away. But instead, the man came out from behind the trees and even stared at us. Judging from his ethnic Li attire, what we uttered was probably entirely unintelligible to him. After a while, he was gone, and we all yelled "hooligan" after him.

The next evening we were in a state of high alert and extreme caution. After a quick dip, we put our clothes back on immediately before settling down to wash our laundry. After a while, we resumed our normal routine. There had been a few "peeping Tom" incidents on the farm, but there was absolutely nothing we could do about it. One of the Guangzhou *zhiqings* observed: "Why should all of us be afraid of just one man? There are so many of us and yet he is on his own. Is it he who is looking at us or we who are looking at him?" We roared with laughter.

One day, we caught sight of a small boat coming toward us. As it got closer, some girls swam farther away, but most just ducked into the water, keeping a watchful eye on him. In the boat was a Li man in his forties, his dark tanned face deeply carved by wrinkles. He nodded at us with a frank smile, devoid of any hint of indecency or lewdness: my eyes followed him until he disappeared. Years later I learned that the ethnic minorities in our country have largely retained a naturalistic view on issues like desire and sex. For them, nudity is a form of natural beauty and many still keep to the custom of mixed public bathing. Nudity in their cultures is nothing unusual or novel: it is only we, the Han-Chinese (especially we Cantonese, I have to admit), who have found it so unnatural or even titillating.

Except during our periods, when we would take a hot bath in the kitchen of a married veteran, most of us, thanks to our primitive living conditions, continued to bathe in the river all year round.

Yet "nature's bathtub" was not always a scene of peace and happiness. The tranquil river, about ten meters wide, was a lovely place to unwind when the weather was fine. Yet whenever there was a flash flood, it would spread to a width of several dozen meters and submerge our "changing room." Littered with all sorts of rubbish and debris, the roaring water could be a horrifying sight. During one of those wet spells when the river was flooded, I went to bathe in the river with my best friend. Though we were both from "politically incorrect" family backgrounds, she had been given a worse deal: denounced as "the offspring of the counter-party and counterrevolutionary" elements, the seven members of her family were dispersed to different parts of the country. Our friendship was toughened by the hardship and unfairness that life had dealt us.

A gentle and popular girl, she loved swimming. That day, she stared at the roaring water and asked all of a sudden: "If I wanted to swim across to the other bank, do you think I could make it?"

I had no idea. "Maybe," I said.

"What if I can't manage to swim back?"

I don't know where my courage came from, but I heard myself declaring: "Then I will come and rescue you!"

With that promise, she jumped into the river and swam to the far bank. On her way back, however, the currents turned into rapids and despite her best efforts, she was carried downstream. I was frightened and yelled at her in panic. Like a fallen leaf, she had been swept farther and farther away from me.

I cried in desperation.

Eventually she clambered out some sixty or seventy meters downstream. I sprinted to her and wrapped her shivering body in a towel.

Her lips had turned dark purple, her breath was uneven, and tears were welling up like raindrops. I was gripped by both guilt and fear. When she finally recovered, I could see in her eyes a sense of triumph and satisfaction! Yet I thought I understood what it meant: despite the disgrace and insults she had endured, she was not ready to surrender to fate just yet. Her attempt to challenge the flooded river was an act of defiance against the injustice that life had inflicted on her.

SKIRT THE DANGER OF CAPITALISM

Rao Ruiguang

Before my rustication, my mother used to dress up her four daughters on special occasions such as Children's Day or Chinese New Year with clothes she had designed and sewed herself. These occasions never failed to excite us.

During the "Up to the Mountains, Down to the Countryside' campaign, we four sisters were sent to different parts of the country as *zhiqings*, and soon even my father was sent away from home to undergo thought-reform in "study classes." Diagnosed with rheumatic heart disease and with many worries on her mind, my mother was no longer inclined, nor indeed able, to make clothes for her daughters.

Life on Hainan Island was tough, and like my fellow *zhiqings*, I rose early and worked for long hours to open up the wilderness, dig holes and build terraces on the hills for rubber planting. At the end of a hard day's work, we were soaked several times over, and because they became sweat-stained and had to be frequently washed, our few clothes wore out quickly. After being mended many times both inside and out, they became rags, almost unrecognizably different from their original appearance. Like everything else in a centrally planned economy, cloth was rationed, but the fact was that although each adult was entitled to four meters of cloth per year, few could afford to make full use of their coupons.

On a home visit, I bought a length of cloth and had a pair of trousers made for myself. Unfortunately they didn't fit and since I was due to go back to Hainan the next day, there just wasn't time to alter them. After returning there, I decided to learn how to sew. Without a tailor or anyone else to teach me, I had to learn by copying from my old clothes. I took out my rags, unpicked their seams, laid them on a piece of the new cloth, traced their shapes on it, and then cut these out piece by piece. I would then sew them together during my spare time. I was clumsy and painfully slow at the beginning, but with practice I gradually built up my skills and was even ready to design several different styles of clothes. I was very pleased with myself: not only could I satisfy my own need and desire for new clothes but I could help my friends. Life was tough, but which of us girls didn't wish to look pretty?

On one occasion I bought a piece of yellow plaid with a pattern of little red flowers and made a lovely pleated skirt for myself. It was a splendid sunny Sunday, so I put the skirt on in order to pay a visit to regimental headquarters and help my friends with their shopping. Soon after I left the dormitory, I met my captain. I thought he would have remarked on how pretty the skirt was, but instead he gave me a stern look and a rebuke: "Wearing a skirt is capitalist behavior!" Thus splashed with cold water, I felt despondent and went back to my dormitory to change. When my friends showed concern and asked what was wrong, I was lost for words. I had spent so much time making the skirt and yet was unable to wear it! I felt terrible. Many days later, I realized I had no choice but to unpick the skirt. Luckily, the cloth was still in one piece and in good shape, so I made two pillowcases out of it. Whenever I slept on it, though, I felt sad: the little girl in me had always been dreaming of gliding, as a fairy might, along a tree-lined path in a beautiful dress. But now the dream had been stifled.

I still take pleasure in designing and sewing clothes for myself, thanks wholly to the skills I picked up during those hard times.

Maoist Propaganda Stars

OASES IN THE CULTURAL DESERT
Zhu Zhaoyu

During the Cultural Revolution, there was a kind of public figure known as a "propaganda performing artist" or, in full, a "Maoist amateur propaganda performing artist," who performed every now and then without a fee. Following Chairman Mao's "Talks at the Yanan Forum on Literature and the Arts" in 1942, in particular his precept that "Literature and the arts must serve the workers and peasants," the propaganda troupes were tasked with using art forms to spread and promote Maoism and communist party principles and policies; to raise the profile of good people and their deeds; and to bring culture to the regiments. The troupe was in reality a study group, a combat squad, and a propaganda machine. A microcosm of the time, it sought, wherever it toured, to make oases in the cultural desert.

The propaganda troupe was a "study camp" and a big family of amateur artists. In our regiment the troupe was normally assembled once a year, required to rehearse a specific project, and toured for two or three consecutive months. It was then disbanded and its "stars" returned to their companies. Chen Longsheng, the "talent scout" and an officer in the political division of the regiment, was responsible each year for assembling from within the regiment and its various companies a cohort of diligent *zhiqings* who showed artistic talent. While the female members had to be eloquent and have the ability to sing and dance, the males were supposed to be able to act or play an instrument, and most of all, to be versatile—to possess more than one skill, such as eloquent speech, singing, dancing, writing, and composition. Most members had never been trained professionally, and their only credentials were a role in a school play or at ad hoc amateur performances before rustication. In the propaganda troupe, it was the first time they would be tasked with putting on a show all by themselves.

To this very day, I haven't a clue why I was picked by Lao Chen. A high school student at the time of rustication, I was first summoned to the troupe in 1970 to be a writer: to invent some patter, rhyming dialogue, and dramas. The following year, I was made leader, likewise in 1973, just before leaving the farm. The troupe was like a boisterous family consisting of nearly twenty *zhiqings* from Guangdong Province and beyond.

Lacking an aptitude for singing or dancing, I started by beating drums and gongs. You mustn't look down on this role, though: drums and gongs are percussion instruments, and the percussionist was the virtual director of a small band like ours. I soon picked up some special techniques from the other amateur stars. I worked on Tibetan dancing, but was so bad at it that I was spared from performing it on stage. I had also been through the basic training for a performance artist but, after several rounds of whirling, got dizzy spells. I even tried my hand at the violin and erhu but made a sound like a cock crowing. As to writing, I took notes from a playwright-actor-poet. Also in the troupe was an actor-musician-playwright-director who picked up mime and turned it into our most popular act. Zhu Jianqiang, a natural musician, could compose on, as well as play, literally any instrument. He was later "discovered," and reassigned to the propaganda troupe of the army corps to compose and direct, a role as senior and prestigious as the membership of an artistic troupe in the provincial army. In the absence of my numerous tutors, it was down to a couple of instrumentalists and me to come up with some tunes for the shows. In addition, there were a couple whose voices were so good that their Beijing opera performance resembled that of professionals—girls who could not only sing and dance but switch easily between characters, such as a young soldier in one scene and a rubber plantation fairy in another. One member had even shot to stardom after she was filmed in a documentary called *Great Fruits on Treasure Island* made in 1972 by the Pearl River Studio.

Don't be fooled into thinking that life in the propaganda troupe was just an idyll. As a combat squad, we often chanted such slogans as "To act in a revolutionary play, one must first act like a revolutionary." We thought that since we were considered the talented and versatile members of each company, it was our duty to improve the decadent image that the artistic community suffered from. We wanted to prove that we were not there to have a good life, or to be pampered, but to work our fingers to the bone like everybody else in the regiment. We strove to uphold the good practices of our companies and even tried to go beyond them. With such a mindset and under the close supervision of the political division, we underwent intensive political study: Communist Youth League classes; heart-to-heart talks, in which a politically progressive *zhiqing* helped out a less progressive one; sessions to learn from good people and good deeds; and democratic discussion forums on everyday life with the aim of criticism and self-criticism. Since the latter addressed genuine and personal issues, their impact was often felt across the whole troupe.

In order to create a wholesome image, we never missed any volunteer work, and we often joined the special task force. When we were participating in the reservoir-building project and the campaign to fast-track the construction of thatched huts, we even competed discreetly with the regimental basketball team to see which was better. We boys were not afraid of our competitors. Although the basketball players were taller and bulkier, tasks such as bamboo breaking and grass cutting, which we would be doing when not performing on stage, were skilled work and demanded stamina. The basketball players, however, had become "non-agricultural workers" and were exempt from such skilled and strenuous daily labor. But for the girls in our troupe, the competition was tough. While they could strike fancy martial arts postures with their willowy figures on the stage, they were no match at all for the strapping female basketball players in the hills. Besides, some of our girls had hardly taken part in the backbreaking "major joint campaigns." Despite this they never wavered, however hard things got. As for us, once we finished our task, we would lend them a helping hand so that our troupe did not lag behind and become a target for ridicule. When the rubber plantation was severely damaged by the No. 13 typhoon, we threw ourselves into rescuing the rubber trees. At the same time we were breaking our backs on this, we gathered good material on site for our shows, and put on spontaneous performances to help boost everyone's morale. We would chant slogans like "The rubber plants were reduced, but not the rubber they yielded," or "The trees were devastated, but not our morale." Bathed in mud and sweat, we looked like monkeys, and our funny appearance produced heartfelt laughter and bravos which helped us keep going. When the typhoon struck again, the river by the regiment became flooded and we all raced to the bank to protect the hydro-electric power station. While we boys jumped into the water to create a human barrier, the girls would pass us sand bags from the flooded bank. At midnight, when the thatched huts collapsed in a thunderstorm, we rescued the rice and other supplies; when the flood crept higher, we jumped into the river to save the pumping machine and other equipment. For our unremitting efforts, we were commended by the regiment and had indeed fashioned a bright new image as "amateur stars."

The propaganda troupe was also a promoter of culture. Barren of cultural life, Hainan Island boasted scarcely any literary or arts events. Though all the artistic activities of that era were bound to be political, what we did in effect was to spread urban culture to the villages, enrich the lives of our fellow *zhiqings* as well as our own, and enliven the culture of the rural areas.

During rehearsals, we were sometimes sent in small groups to help various companies with their propaganda campaigns. This not only helped us to keep up with good practice at the grassroots, but to improve the skills of their "singing ensembles," a much welcomed and commended aspect of our visits. Since all artistic and literary activities had to serve political purposes, creative staff would also pay visits to the old hands and *zhiqings* so that their good deeds could be written into our plays. My first attempts to write plays were shallow, slogan-driven, unrealistic and inartistic, but with the help of my colleagues and after in-depth interviews with role models, I became much better at it.

Though rehearsals were exhausting, performances, the highlight of our stint as theatrical artists, required even more exertion. As well as performing in the regiment and participating in the major arts events in the division, our role was to tour all the companies, and sometimes even take our shows to the Li villages in the hills and to factories, mines and other enterprises, as well as to the military posts. The toughest task of all, owing to the lack of any form of transport, was the visits to the companies and Li villages in the hills, for which we might have to trek anywhere between two and ten kilometers, or even farther. With a red flag reared high above us and with props on our backs and instruments on our shoulders, we marched along dusty and weedy tracks. We laughed and we sang; we went out in twilight and returned under starry skies; we tried to find fun amid hardship. On one occasion, we were caught by a heavy downpour during our longest trek to the north, to No. 6 Company, and in our efforts to protect the instruments and props on a flooded trail, we quickly became soaked. What were we to do? We had to decide on the spot whether or not to soldier on. At a previous political study session, we debated which was the more important: to participate in the arts events in the division or to take shows to the companies. Most decided that the latter was. Chanting "Forge forward," we rolled up our trousers, removed our shoes, and plodded ahead on the slippery trail, which because of the color of the local soil was covered by a red flood. On arrival, we were immediately greeted with bowls of hot ginger tea sweetened with red sugar to help dispel the cold, and a log fire to keep our bodies warm and dry our clothes. As soon as the rain stopped, puddles were swept away and gas lamps lit, and although it might rain again, the ground was packed with old hands, *zhiqings* and children. We gave our most enthusiastic performance and were rewarded with laughter and thunderous applause. On another occasion, after trekking more than five kilometers to a Li village, we were greeted by fireworks, gongs and drums and, on entering the village, by a traditional welcome from the Li people—splashes of water on our bodies from the Li girls. We were then ushered into their communal area for a treat of pork and dog meat, though some of us dared not touch the latter. Our stage was the grain-drying ground, and awaiting us were hundreds of Li from the nearby villages. It was a chilly night, and the Li tried to keep warm by wrapping themselves in ragged blankets. Looking at these bewildered spectators, we were not sure how well they could understand us. But we were prepared for such occasions, and we put together a show with little dialogue but much singing and dancing, and with revolutionary model operas,[9] which were the staple of radio at that time. When we heard laughter and applause from the Li, we were greatly relieved. By the time the show finished and everything was packed up, it was already midnight. The village chief and two of his militia insisted on escorting us all the way back to regimental headquarters to spare us possible attacks from poisonous insects, wild animals, or other dangers and inconveniences. Incidents had sometimes occurred when we were returning late at night. A watch was a luxury item, and because one of our members had not been careful to hide the fact that he owned one, we were once followed home by a would-be thief.

Every year when the troupe assembled, we would tour with nearly twenty shows. The day after each performance, there would be a critique to identify areas for improvement and then more rehearsals to get it right. While a real star can easily fetch thousands or even millions of *yuan* in fees, we amateurs did it as voluntary work—our salary was the same as everybody else's in the regiment, 28.60 *yuan* each month in the later years. On our return from a show with empty stomachs, we would usually receive, as our "fee," a pot of sweet potato congee or sweet noodles. Sweet noodles were a Hainan delicacy. Short of oil, meat or vegetables, what cooks would improvise as a treat was boiled noodles with sugar and minced ginger. We thought it was a delightful

---

9. In 1967, six revolutionary operas and two ballets were chosen as "model plays," the template of which must be adhered to in all art forms. To help their promotion across the country, they were turned into films between 1969 and 1972 by state studios. Spearheaded by Jiang Qing, the wife of Chairman Mao, the eight revolutionary model plays were among the few entertainments allowed during the Cultural Revolution.

snack and were most grateful to the cook for staying up to make it for us. In October 1973, we joined a school troupe in a performance at the division on an open-air stage in an iron ore mine. There was an audience of over four thousand consisting of officials, soldiers, workers, and peasants. We put on a fantastic show and were commended for it. On our return to regimental headquarters, we were offered the highest "fee" ever—a farewell dinner party. It was a scrumptious meal with fish and meat. The next day, the political division of the regiment had a photograph taken of us, and we were then dismissed and sent back to our respective companies.

Nearly four decades later, in April 2010, some of us propaganda artists got together at the fortieth anniversary of rustication held in Meizhou. We put on a show without much difficulty and were quite pleased with it. The resounding poetry recitals, the beautiful melodies, the graceful dances, and of course the laughter, transported us back to our youthful *zhiqing* days. Our "fee" this time was the heartfelt cheering and applause from our ex-*zhiqing* friends.

A BROADCASTER AHEAD OF HER TIME
Yang Heping

It was autumn and I was working as a telephone operator in the security and messenger squad of the regiment. One day, a political officer asked to speak to me. He told me that now that Xiao Han, our only broadcaster, was returning home to the city, a decision had been made that I should take her place. It was unprecedented: each year, when the broadcaster visited home, somebody in the political division would merely cover for her. Why was I chosen now? I have a vivid memory of that conversation: it took place under the magnolia tree in front of the telephone operators' room, and I had little choice but to accept the arrangement.

The studio shared a room with the telephone operators' room: they were divided only by a wooden partition. While the latter took up the outer compartment, the studio occupied the inner one. I don't recall getting much training before I started my career as a broadcaster.

Every morning, when the power generators roared into life and the lights came on, I would get up swiftly to prepare for the morning session of cable broadcasting. My dormitory was in the same single-storey building as the studio, only a few steps away to its left. When I arrived, I would first of all turn on the main switch to warm up the machine, and then throw the line of switches on the wooden panel to the upward position. The broadcasting system shared a cable with the telephone system: when the switches were in their default—downward —position, the telephone system was in operation; when they pointed upward, the radio was connected to all companies and the phone lines were cut off.

Five minutes later, with the microphone on and to the tune of "The East Is Red," I would announce: "No. 13 Regiment's Maoist Radio Station will now broadcast"; and the announcement would ring through regimental headquarters and the fifteen companies, including the remote one based on Keling Hill. Though I only played the tune, the lyrics of "The East Is Red" could be recited by the whole nation:

> The east is red, the sunrise strong,
> Hail China's offspring, Mao Zedong.
> He seeks the good of one and all,
> Hurrah, and frees us from our thrall!
>
> Our Chairman holds the people dear,
> In him our destiny shows clear.
> His aim, to forge a nation new:
> Hurrah, let's praise our leader true!
>
> The Communist Party, like the sun,
> Where'er it goes, lights everyone:
> On mountains, valleys, rolling sea,
> Hurrah, it sets the people free!

Live broadcasting follows fixed schedules and provides accurate time checks. But during my stint at the microphone, my work could only start when the power generators were switched on in the regimental power station. I was not only a presenter but a technician: while broadcasting, I would also be checking the meters of the transmitter and adjusting the knobs to keep the voltage steady. There were no recording facilities; everything was presented live in front of a microphone wrapped in a piece of red cloth, the politically correct color for propaganda.

There was a rudimentary cable station in each company, a tall wooden frame made by tying several tree trunks together and fixing them into the ground. After work each evening, the company broadcaster, armed with a tin loudspeaker, would climb atop the frame and make various announcements, such as naming the good people of the day and their good deeds, along with other items.

In the morning, most people would listen via the loudspeakers to the regimental radio broadcast while getting up and eating breakfast. At night, as well as relaying news programs from the Central People's Broadcasting Station and the Guangdong Provincial People's Broadcasting Station, it would include live features about various people whose good deeds each company had reported to regimental headquarters, along with newspaper extracts, and so on. Whenever there was a crucial item, such as the joint political commentary by the three main news publications—the *People's Daily*, the *People's Liberation Army Daily* and the *Red Flag* magazine—everybody would bring a small wooden stool out from their dormitory to sit in front of the loudspeakers and listen attentively. The next day, each squad would hold discussions on that piece of commentary during the one-hour "daily study" session, which was held after lunch. In those days few people could afford their own radio set: the relays from the Central Station and Radio Guangdong became a crucial way for us to keep up with news outside the remote and isolated regiment.

The studio contained a modest collection of 72 rpm vinyl records and 36 rpm red, blue and green plastic records. If one was not vigilant, it was easy to forget to adjust the speed of the turntable to correspond with that at which the records were meant to be played, resulting in something which sounded either like Donald Duck or the groans of a dying man. I never made such errors, though. Many of the tuneful songs written before the Cultural Revolution were banned and stored away: the Central Station had approved only a few communist and revolutionary tracks for the public to listen to, such as "Sailing the Seas Depends on the Helmsman," which affirms the absolute leadership of Chairman Mao, and those laced with Chairman Mao's quotations. Only a handful of artistic songs survived the censors to make it on to the playlist: these, such as "Horses, Please Slow Down;" "Rambling in the New City;" "Please Come to the Youth Task Force" and "Many Hands Water the Flowers of Happiness," either praised socialist innovations or our dedication to socialist construction. Thanks to repeated playing and an absolute lack of choice, I could sing all these songs by heart. Although the playlist was so limited, I still tried my very best to match the songs to the content of the script.

Just before signing off the morning or evening session, each lasting for one to two hours, I would make a request: "Will each company please turn the main switch down to the telephone mode so that the telephone line at your company is restored."

Besides presenting, I also prepared scripts. Of course, most of them were written either by the regimental correspondents or the reporters in each company. Largely because of the shortage of supplies, the regiment became virtually self-sufficient: a vegetable squad in regimental headquarters and in each company supplied all the vegetables we consumed. On one occasion we wanted to comment on the "rich" variety of the vegetables that were served in the regimental canteen. As soon as I had finished the morning broadcast, I took a pen and notebook to conduct an interview with the leader of the vegetable squad. I asked him how many members were in his squad, how large the field was, how they combated typhoons and repaired their damage, and how they tackled the various issues in vegetable growing in order to maintain a steady supply to the troop. I even went to the field to see how they watered and applied fertilizer. After viewing the rows of fresh vegetables such as water spinach, lettuce, spring onions and leeks, I wrote "Red Hearts, Green Leaves"—"red" being the correct color of one's political position and "green" being the color of the army uniform—and delivered it on the radio to eulogize the vegetable squad. More than a decade later, when Radio Guangdong was pioneering China's first live radio in 1986, broadcasters who had previously worked in clearly demarcated roles were now required to combine the jobs of interviewing, editing and presenting, and at the same time to operate the desk. When I heard about it, I exclaimed: "But, hold on a second, wasn't that exactly what I was doing more than ten years ago as a *zhiqing*?"

We also made broadcasts outside the studio. Whenever the regiment began a major joint campaign, we would move our equipment to wherever it was being conducted. With the console carried to a makeshift command office, loudspeakers hung on trees or up in the hills, and cables all connected, we could broadcast live. On such occasions, the regimental commander or political commissar or the deputy regimental commander responsible for production would launch into a cliché-ridden, morale-boosting oration. Their speeches would unfailingly be larded with slogans or Maoist quotations such as "Let's put an early end to rubber importation" or "Be resolute, conquer all difficulties, fear no sacrifice, strike for success." Of all the songs featuring Chairman Mao's quotations, the one most frequently chosen was "Be resolute, conquer all difficulties, fear no sacrifice, strike for success." The clerks and reporters of each company would keep sending in articles on the "achievements" of their respective companies during a major joint campaign, and the "frontline broadcasting station" of each troop would send in reports on the good people and their good deeds. Combining bits of material from all the reports, I once made up a piece of doggerel and presented it during a broadcast: "Comrade X in No Y Company is outstanding, building Z hill terraces in just one day. Let's all learn from him, devoting ourselves to the revolutionary cause."

My broadcasting career at the farm lasted until my final day on Hainan Island. After returning to Guangzhou, I was soon assigned to work as a journalist at Radio Guangdong, a post I held until my retirement.

PICTURES AND MEMORIES

Lu Zhongmin

There is an old cardboard box in the corner of my apartment that has been lying undisturbed for years. It contains all the stuff I brought back from Hainan as a *zhiqing*. When I opened it the other day, I found an old and fading anthology that transported me right back to the Daling of several decades ago.

A book of propaganda edited and published by the best-known Red Guard "rebel group" at the leading edge of the Cultural Revolution, its content at that time couldn't have been more familiar to the entire nation: a collection of Chairman Mao's pictures and sayings which swamped all the newspapers, books, and magazines and were plastered on the walls of every street corner. Having been bombarded with its content in their youth, many may well have lost interest in this book; but it still occupies a special place in my memory.

Drawing has always been my passion. At primary school, it got me noticed, and my class teacher would nurture it by way of letting me draw a picture for the headline article of the bulletin board in the classroom. When the Cultural Revolution broke out, I was a mere junior secondary school student, and like those with a little bit of artistic talent to show off, I designed posters and drew caricatures to campaign for bringing down the "capitalist-roaders" of our country. When this collection of paintings of Chairman Mao was published, for me it was like discovering a treasure chest.

I had learned at a young age that without a prestigious family background I would have to work my way up on my own. To make my progressive tendencies known, I approached our political instructor soon after my rustication on Hainan Island and placed my unique skills at his service. I had a hidden agenda—to escape the backbreaking manual labor in that tropical climate. On arriving at the farm, I had been assigned to the jungle squad and tasked with chopping down bushes, young trees, and creepers. In those first days, after a few hours of toiling in the fierce sun, we suffered from severe dehydration and headaches. We were soaked in sweat, and we wept: as fresh urban school leavers, we were in no way built for the tropical climate and such hard work.

Before the influx of *zhiqings*, there were barely any educated employees on the state farm: the childish graffiti on the walls was a tell-tale sign of just how low the level of literacy had been. My offer to help out with the propaganda effort was readily accepted. Armed with my (rather modest) experience with the bulletin board at primary school and with the anthology of Chairman Mao's paintings and quotations, I never let the political instructor down during my time as the company's propaganda officer.

Before we got started, the political instructor showed us around the premises and gave us a thorough briefing. Our priority was to increase the coverage of Mao quotations and to add more propaganda paintings and motifs which would display our allegiance to Mao. Our "canvas" was the hall, the walls—literally all public spaces. He pinpointed for us the most important space for Mao's highest instructions and his classic propaganda slogans such as "Be resolute, fear no sacrifice"; the places where we should copy his other quotations; the spots where we should set down the appeals from Lin Biao, his then heir-apparent; and the walls where we should paint Mao's life-size figure, his portrait and a motif designed to show our dedication, which would consist of the word "loyal" and a drawing of a chrysanthemum and Mao himself. All of these drawings aimed to give the public a convenient opportunity to express their allegiance to Mao as frequently as possible. On top of that, we had to observe the political climate of the day by publishing a wall newspaper and creating posters on a regular basis. Eventually, we also ran the company radio station.

It was no small job. But when we were asked if we had the confidence to carry it out, I heard myself responding without a hint of hesitation: "For the sake of the revolution, absolutely no problem!" Although I accompanied it with an invisible sneer, I was quite satisfied with my straightforward, politically correct answer.

Professionally I was less easily satisfied, but with the basic training and practice that my school had given me in the different styles of calligraphy, and my sheer determination to do a good job, my mural representations of political slogans and Mao's sayings were never criticized.

The challenge was to paint Mao's figure or portrait on a wall. To imitate what was perceived as the correct style of depicting our great leader, I first copied his image from the anthology on to a piece of glass. Then we used a flashlight to project the image on to the wall and traced it there with a pencil, something we could do only at night. We then applied colors to the drawing during the day: the most challenging procedure of all, since it was a real test of one's artistic training and talents. Fortunately, we always managed to satisfy public scrutiny, and our depictions of our great leader were never censured for not being "real" enough.

During one of our nocturnal working sessions to re-capture the image of Mao that had been projected on to the wall, we suffered a glitch. While we were absorbed in copying Mao's portrait on to the wall, some of those who were walking home after a prolonged political study session stayed to watch us. Noticing that we were fiddling about in the dim light, one of the old hands removed the flashlight that had been fixed at a certain angle for the purpose of casting Mao's figure on to the wall, and held it right behind us. When we saw the glaring light on the wall, it was too late and all our efforts were ruined. We groaned in frustration but dared not utter a single word of complaint.

As to the "loyal" motif, we would first draw a picture on a piece of brown paper, cut it out, stick it on the wall and then spray the outline on to the wall. The character for "loyal" and the drawing of a chrysanthemum were relatively easy and could be drawn on a single piece of brown paper. As for Mao's portrait, wanting to avoid using the same one over and again throughout the premises, we chose variations from the anthology and made five separate versions. This was no laughing matter and had to be meticulously executed. Any error, even the slightest one, could be deemed a political matter, epitomizing one's ideological position and expressing a negative attitude toward the class struggle, with the offender liable to be sent to prison. With no electrical device available, all that we had to enable us to complete a vivid portrait of Mao was a hand-held spray.

To consolidate the relationship between us Han-people and the Li, our "advanced methods and technology" were recommended to a local Li village. Armed with my own supply of blueprints, colors, brushes and a spray, I went to the village one night to supervise a painting. In return for my trouble, I was treated to a feast of sweet potato, cassava, rice, muntjac, and sweet potato wine. Unfortunately, the wine was wasted on me, for I had yet to acquire a taste for it.

Our captain bought a three-in-one transmitter with a record player during one of his visits to Haikou City. After some rudimentary but ingenious adaptations based on a limited knowledge of transmission technology, we hastily set up a simple radio station for our company. Every evening before the regimental cable radio came on air via the telephone line, we made our own broadcasts. We played revolutionary songs such as *The East Is Red* and read the political commentaries from the state news agency, articles on anti-capitalism and anti-revisionism, and some thoughts from the troops after they had undergone yet another study session.

For the most part, my work as a propaganda officer was far less strenuous than toiling in the jungle. But not always.

One day, while we were preparing to welcome some senior figures who had come to inspect a major joint campaign, the regimental headquarters borrowed our transmitting facility with the aim of broadcasting a fanfare on the newly completed terrace. It was considered an honor to be entrusted with such a "glorious" political task. Unfortunately, the only vehicle in our company, the ox-cart, was needed for transporting meals to those working on the terrace, leaving me with no choice but to resort to a shoulder pole to carry the equipment there. In one basket was the transmitter, record player, microphone and broadcasting scripts, in the other, four large dry-cell batteries and the loudspeakers. As I was tottering along the hill track with this heavy load, I must have resembled some street hawker of pre-liberation days on his way to market. I became the butt of many jokes.

I set off early—at eight o'clock. After a while, I was so sweaty that I began to strip off my clothes, until all I was wearing was a pair of shorts. When I eventually reached the terraces more than an hour later, I was bathed in sweat and exhausted before I could even set up the equipment.

For the majority of my time as a propaganda officer, my skills in fine art spared me from physical labor. But during the later stage of my life as a *zhiqing*, propaganda officers were no longer exempt from toiling in the open air, and eventually I had my fair share of hard labor in the rubber plantations and vegetable fields.

SALUTING THE MORNING SUN

Huang Ronger

In 1972, I was assigned to the political division of the regiment to work as a propaganda officer. The political division was a place known for the versatile talents of those who worked there. Some came from the army, some from the local communities, and some from the *zhiqings*. I couldn't compete with them, but I knew my role: my strength was to mobilize them.

I wasn't well read or versatile. When I was studying in Guangya Secondary School, we had a half-day off on Saturdays. My sister and I would go to the *Nanfang Daily*, the newspaper where my father worked. But while she would go and read in the library, I would play table-tennis just outside it. At senior secondary school, my classmates were all preparing to gain entry to the top universities, but I didn't give a damn and preferred to play ping-pong. I wasn't a keen reader, and after I took up my new job at regimental headquarters, I soon made myself a laughing stock. I composed a poem about the Paris Commune, and in it I wrote that the soldiers were singing "The Internationale" when they marched to Versailles. The error was soon spotted: the song had not been written until after the Paris Commune was destroyed. I was ashamed of myself. I knew that by nature I preferred outdoor activities to sitting down quietly with a book. But I was a natural born organizer, and I decided to exploit my strength.

Before being promoted to work in the regiment, I had already experienced some successes as a clerk in No. 9 Company. I tried every trick to enliven the leisure of the troops, such as organizing night schools, publishing a regular wall newspaper, holding parties, getting back the football which had been confiscated from its owners by our supply chief, and getting a ping-pong table built from scratch. As the propaganda officer of the regiment, I now had a much larger platform. I headed the Maoist propaganda troupe when it toured the regiment, the Li villages, and the naval outposts on Hainan Island. On one occasion, we were even chosen to give a public performance to the army corps on behalf of No. 4 Division. And while most *zhiqings* were feeling disoriented a few years into their rustication, I organized the writing and performance of the suite of songs, *I Love My Army Corps*. But of all the schemes I tried out in the regiment, there was one which made the greatest impact on my life: the publication of an anthology of poems and a periodical named *The Morning Sun*.

In the regiment there were many gifted and talented *zhiqings*. When they had time on their hands, some would write, some would draw and some would contribute to the radio station. A number of them had even had poems published in the *Regimental Soldier's Paper*, *Hainan Daily*, and *Hainan Youth*. As soon as I told the Daling *zhiqing* poets that I would like to compile and publish a collection of their work, they were most enthusiastic, and I shortly received several dozen new poems from them. The collection was swiftly printed as a mimeograph. It didn't cross our minds to give the anthology a name: the cover was a piece of plain white paper stamped at the top with "PP," the initials of the political propaganda unit. Copies of the anthology were distributed to all *zhiqing* poets across Daling Farm.

By then, my father had been reinstated to the post of deputy director of the Guangdong Provincial Propaganda Department, and he was also the director of the Guangdong Press. I decided to exploit our relationship and get the Guangdong Press to publish the anthology.

Carrying a copy of it, I paid a visit to my father in Guangzhou. After flicking through it, he told me bluntly that it was unlikely that the press would publish the anthology on its own. He added that the press was compiling a general anthology of work by young poets and suggested that I submit the Daling anthology to the editorial department. Bearing a handwritten note from my father, I went to visit the editor-in-chief. The editor took our anthology and asked if I had contributed to it. I pointed out my own contributions, knowing them to be inferior to those of my fellow *zhiqings*.

After my return to Hainan, I waited anxiously for feedback. I felt certain that in order to ingratiate himself with my father, the editor-in-chief would publish at least one poem from each of my poet friends. After much apprehension on my part, the anthology appeared. It was called *Years of Flame!* It contained the works of some famous young poets, but only three pieces were reprinted from the Daling anthology, and one of those was mine! I didn't know how to explain this embarrassing situation to my fellow *zhiqing* poets but they all took it in stride and offered comfort to me. In fact, the editor-in-chief had not made a wholly unwise choice: the other two pieces from the anthology were by two of the best-known poets in Daling.

The publication of *Years of Flame* boosted morale and encouraged poets to write more assiduously: I felt that there should be a forum to help them develop. I gathered a few like-minded *zhiqings* for a meeting and announced the formation of *The Morning Sun Creative Group* of No. 13 Regiment, No. 4 Division. A group consisting of myself as head and eight or nine active members in support decided that we would publish a periodical entitled *The Morning Sun*. Chairman Mao had once said that the world belonged to the young because they were like the bright rising sun at eight or nine o'clock in the morning. By naming our periodical *The Morning Sun*, we wished to be entrusted with the great revolutionary cause.

Most of the contributions reflected on our daily manual labor and ordinary *zhiqing* lives: they expressed our revolutionary ideals and ambitions, and celebrated the flame of communism. Inevitably they were tinged with politics. I entrusted the versatile Guangzhou *zhiqing*, Ou

Nianzhong, the composer of *I Love My Army Corps*, to design the cover, and he came up with some designs that vividly captured the passions and ideals of the young Daling poets.

As to printing, all we had access to was a mimeograph. Luckily, Zhang Huixin, then a teacher at No. 7 Company and also my Guangya ex-schoolmate, was good at making stencils. She rose to the challenge brilliantly, and every night after she had finished marking student papers would work on the stencils in the dim light of an oil lamp until midnight. She had fine, distinctive handwriting, and I was grateful for her hard work and commitment. Without such talent and dedication, the periodical would never have appeared, and I decided that if these people should need any help in the future, I would take it as an opportunity to repay them. And so with enthusiastic and voluntary contributions from all sides, we published a number of issues of *The Morning Sun*.

In early 1975, a friend informed me that the Guangzhou Municipal Cultural Bureau was about to recruit six well-trained *zhiqings* or cultural officers from Hainan, and he instructed me to send him some samples of my writing. Writing had never been my strength and besides, I was tied up with so many duties, whether political or related to production campaigns, that I passed up the opportunity. To my surprise, however, an order was soon delivered to the farm for me to work in the Guangzhou Municipal Cultural Bureau as its creative writer. I was intrigued and didn't know how it had happened.

It turned out that after I had turned down that not-to-be-missed opportunity, my friend paid a visit to my father about it. My father told him that as my father he knew for certain that I was not a good writer. My mother, however, thought differently and didn't want me to lose the opportunity: she took it upon herself to find samples of my writings. By chance, a good friend of mine was returning to Guangzhou to study at a polytechnic institute, and at about that time he paid my mother a visit. Although he had worked as a carpenter at No. 9 Company, he had kept a copy of *The Morning Sun* and had even taken it back to Guangzhou. He gave it to my mother, but it would take more than a single copy of the periodical to persuade my father. Nevertheless, one of the best-known Daling ex-*zhiqing* poets studying in Guangzhou managed to get hold of several issues and give them to my father. My writings weren't any good, but my father forwarded them to the director of the Guangzhou Municipal Cultural Bureau, who happened to be a friend of his. I wouldn't be surprised if the order for my return to Guangzhou was issued before he got around to reading a word of what I had written.

At that time, China was in the midst of another political campaign, this time to criticize the traditional novel *The Water Margin* for the appeasement and revisionism displayed by one of its leading characters, a rebel. My first assignment as a state-employed creative writer was to write an article criticizing the novel. I pieced something together by copying from here and there and submitted it as mine. Before I knew it I was transferred from the creative writing sector to a managerial role in the training sector.

I can't remember how many issues of *The Morning Sun* were published, but what I know for certain is that many of those involved made good use of their energies and talents. Among its active members and contributors were those who would later make their mark in various fields, such as radio, television, newspapers, further and higher education, and the commercial sector. As for me, I have always treasured the friends I made during those days when we worked together to get the periodical published, and throughout the years I have stayed in touch with them all.

For me, *The Morning Sun* encapsulated the passion of our *zhiqing* age.

TRUTH WAS THE LEAST CONCERN

Cao Nancai

Rusticated from 1968 until 1975, I had a long spell in my *zhiqing* life when I was working as a correspondent. In theory, our job was to report on grassroots activities, act as the voice of the troops and express the attitudes of the masses, a task we took seriously. However, in an era when ideology was dominant and theories with no factual basis were rampant, journalism and writing as a whole were hit by a tsunami of vapid formalism, from which few emerged unscathed.

The prevalent practice in writing was fabrication, stealthy substitution, hyperbole and glorification, plagiarizing, and muddling. To ensure that our writing was sufficiently mendacious, fraudulent, bombastic and insubstantial, we took to inventing sensational "news" and infusing our writing with fancy alliteration, elaborate rhyming couplets, parataxis, and doggerel. A typical example of such nonsensical output was: "Master three syntheses, establish four connections, grasp five steps, excel at six words, compose seven articles"—all done in the name of literary "refinement."

In our effort to stay up with the game, many of us kept a notebook and would copy from newspapers and other sources the titles and propositions of the "exemplary" pieces, search for something to fill gaps, throw in some cooked evidence and a bit from our own imaginations, retitle and package it, and then submit this farrago as our own work. To elevate it to new heights of fabrication and grandiosity, many dedicated correspondents would spend long hours chained to their desks, and hence sport panda eyes and prematurely gray hair. We described our job as "playing with words" and ourselves as "plagiarists." Indeed, we were often mere monkeys fooling with language. A long-standing joke epitomized our typical mind-set and style of work: A correspondent went to interview an old timer who had been driving an ox-cart for years on end. When asked what he thought about while he was working, the old timer replied: "Nothing really, I just want to get home soon." The correspondent would not accept this as an answer, and said: "No, that can't be the case: you must have something profound in mind." The old timer was baffled and replied: "I'm only driving an ox-cart. All I care about is whether the cart is in good condition and the ox is fed. If I had too much on my mind, I might be distracted." The correspondent was anxious and said: "Aren't you wondering if you can drive the ox-cart until the dream of communism is realized?" The old timer was even more confused . . .

As well as reporters, we were the ad hoc ghostwriters of the regiment. One of my assignments was to write a speech for Lao Quan, the political instructor of No. 3 Company, who needed to explain how his troop had turned into a model company. As it turned out, the toughest challenge was not to get my paper approved by the authorities but to coach Lao Quan, who without the aid of my script was to get up on the podium and give the speech as if it were his own. A few days before the assembly, I was tasked with helping him to understand and memorize it. A down-to-earth veteran, he got on with it immediately. He would consult me whenever he came across a new word or bit of jargon. It seemed like a cakewalk: after all, the speech was only a few thousand words long. But what I had underestimated was not only the challenge that my faultless writing posed to a grassroots cadre with little education, but the extent to which I had been carried away in my pursuit of the perfect style for the occasion.

After struggling with my script for a whole day, Lao Quan asked me some tough questions, such as: what did I mean by "guiding principle." In the speech, I had laid down three propositions: First, adopt Maoism as the guiding principle, so as to set the helm on the right course; second, apply Maoism in rubber tree planting, so as to retain control of production and construction; third, adopt Maoism for indoctrination, so as to complete the program of thought education. I was secretly rather pleased with it: it came as a shock that it was not to Lao Quan's liking. I thought that my script had not only captured the essence of the topic and built on the argument layer by layer, but that the structure of parataxis and antithesis was simply impeccable. But Lao Quan didn't buy it: the more I explained, the more confused he got. In the end, he threw in the towel and said: "To be perfectly honest, who the hell has time for this crap? At our level, we just do as we're told. You people with pens are just full of bullshit. But I can see how tough it must be to write to the order of the authorities. I'll just have to play along." A few days later, he finally mastered my script and the day after he delivered the speech, he told me: "I thought that the toughest job was to work at the grassroots, but now I know that the job you guys have is even tougher. Who would have imagined that it was going to be even harder for me to memorize your script than for you to write it!"

Elated by that particular effort, I imagined that in the division its exceptional quality would lead the field. But to my surprise, a rival outdid me. Although I can no longer remember its peerless parataxes and antitheses, I have a vivid memory of its grandiloquence. "What is the priority in the construction of a troop?" it asked, "Politics or production? Politics! What is essential to the construction of a troop—the nurturing of its workforce or its trees? The workforce! What kind of troops do we need to nurture—Li Yuhe or Wang Lianju? Li Yuhe!" These were both undercover revolutionaries from *The Legend of the Red Lantern,* one of the eight revolutionary model plays. As a result of being betrayed under torture by Wang, Li became a martyr. Such well-turned phrases were apparently inspired by a recent re-staging of the revolutionary opera.

I HELPED CREATE A HERO

Chen Hongbo

In early 1974, a striking role model who dared to "swim against the tide" was created in our regiment.

Then a regimental correspondent, I first learned about him from an official when I visited No. 15 Company to compile a report for the regiment. His name was Zeng Ruijie, a *zhiqing* from Jieyang County.

No. 15 Company was a newly established troop which was based in a remote and poor area and with the worst living conditions in the regiment. So that it could become self-reliant, Zeng was charged with growing vegetables for the whole company. He rose early in the morning and worked long hours every day to cultivate the fields, to set up an irrigation system, and to tend the vegetables with great care. As a result, they were available to the troop all year round, no small feat in those days. During spells of bad weather, when other companies were deprived of vegetables, the fields he tended were still yielding a decent harvest. He combined diligence and resourcefulness in a way that typifies the Chaoshan people from whom he came. On many occasions his achievements were highly praised by his company, yet he always turned down the bonus that was awarded to him.

I submitted an article about him to the *Regimental Soldier's Paper*. The article, however, didn't get published and according to my superiors and those in the political division, there were three main reasons. First, they said, there was no shortage of people like him in the regiment—people who worked their socks off in times of hardship. Second, my article had not sufficiently explored the way in which Zeng differed from other exemplary figures. And third, my article had not struck the right chord in the current political climate. They decided, therefore, that the article should be scrapped and rewritten.

In my second attempt, I highlighted the fact that Zeng had not only never asked for any favors in return for his achievements but had turned down all rewards and bonuses. In other words, his dedication to the job had been entirely selfless. I also changed the style of the piece, writing it as if it were an argument expressed by Zeng himself and entitling it "Why we should focus on what contribution we can make and never ask for rewards of any sort." After submitting the article, I followed in the footsteps of our political commissar by staying at No. 14 Company in order to gain first hand experience at the grassroots.

Three days later, we received a phone call informing us that a high-ranking army corps official was paying a visit and that we were to return to regimental headquarters without delay. It turned out that the second version of my article had attracted a lot of attention at the *Regimental Soldier's Paper*. Led by a political official of the army corps, the editor-in-chief and a dozen or so reporters decided that they should pay us a visit. They believed that Zeng's case embodied certain principles of great political significance. These included: the importance of working hard yet never asking for rewards; a high level of political awareness in channeling one's efforts in the right direction; the need to be heroically ambitious by swimming against the tide. The purpose of their visit was to interview him in person and check the facts so as to promote his good deeds throughout the army corps. Following a briefing by the regimental officials, they worked in groups: some to visit No. 15 Company to talk to his captain and get feedback from his fellow *zhiqings*; some to take a good look at the vegetable fields he tended; and some to interview him in person.

A week later, under the headline: "To Fight for the Consolidation of Proletarian Rule, Never Work for a Bonus," a letter to the editor under Zeng's name occupied the front-page spread. The following two pages gave a detailed account of Zeng's achievements. All this coverage vividly reflected the political atmosphere of the time and highlighted his determination to "swim against the tide" by working hard and never expecting recognition or rewards. It caused a major stir in the regiment, and a movement to learn from him was launched. The Party committees of the army corps and the regiment jointly issued "The decision to learn from Comrade Zeng Ruijie," Soon afterward, Zeng was chosen by the regiment, the division, and the army corps as the proactive member to learn Maoism, and the Communist Youth League awarded him a Grade Three Medal. *Nanfang Daily*, the provincial Party paper, ran his story in a prominent position and at great length.

Without any doubt, Zeng had done a great service to his troops in improving their diet, and in never thinking about what he could gain from his hard work; he was unselfish and a very valuable exemplar. Yet his story was also somewhat helplessly shaped by the time he was living in, a time when he had absolutely no control over his own destiny. He had been manipulated by particular political needs and quite gratuitously turned into a hero who dared to "swim against the tide."

THE STRUGGLE TO GET INTO PRINT
He Qinghua

After graduating from Guangya Secondary School in 1967, I was rusticated to Hainan the following November. Assigned to No. 3 Company, I worked first in the jungle, then in propagation, and finally in the rubber cutting squad. When the management of the state farm was handed over to the army a year later, I was reassigned to regimental headquarters to work in its newly formed correspondence squad, which, managed by the political division of the regiment, was charged with providing articles for the *Regimental Soldier's Paper*.

Published by the Guangzhou Army Production and Construction Corps, it was distributed, along with the Guangdong provincial newspaper *Nanfang Daily* and the Hainan official newspaper *Hainan Daily*, to each company. It was a compact four-page weekly, and its main readership was supposed to be the *zhiqings*-turned-regimental-soldiers. Since it was kept in the office, most *zhiqings* didn't get around to reading it. However, during that closed era, in particular, the circumstances we were trapped in, the paper allowed a glimpse of a world outside our isolated regiment.

There were four regimental correspondents in the squad. Although we all liked to consider ourselves adequately prepared for our new jobs, none of us was a trained journalist or knew much about feature writing. And it showed! Even though we did our very best and submitted over seventy pieces in our first year, only two got published. Yet despite the recurrent disappointments, and despite the fact that all of our contributions were anonymously signed off as "No. 13 Regiment of No. 4 Division," we never hesitated to grab the paper as soon as it was delivered to the office and scan it for our individual contributions. To tell the truth, the average article was so short that it was termed a "tofu piece." But through hard work and sheer determination, we gradually picked up some trade secrets on how to write for the *Regimental Soldier's Paper*.

Two success stories stand out in my memory. The first was a report on how a Party branch had changed its management style to that of collective leadership. Led by our political commissar, a colleague and I went to stay in No. 5 Company for a whole week, during which we shadowed the rubber cutters in the mornings while they worked on the plantation. In the afternoons, we conducted interviews with branch members, company officials, and the *zhiqings*. We also sat in on the branch meetings. After collecting sufficient materials, the political commissar drafted an outline for us: we needed to focus on how the branch had diligently studied Chairman Mao's works on the democratic centralism of the Party; to explain how it had put Mao's theory into practice by no longer allowing just one person to lay down the law; and to describe how such a new practice was applied to the management of the company in order to strengthen the Party leadership of the troop. After many drafts, we submitted it to the political commissar for his approval. He added a paragraph to point out that the collective leadership of the company was not a one-off exercise, but had been built into the system. We were enlightened by this concluding paragraph and thought it lifted our article to a new height. And, indeed, it was published as the headline report and spread across half the first page! For our young squad it was a real morale booster. In our second year, we were able to get more than twenty articles published by the *Regimental Soldier's Paper* and on one or two occasions, they were even reprinted by the provincial newspaper, the *Nanfang Daily*.

The second success story was when two of our contributions were published in the same issue, one of them written by me. We were thrilled, and I can still remember my efforts on that particular piece. One of our *zhiqings* was promoted to deputy captain. After interviewing him, I wrote a feature on the path he had taken to become a role model. It didn't get published. I went to interview him again for more details, but the second effort got nowhere either. After a couple more tries, it struck me that perhaps I should rewrite the article from a different perspective: on how an ordinary *zhiqing* had been mentored by the regimental officials and transformed into leadership material. This time, it got published.

The role of a correspondent left an indelible mark on me. Correspondents were supposed to be out and about to report on the progress of all the companies. The trip from regimental headquarters to its fifteen companies varied from a mere ten-minute walk to a trek of a good two hours along deserted hill trails. Until my rustication, I inhabited a narrow world between home and school and had never been allowed to escape the vigilance of my grandmother: I was shy, timid, and scared of all dark corners. However, after exchanging my pickaxe and machete for a pen, my first assignment required me to visit a remote company by myself. It was in the afternoon when I set off, a sack with a few days' clothing on my back. To boost my courage, I sang one song after another as I strode along the eerily quiet hill trail. Then all of a sudden, I caught sight of a bare-chested *Leilo*, the name that the Cantonese *zhiqings* had coined for the Li men. He was striding toward me with a machete on his shoulder. Although I had never heard of *zhiqings* being abused or attacked by the *Leilos*, his relatively large build and the "weapon" on his shoulder scared me to death. My singing died away; I held my breath; my steps became mechanical and leaden. It was not until he had walked past and after I had cast a timid glance at his retreating figure that I could take a deep breath and realize that my whole body was trembling. I was ashamed of myself and never told anyone about this incident for fear of becoming a laughing stock. The experience eventually helped me to overcome my timidity.

As the only woman correspondent, I sometimes got special assignments. No. 8 Company had just built a pig farm run solely by female *zhiqings*. It sounded interesting, and it fell to me to cover the story. I stayed at their dormitory in order to shadow them. Their jobs, they told me, were straightforward: prepare the feed, feed the pigs, and clean the sties. When I picked up a cleaver to chop vegetables for the feed, I realized that for an urban young woman like myself who had never been needed in the kitchen at home, chopping efficiently was no mean feat. Despite my best efforts to learn their craft and to work up an interesting story, my article didn't get published. Years later, after my return to Guangzhou, I was sent to work on a chicken farm. During a New Year's party, I produced a song-and-dance routine based on that experience at the pig farm. It was well received and even won first prize—a reward that was somewhat belated!

Besides writing for the *Regimental Soldier's Paper*, we wrote reports and speeches on behalf of the regiment. Sometimes we were also invited to training programs organized by the division to learn from the more senior correspondents whose contributions had been reprinted in the national press such as the *People's Daily*.

The *Regimental Soldier's Paper* folded in 1974 when management of the regiment was returned to the local authority. I was given a new job of secretary to the Party committee of Daling Farm. During my four years as a regimental correspondent, I went to many companies and learned about how things got done at the grassroots. I also overcame my shyness and grew more outspoken, confident, and independent. My experience not only changed my perspective but my status: a fellow correspondent became my husband. It was a life I shall never forget.

Bringers of Arts and Knowledge

TENDING THE LAMP OF LEARNING

Zhu Zhaoyu

From the late 1960s to the early 1970s, the influx into Hainan Island of *zhiqings* from the urban areas of Guangdong Province and beyond brought new life to its agricultural development. Alongside it, the island also experienced a tremendous transformation of its cultural scene. The *zhiqings*, or "educated youth." were in fact educated only to secondary school level, some with nothing more than a primary qualification. Nevertheless, while being instructed by the workers, peasants, and soldiers in how to transform their petit-bourgeois values, these not-so-highly-educated youngsters brought knowledge and technology to the farms they were living on.

Studying at night

Of all the re-education we received as *zhiqings*, the one deemed most important was in ideology. Most of us went to Hainan with the idea of receiving re-education from the poor and lower-middle peasants and the aspiration of opening up the nation's treasured frontier island. Yet reading was a vital part of our lives.

I built my own desk. Gathering bamboo and tree trunks which had been chopped down in the hills, I trimmed and smoothed them with an axe before joining them with white canes and fixing the structure to my bed, something else that I had made with tree trunks. After toiling all day in the elements and then undergoing hours of voluntary work organized by the company, we would sit at these homemade desks to read from the dim light of an oil lamp. On my desk I kept a jar of sugar, which in Hainan cost as little as six to ten *jiao* per kilo: it served as a snack and as a stimulant to relieve night-time fatigue. When we first started, the books we could find were mainly *Mao Zedong's Anthology*, *Memories of Lenin*, *The State and Revolution*, *The History of the Communist Party of the Soviet Union*, *The Communist Manifesto*, and the like. A few official newspapers, such as the *People's Daily* and the *People's Liberation Army Daily*, were also available. Later on, when we were running night schools, there were also elementary textbooks of arithmetic, history, geography, Chinese, and so on. Still later, when we were preparing for the college entrance examinations, some secondary school textbooks for mathematics, physics, and chemistry became a must for us.

Our dormitory was a low-ceilinged thatched hut we built out of trunks, branches, and grass. Drafts came in from all sides, and besides bombardment from the mosquitoes, which were known as "Asian tiger mosquitos" because of their pattern and huge size, our daily nocturnal visitors included snakes, centipedes, "mountain lobsters" (scorpions) and all kinds of ants. One night, just as I was sitting down at my desk after lighting the oil lamp, I felt a stab of pain in my backside. When I looked down, I saw on the bed a monster with claws: it seemed to be staring up at me triumphantly. A mountain lobster! I saw red. At once I snatched up a book and struck it to the dirt floor before chopping it with an axe. The pain soon shot down to my thigh, and seemed to be affecting my heart as well: I was trembling. As primary students in Beijing, we were warned that scorpions are poisonous and that their sting can kill. Luckily for me, a roommate had learned from one of the old hands that despite the pain, it isn't fatal. He raced to the thatched shack where fertilizer was stored, brought back a glass of ammonia, and applied it to my wound. The pain was relieved soon enough but it was a week before it had gone entirely. I always wondered if the mountain lobster had been lured to my desk by my one snack, the jar of sugar. Later on, we built tiled-roof houses as a dormitory, which much improved our living conditions. We also made wooden desks and even organized special-interest groups.

Bringers of Arts and Knowledge

Entertainment at night

When we first arrived on Hainan Island, there were barely any leisure activities. A film projection squad in the regiment that toured the companies every now and then provided the only source of official entertainment. Wherever there was a screening, we would hike through the hills and cross the streams, bringing along wooden stools which we had made for ourselves. Our leisure hours were mostly filled by reading, running night schools, attending Communist Youth League classes, and paying visits to the old timers and helping out with their household chores (such as carrying water, chopping firewood, and washing their children's laundry). We were desperate for fun and entertainment of some kind. That was how we began to create it for ourselves. Every company boasted a "singing ensemble," and among all the *zhiqings*, there were always some who were especially artistic or had a talent for performing. Besides entertaining their own troops, the singing ensembles toured other companies, the regimental headquarters, and even the Li villages and military outposts. In addition, we organized parties at festive seasons: we did all we could to liven up the torpid farms and villages. My diary for the time contains a list of the various ways of partying: performances for the troops; talent shows, singing competitions, local operas, story-telling. sharing letters from home, poetry recitals, performances on musical instruments. Furthermore, we devised the kind of activities you might perform in a modern theme park, and even played musical chairs. We came up with quizzes and held quiz parties. Such activities helped us to forget our harsh environment, the toil and hardship we endured. They dispelled our fatigue, worries and loneliness, and even the thoughts of our faraway families. And they helped our fellow *zhiqings*, the veterans and their children, to immerse themselves in an atmosphere, however contrived, of peace and prosperity and to feel part of a big family.

Night schools

Although most *zhiqings* had not even completed their secondary education when they were rusticated (I myself was only a seventh-grade student), we were dedicated to voluntary work to promote literacy and impart knowledge. In those days, the old hands (we called them "old workers" although they were only in their thirties) were mostly from the rural areas, or they were ex-servicemen who had received little education, never mind their rustic spouses. Even among the *zhiqings*, some were from rural townships or villages and had received only primary schooling. Under Party leadership, the Communist Youth League in my company organized tutorial groups for the night school and study groups. My diary records that the night school was intended to promote "literacy, culture, and research" in four phases. First, the promotion of literacy and numeracy: the teaching of reading and the *pinyin* system, use of the dictionary, letter writing, newspaper reading, and arithmetic in everyday life. Second, primary education: the teaching of Chinese, how to structure articles, the principles of science and geography, the use of the dictionary, arithmetic. Third, junior secondary education: phrases, terms and terminologies in the works of Karl Marx, Lenin, and Mao Zedong; literary quotations, social and communist history, mathematics, physics, chemistry, literature, meteorology, astronomy, and so on. Finally, research into fruit and rubber; the development of technology such as soil cultivation and fertilization; the construction of terraces for cultivation in the hills; the eradication of couch grasses, weeds, and so on. Looking at these notes now, I find it hard to imagine how we planned the curriculums and prepared the teaching materials: neither have I kept any of these materials. What I can recall clearly was the "textbook" we consulted at all times: *Ten Thousand Whys*, the then best-selling science title for children which my family sent me from Guangzhou. In my company alone, there were eleven old timers and *zhiqings* who signed up for the literacy group and, in addition, six reading groups. Like everybody else in the company, we rose early to toil in the fields all day and then took part in the after-hours voluntary work to improve our living conditions: it was not until the evening that we could find time for curriculum development and to prepare ourselves to teach. We organized study groups, tutorial sessions, seminars, tests, and exams—despite its voluntary nature, we took this job seriously. Though we were provided with some basic equipment, such as desks, chairs, blackboards, paper and gas lamps, no extra resources were available, and the night school was run on a shoe-string. To subsidize its tight funding, we had everybody go round the companies and even the Li villages to collect reclaimable waste such as newspapers, bottles, plastic, rubber, copper, iron and so on, and then exchanged them for money at the collective reclamation store.

When higher education was partially reopened in the early 1970s,[10] I and many other *zhiqings* seized the opportunity to recharge ourselves with the will and stamina we had expended during the years of toiling on the farm. In December 1973, I fulfilled my childhood ambition to become a geological researcher. The day before I was to leave Daling, officials, old timers and fellow *zhiqings* all came to bid me farewell. Among their presents were a notebook from an old timer who asked me to "Study hard and work for the people"; a bamboo plate, which is a Chaozhou speciality; towels and more notebooks; and a bamboo flute from a fellow *zhiqing* with the inscription: "A small bamboo can launch a thousand words. I hope you can carry it with you at all times. Play it during your breaks from study: its tune can carry your thoughts to friends afar." I was also reminded to preserve the good practice of working hard wherever I went and to make the most of myself. The following spring, I received a parcel from the regiment: it contained a certificate of merit from the Communist Youth League, a towel, a pen, a notebook, and an enthusiastic letter to my parents commending my conduct. I was deeply moved: Daling had not forgotten me.

Years later, I was awarded a PhD in Geology and became, at last, a genuinely "educated" youth!

---

10. All schools and colleges were closed down soon after the launch of the Cultural Revolution in 1966. Schools reopened a year later, but it was not until 1970 that some institutions of higher education were allowed to follow. However, they were accessible only to workers, peasants and soldiers with "politically correct" backgrounds, and it was not until 1977 that higher education was officially reestablished.

TEACHING TWICE AS HARD

Feng Qiqin

I was rusticated to No. 7 Company of Daling Farm in November 1968. In my troop, I was the first *zhiqing* to be asked to be a substitute teacher at the company school. Housed in a tiny tiled building in the hills between two companies, it catered only to lower primary students from the local areas. The older students attended the more formal regimental school, which employed trained teachers. The teaching at the company school was casual, since it offered neither a trained nor a permanent teacher, nor even a formal curriculum. All the substitute teacher could resort to was a set of primary textbooks of Chinese and arithmetic: everything else was left to her or his own devices and had to be improvised.

My pupils were all local kids. They were divided roughly by age into two groups and shared the only classroom on the premises. The two groups sat back to back: before I finished with one group, I would assign them some classwork, and then walk to the other end of the room to teach the other group. There was a blackboard at each end of the room. At such a tender age, the kids were easily distracted by what was going on behind them and would often turn round to see what the other group was up to. Because there was always only one member of staff in the school, the supply teacher had to become a sort of polymath: besides teaching Chinese and arithmetic, she or he was also obliged to teach singing, drawing, manual labor, and physical education. Short and rather weak, I was no good at physical education. Outside the one-room premises, there were no playground or sports facilities to assist me. All we could do in physical education was to practice lining up, turning right or left, coming to attention or standing at ease, and marking time. The youngsters were so docile that they excelled at the limited exercises, and on their way back home along the hilly paths, would usually walk single file. After school the pupils were required to go over what they had learned in the classroom, and they would do so by the dim light of an oil lamp. I inspected them regularly, chatting with their families in order to check how they were faring at home.

Because of the extreme isolation of the region and the low literacy rate, the youngsters were largely untutored; but they were also adorable—unaffected, brave, and funny. One day, as I was absorbed in helping one group to read a new text, some of them suddenly leapt up and threw their shoulder bags and small wooden stools to the floor. It turned out that a huge centipede had crept into the classroom and, thanks to them, I had a lucky escape from it. It was said of this monster that it could make even a strong man cry.

I left Daling Farm to return to Guangzhou in 1975 and lost touch with my pupils, but in 1998, and with the help of some of the ex-*zhiqings*, the son of the deputy captain managed to track me down. He paid me a visit, bringing bags of fresh lychees and rice from his new home, a satellite city of Guangzhou. What he remembered about me the most, he revealed, was that it was I who taught him pinyin, and through it, he was able to develop further. Learning pinyin is the most basic step toward acquiring Mandarin Chinese, and yet in those days it was not until the *zhiqings'* arrival at the state farm that the system was introduced to the remote mountain schools. Educated only to junior secondary school level, and without any formal training, I am not qualified to teach. But even under those austere conditions, some of the mountain children grew up to be academics, civil servants, and entrepreneurs. I am glad my efforts bore some fruit.

SOWING THE SEEDS OF THE ARTS
He Yancheng

When we were rusticated to Daling Farm, some "Guangzhou boys" were regularly dispatched to the "big school"—the only school—in the regiment. Located in Baisha County, one of the poorest and hilliest areas of Hainan Island, the underdeveloped Daling Farm had little to offer in cultural terms. Due to the primitive roads and transport system, some companies, especially the really remote ones, would set up their own school for the convenience of the youngsters, using a small thatched hut or a run-down tiled building. The dozen or so primary-age pupils shared not only a single classroom but a single substitute teacher, who taught all subjects to groups of different ages and different abilities. After a few years, they would be sent to the regimental school for upper primary and secondary education, and that was why it was called the "big school."

The reason we were regularly assigned to work at the school was to facilitate the rehearsals and performances of its Maoist propaganda troupe. The repertoire of the troupe was original in the sense that it was largely inspired by "real lives" and created by us. For us, the best reward for our efforts was the warm reception the performances usually received.

It was a common belief that we had an easy and rosy life working for the school troupe. To some extent this was true, especially at the beginning, when we were given the incredible privilege of being driven everywhere we toured. But the favorable policy was discontinued when, with the development of production and construction, the demand for vehicles grew. No matter how far our destination was, we then had to trek across hills and valleys, and to ford streams with musical instruments and props on our shoulders. And, thanks largely to the fickle tropical climate of the island, there was no shortage of occasions when we were caught by thunderstorms halfway through a trek, and arrived at our destinations like drenched chickens. In our first encounter with such conditions, the youngsters in our care turned out to be our guardian angels because, thanks to an early exposure to thunder and lightning in the hills, they had learned how to dodge them.

Our repertoire included ballet and performances on musical instruments. For ballet, the youngsters were sent for training to the propaganda troupe of the state farm bureau in Haikou, where they underwent strenuous ballet classes by day and received normal schooling at night. All the ballets were "modern" in the sense that they had communist and revolutionary themes and were based on the template of the eight revolutionary model plays. Sometimes we would even stage the whole of *The Red Detachment of Women*, one of the eight model plays.

The troupe was usually the first place that the youngsters came across any musical instrument, let alone played one. When the troupe was set up, the job of both playing and teaching musical instruments fell to us, their *zhiqing* tutors. Like white blotting paper, they absorbed everything we taught them, from the basics of how to handle an instrument to the skill of reading music. We had only a few instruments at our disposal: a flute, an accordion, a dulcimer, a violin, and an erhu. There was no bass, so its sound was missing. Although none of us had ever seen a real cello, this didn't stop us from having a bold idea—to get one made locally! We had seen it in films and that was sufficient for us. It looked to us like an enlarged violin, and with this impression in mind, we asked some skilful carpenters to make one for us. None of them took up the challenge, so in order to realize this dream, we searched the hills for the finest wood possible and spent days persuading some of the best carpenters to make it for us. Our cello, a labor of love, looked somewhat rustic and didn't sound perfect either. But that was what we had: we cherished it and tried to get the most from it.

From performing in the big school to touring Daling Farm, from an unknown ensemble to one that was warmly received everywhere, the troupe gradually built up its repertoire and reputation and even toured beyond Baisha County. It matured quickly, and we were very proud of it. We hoped that what we did was not just to train a few artistic talents in the school but sow some artistic seeds in the cultural desert of Daling Farm.

Come to think of it, among us "Guangzhou boys" there was a female *zhiqing* from Meixian who was captured in the documentary film *Great Fruits on Treasure Island*.

Living with the Li

INTOXICATED BY THE GIRLS

Huang Ronger

Some twenty kilometres from the west coast of Hainan Island is a hill. The trees there are so green that from afar it looks dark. The word "dark" is not auspicious for the Chinese. We named the hill Keling (the "*ke*" hill) because the Chinese word *ke* sounds like the word for "dark" in Cantonese. From its foot to the west coast of the island is a vast plain. The peak of Keling is only slightly over two hundred meters above sea level, but being the highest in the area it looks grand and majestic—like a stately king surrounded by an entourage of bodyguards. Interspersed among Li villages, the fifteen companies of Daling Farm were scattered along the range.

The Li people in the area retained many characteristics of a primitive tribe and, as I recall, even those of a matriarchal society. About an hour's walk from the Red Star Company that I was initially assigned to was a Li Village called Rongbang. Together with some old schoolmates, I had once been there to have a look round. The Li men didn't wear their ethnic attire, but instead put on old People's Liberation Army uniforms and Liberation shoes. They appeared to have been assimilated into our Han-Chinese culture. While many children wore Han-Chinese attire, some were naked even on the wintry day that we visited and, to keep themselves warm, were cuddled by the elders. As for the women, they wore plain black close-fitting skirts and open-front blouses without underwear. As we walked by, they would pull their blouses closed to cover their breasts. On a rainy winter's day, the temperature in the area could drop below ten degrees Celsius. Although it was sunny when we were there, it felt chilly. To keep warm, most of the women and children stayed by the fire in their pyramid-shaped thatched huts. When we glanced into one of them, we could see a fire in the middle of the living area and the villagers sitting round the fire on the dirt floor and wearing little, except for a few who had blankets wrapped round them. The smoke of the fire was so pungent that most kept their eyes shut. Some elderly women were sitting by the door in the sun, chewing something that dyed their teeth black and which turned out to be betel nut. With black teeth and blue tattoos on their faces, they looked rather terrifying. Later on, I learned from some of the old timers that a tell-tale sign of whether a Li woman was born before or after the 1949 Liberation was her facial appearance. Since tattooing was considered primitive and backward, a symbol of how women were exploited and tortured under the old customs, the practice was banned after Liberation. To abolish the customs was perceived, at least by the Han Chinese, as a step toward the modernization of a primitive tribe. In Rongbang, most of the teenage girls we came across didn't sport any tattoos on their faces.

My most striking memory of Rongbang Village was a party that we had with the Li.

Before the Spring Festival of 1969, our captain assembled all the *zhiqings* under his command and announced that, as part of our effort to cement the all-important union of workers and peasants, we were to have a get-together with the Li people of Rongbang. Such a union was crucial for our survival, he said. During the Cultural Revolution of 1967, the fighting between different factions had been fierce, and due to a particular dispute our company was in danger of being annihilated by a nearby farm on the plain. The Li, however, came forward to make peace between us: they maintained that the workers of Daling Farm were their friends and shouldn't be attacked. Owing to their fear of the Li, those who had plotted to attack our company changed their minds. Although the Li villages were small, their bonds were so strong that if a roll from a wooden drum was sounded, several thousand Li from the nearby areas would mobilize within no time. It was vital for us to secure their protection.

After hearing this, we all became enthusiastic about the idea of having a party with them. But we had one slight concern. It was said that the Li people did not care much about food hygiene—that they caught frogs, snakes, and even mice and kept them in a clay pot until they rotted, treating them as a delicacy which they reserved only for their honoured guests. However, we were assured by our captain that some of the young Li men who had been working as technicians in our company would instruct their tribesmen on how to cater for us according to Han Chinese customs.

Led by our captain, we went to Rongbang Village on the second day of the Lunar New Year. Hanging on his chest was a piece of cardboard that measured thirty centimeters in width and twenty centimeters in length, on which was Chairman Mao's portrait and the Chinese character "loyal." Since such placards were commonly hung on those denounced at class-struggle rallies as "capitalist-roaders" or "monsters and demons," we thought this somewhat ludicrous. On the placard was the name of the accused with a big black cross on top. But none of us dared to vent our feelings, let alone mock such a typical Hainanese way of pledging one's allegiance to Chairman Mao.

At the entrance of the village were two lines of Li men with their hunting guns. As we walked down the lane, they fired in the air and the whole lane instantly smelled of gunpowder. Once we were past them, we heard drum-rolls and saw that those who were hitting the drums were the Li women. The small round drums were hung on their fronts, but I had to keep my eyes ahead and dared not look sideways: under the open blouses of their ethnic attire, none of them had covered their breasts with underwear. When we reached the front of a big thatched hut, we saw on a high platform a tattooed elderly woman. With her black blouse wide open and her breasts exposed, she looked grand and majestic. She was hitting a huge drum, which produced a solemn sound. It felt as though we were entering the tribe of an ancient matriarchal society. In such societies, the men fished or hunted while the women harvested crops. Women were the most important figures in the family and also the most revered in the tribe. These Li women were indeed held in high esteem, and they shared the harvest with their hunter-menfolk. To me, the Rongbang villagers were still by and large a matriarchal tribe, and on that day we were interacting with a truly ancient people.

After we had entered the large thatched hut, we were seated on rough wooden stools. Our captain handed over our gifts and then the village chief made a speech, which was interpreted by a young Li technician working in our company. Our captain returned this courtesy with a few simple Li phrases he had picked up. After the brief formalities, some teenage Li girls brought in food on large plates and laid them on the table positioned in the middle of the room. The tabletop looked like a raft made from several tree branches which had been bound together, and the plates were piled with large chunks of meat. They then brought in two pots of sweet potato wine. Our captain announced at the top of his voice that for this occasion, our Li brothers had hunted wild boar and muntjac, and that to show our appreciation of their hospitality we should eat to our hearts' delight. But he warned us against the sweet potato wine: it could easily make us drunk. Since most of us had never touched alcohol before, we decided to take only the meat and steer clear of the wine. Boar's liver cooked with vermicelli was a dish that I had always relished: that night it was the freshest and most delicious I had tasted. Serving us at our sides were the Li girls, their faces free of tattoos. We were not sure where the Li men had suddenly vanished to, but the girls started to serve us the sweet potato wine, and when they found that none of us were drinking, began to urge us. If you took just a sip whenever a big bowl of the wine was held before you, they would leave you be; but if you didn't play by their rules, two of them would coerce you. One grabbed your waist from behind while the other would hold your ear or nose and force the wine into your mouth. When it was my turn, I accepted the bowl at once and took a mouthful from it. Some *zhiqings* managed to escape by pretending they needed to relieve themselves and leaving their straw hats as a pledge of their speedy return to the table. A friend who sat next to me refused to follow the rules and was forced to finish a full bowl in one go, which must have been about half a liter of wine.

On our way back, our only vehicle, the ox-cart, was packed with drunken *zhiqings*. They were so senseless that they could have been corpses. There was no room left for my friend on the ox-cart: I had to carry and drag him all the way back to our company. For many of us, that was our first experience of getting drunk, all courtesy of those intoxicating Li girls.

PULLING-POWER WITH THE LI
Zhong Enming

While working in No. 7 Company, I did everything a *zhiqing* could possibly do on Hainan Island: cleared the jungle, felled trees, set fire to hills, removed tree roots with explosives, planted and harvested fruit, made mud and fired bricks, drove an ox-cart, patrolled at night to keep wild boars at bay, and even did substitute teaching at the primary school.

In the second half of 1970, I was reassigned again, this time to drive a tractor in the transport company. This was a great opportunity for a *zhiqing*, no less so than when a new university graduate lands a good job. You see, we were all rather simple and pragmatic: to drive a tractor was far less exhausting than engaging in the physical labor most of my peers had to do. Besides, it was a chance to equip myself with some technical know-how. Those were the days when the main form of transport from a company to regimental headquarters was an ox-cart. In 1972, I was qualified to drive a tractor on my own. It was the renowned Harvest brand made in Shanghai, then the industrial powerhouse. With a plow behind, it could plow the fields for any company; with a trailer, it could transport rubber, cement, rice and all sorts of building materials. And so I drove the tractor until 1976. During this time, I was also called up by the regiment to be a member of the Maoist propaganda troupe, to rehearse and tour for about two months at the time of the Spring Festival.

In 1973, to strengthen the relationship between the regiment and the Li people, I was sent for a week to the Rongbang Commune of a Li tribe to help build sties by transporting stones.

Remembering how poor the roads in all the Li villages were, I took a one-and-a-half tonne, two-wheeled trailer with the tractor. When I arrived, the village chief, the accountant, and the director of women's affairs were already waiting at the entrance of the village, together with some villagers. Li over the age of thirty normally bared their upper bodies, regardless of gender, and even if they wore something, their chests were left uncovered. The elderly women also had geometric blue tattoos on their faces.

It was not yet noon and I proposed to start work immediately. But they would not let me. They insisted that I must first take a break and have some lunch. The accountant then took a forked stick with him and when he spotted a big chicken in the village, he pinned it to the ground: as payment for the chicken, the owner would then be entitled to collect two *yuan* from the village committee.

At noon, they served me with a simply cooked yet most delectable chicken. Accompanying me at the table were the village chief, the accountant, and the director of women's affairs. The latter was in her twenties and, speaking fluent Mandarin, didn't seem like a typical Li at all. We drank the local wine, a sweet potato wine, from a big bowl. With the help of an interpreter, I communicated with them in basic Li language.

Most of the Li lived in low-ceiling thatched huts and their living conditions were wretched. After lunch, the director of women's affairs ushered me to a small thatched hut. It was tidy: the wall was plastered with old newspapers. The room was bare; there was nothing but a small table, a stool, an oil lamp, and a thermos flask.

After a nap, we set off for work. The women's affairs director took four or five women with her into the driver's cab: some sat, some stood. We drove to where they had collected stones in the jungle.

Every morning before I left the village, they would put some coconuts on the tractor. They also put a machete next to them so that during the day I could cut one open for a drink. The work was hard, especially for those young women who were passing and lifting the stones on to the trailer. And yet every day they maintained their high spirits. In those days the Li were rather isolated and seldom came across such modern technology as a tractor. Our presence in the Li community pleased them. The women's affairs director was herself a pretty and cheerful young lady.

Every day, the accountant would use his forked stick to catch a chicken in the village. I never stopped him from doing so because I dared not try the only other dish on the table, roasted mice. And accompanying me at the meals were the village chief and the accountant. We drank the sweet potato wine together.

After seven days of hard work, we had finally gathered enough stones for the sties. On the day of my departure, they wrote a thank you letter on a piece of red paper, slaughtered a pig, and put half of it on a banana leaf on the trailer. Next to it were some bananas as well. The village chief thanked me for my hard work and invited me to visit again for a feast of chicken. I was delighted and drove swiftly back to my company so that the cooks could serve us pork for supper.

Illustrations

Figure 1 Zhiqings aboard a Red Guard ship at Guangzhou and about to sail for Hainan Island.

Figure 2 "With Chairman Mao's badge on my chest, a red sun arises from my heart." Too heavy to be pinned, the badge had to be hung from the neck.

Figure 3 Painting Chairman Mao's portrait. "Any error could be deemed a political matter."

Figure 4 "Our hearts stand by Chairman Mao."

Figure 5 Reading the People's Daily during a study session. A typical propaganda photo conveying popular delight at the nation's socialist development.

Figure 6 A Daily Study session at Daling Farm.

Figure 7 A Zhiqing following Chairman Mao's instruction to learn from Comrade Lei Feng, a hero of the revolution.

Figure 8 Toiling under the tropical sun.

Figure 9 Learning to love pigs.

Figure 10 Making bricks for the construction of headquarters and dormitories.

Figure 11 Felling and gathering tree trunks to build dormitories.

Figure 12 Assistant nurses were not exempt from laboring in the wilderness.

Figure 13 Iron girls: undergoing military training.

Figure 14 "I love my motherland": bringing arts and culture to the rural areas.

Figure 15 Children and zhiqing teachers at an assembly to learn Maoist thoughts.

Figure 16 A familiar scene from "The Red Detachment of Women."

Figure 17 Despite the limited choice of fare, movie nights created huge excitement.

Figure 18 Studying Marxism and Maoism was the main task of the zhiqings.

Figure 19 Wells, dug by the zhiqings themselves, were the main source of water.

Figure 20 The ox-cart was the main means of transport.

Figure 21 Getting a kick out of life: a game of football in front of the thatched cottages.

Figure 22 Nature's bathtub: frolicking in the river was the cheapest pastime.

Figure 23 An old hand and her children. "We saw our future in them: we had to escape."

Figure 24 A rare visit home. Early in the morning, zhiqings waited by the main road to start their long journey by bus.

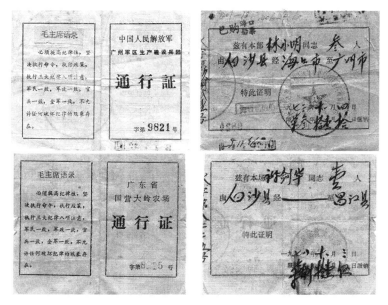

Figure 25 Travel passes issued by the Guangzhou Army Corps and Daling Farm, both containing Chairman Mao's quotations on the left.

Figure 26 Just one memento: Ou Nianzhong conducting a rehearsal of "I love my Army Corps."

Home and Back

WRITING HOME

Lin Yuhua

21 March 1973

Dear Mom and Dad,

It's ten days since we parted. How are you doing? I had a safe journey back to the company on the eighteenth. Don't worry.

I had been instructed to report back to the troop on the eighteenth. I had assumed that by setting off a week early, I wouldn't have a problem arriving on time. When I got to Guangzhou, however, the first ticket I could get for Hainan was for the nineteenth, and this was in spite of all my efforts during a four-day stopover to find an earlier ticket. I panicked. What else could I do?

There would be a Communist Youth League study session on the twentieth which I simply could not miss. The day before my departure for the visit home, our captain had made a point of reminding me about it: "Please make sure you return on time. No one is to miss the study session!" If I couldn't keep my promise, not only would I be criticized but my next application for home leave would be jeopardized. Just as I was plunged into the depths of despair, a fellow *zhiqing* (he's from Guangzhou) came to my rescue. An aunt of his worked as a doctor on one of the ships, and through her, I was allowed to board on the sixteenth and pay for the ticket afterward. I was thus able to arrive at Haikou City on the seventeenth and make it back to the company just in time on the eighteenth.

There is some good news I would like to share with you: a regimental official informed me the other day that I might be reassigned to No. 4 Company to work as a substitute teacher in the primary school there. He asked me to get ready for the move. I am so pleased and yet also extremely anxious. I am pleased because it is such an honor to be trusted and promoted by the regiment to that position. I am anxious because with my rudimentary education I am not sure that I am cut out to be a teacher. It is also said that instructing the mountain kids is quite a challenge. Nevertheless, I am determined to learn from practice, and hope that my dedication will pay off. What do you think?

Dad, you should have taken a good rest to recuperate after your kidney operation, but instead you wasted your hard-earned savings on such a fine length of corduroy for me. It is indeed rather windy here on Hainan and I know you worry that I might catch a cold as result. You've designed such a fine jacket for me. When I saw you spreading the length of corduroy on the dining table, putting on your pair of reading glasses, taking up the scissors and cutting the corduroy under the dim lights after supper, I thought your dedication made you look every bit the master tailor! The way that mom worked on the machine to sew the jacket was also unforgettable! I will forever treasure the scenes in my mind and will never forget your love and care for me! As your daughter, how I wish I could stay behind and look after you. And yet here I am in the back of beyond, hundreds of miles away from home. I am stricken with a strong sense of guilt whenever I think about it. All I can offer you is a mere "thank you!" in a letter.

The boxes of sore-throat powder that I brought from home are extremely popular and have all been snapped up. Everyone says that the powder made in our own Meixian is the most effective. My friend Peng Lijia is now on home leave and will return to Hainan by the end of the month. Please ask my sister to buy a few boxes of the sore-throat powder and pass them on to Peng so that she can bring them back. She lives in Peng Village (near the People's Primary).

More next time.

Take care!

Daughter Yuhua

THE HARD ROAD HOME

Huang Jian

My first home visit

"A mother whose offspring are far away has an unquiet mind." This saying expresses that undying maternal love which is felt for a child who is away from home. Much could also be said about how we *zhiqings* missed our parents and sweet homes during the time of our rustication. Being granted home leave was one of our shared dreams, regardless of the trouble and hardship each home visit would always entail.

To realize the dream was no simple matter: there were more than two hundred *zhiqings* in each company, mostly adolescents or young adults, and every single one of us wanted an early reunion with our families. However, it was said that each year only about four of us would be given the chance. In desperation, many would make up some excuse such as "My grandparent is ill," or even "critically ill." I disliked such tricks: I believed in fair play—when it came to my turn for home leave it would be granted to me.

Yet after two and a half years, when many of my contemporaries had already been on home leave, my patience ran out. Against my better inclinations, I asked my father to send me an express telegram: "Father critically ill return immediately," and when it arrived I was finally granted a chance to visit home. I was so exhilarated that I couldn't sleep: I was the last one of our group to visit home since our rustication began. The night before my departure, I dreamed of my home, my parents and younger siblings: when I had left more than two years before, my younger sister was only six months old.

The next morning, two *zhiqings* and I walked to regimental headquarters before dawn, our flashlights lighting up the path. We would join many others there to take a truck to Haikou City. This had been arranged by the regiment for those who were visiting home for the forthcoming Spring Festival.

It was a rough and tedious ride of about two hundred kilometers: the dirt road was narrow, winding, bumpy, and dusty. With about twenty-five to thirty of us on the truck, there were few seats available and there wasn't much legroom either. I spent most of the eight-hour ride standing among the other *zhiqings* and our luggage. Some of the female *zhiqings* became so travel-sick that on reaching Haikou City they were too feeble to walk.

The next morning, after spending a night in the army corps hostel, we took an early train to Xiuying Pier. Since this was the first long journey on which I was traveling alone, I was both excited and a bit frightened while mingling with the crowds and gazing in awe at the huge Red Guard ship that would take those who could afford to travel directly from Haikou to Guangzhou. I was, however, one of the less fortunate ones who would have to travel in a more economical and time-consuming way.

After being ferried across the Qiongzhou Strait, the first thing we saw lining the road were rows of Liberation trucks bearing the name of our army corps. They had been sent to take us across to Zhanjiang, and all that was required for a ride was a regimental soldier's pass issued by the regiment. It was the pre-Spring Festival season and to relieve the pressure on local transport, the army corps had taken special measures to transport us. And indeed when so many others failed to get tickets, we felt immensely privileged to be regimental soldiers.

Although each truck was packed with several dozen strangers, most of them standing, the journey didn't feel too rough, especially in comparison to the ordeal we had been through the day before. Road conditions on the Leizhou Peninsula were much better than on Hainan.

On reaching the Zhanjiang bus terminal, everybody rushed frantically to the ticket office: the rudimentary station was packed and chaotic. When it was my turn to buy a ticket, the earliest available was in five days' time. With little money in my pocket, I could not afford to stay in Zhanjiang for five days. Frustrated, I would have to try my luck first thing the next day: I would try to get a ticket for standing room only, which was not for sale at the ticket office.

I arrived at the station at five o'clock the next morning. With many buses departing at around six o'clock, I thought I stood a good chance of catching someone who wanted to get their tickets refunded. But that didn't happen. After everyone had boarded, I went to the ticket collector and asked for a standing-room ticket. Having the fresh face of an eighteen year-old and an army shoulder bag was an advantage for me: I was allowed to board a homebound, long-haul bus.

Though I had to stand in the crammed bus for the whole journey of more than seven hours, the image of home and my family and the thought that I was getting ever closer to them kept fatigue at bay.

My second home visit

After toiling in hard conditions for a few years, I had grown from a naïve adolescent into a curious young adult, eager to extend my horizons by visiting the many beauty spots in the country. By mid-May 1975, when I was granted my second home leave, I had managed to accumulate nearly 200 *yuan*, some saved, some borrowed, for a long-anticipated tour.

Traveling by both bus and ferry, I eventually arrived in Zhanjiang where I purchased a train ticket to Guangzhou. The train took a detour in those days, stopping in Guangxi Zhuang Autonomous Region and Hunan Province. The ticket cost slightly over twenty *yuan* and was valid for seven days. My plan was to take a sightseeing trip to Liuzhou City, Guilin City and Hengyang City, followed by a visit to some former classmates in Shaoguan City on my way to the famous Southern China Temple. I would also take the opportunity to tour "The City of Five Goats," Guangzhou.

The view from the terrifyingly high Liuzhou Bridge was breathtaking: I hadn't expected to see such a high bridge. In Liuzhou People's Park, I paid a tribute at the tomb of Han Yu, the great essayist and poet of the Tang dynasty. After supper, I boarded a train to Guilin.

It was warm when I left Hainan in mid-May, and I had only packed two white shirts for the trip, but unfortunately I left one of them behind in a hostel in Zhanjiang. I thought the climate in Guilin must be similar to that of Guangzhou and Hainan, but how wrong I was. It was seven o'clock in the morning when the train arrived at Guilin. A wet day with a northerly wind, it felt cold. The locals were wearing warm jackets, coats, Mao suits, or sweat suits. Wearing just a shirt, I turned many heads as I walked along the streets.

To keep warm and also to avoid the curious looks, I walked fast to find a place to stay. However, all the hostels were full. Guangzhou was hosting the annual Spring Trade Fair. During this period, none of the more than two hundred thousand people working on rice propagation on Hainan Island were allowed to travel via, or stop over in, Guangzhou. To relieve the pressure on Guangzhou, they had to make a detour through northern Zhanjiang, and therefore most travelers took advantage of this temporary measure to visit Guilin for a view of its famous "unsurpassed scenery". Adding to the stress on Guilin's tourist resources was a concurrent event that it was hosting: the national youth volleyball games. I spent a whole day walking around the city to find a place to stay, but to no avail.

Every time I came to a shop, I would go in hoping to get something warm for myself. But I didn't have what every shop assistant asked for, the then all-important ration coupon for cloth: all I had was the national food coupon which would only allow me to buy food. I could do nothing but brave the chilly wind and continue to hunt for a place to rest my head.

By eight o'clock, all the shops were closed. I returned to the train station with sore feet and an aching body. Just as I was about to abandon my plan for Guilin, someone sitting next to me asked if I was from Guangdong, something he picked up from my attire. Like me, he had wasted a whole day trying to get a roof over his head but without success. He was on a business trip to the south from Henan Province and had wanted to spend a couple of days in Guilin before returning home. We had a great chat and decided to tour Guilin together.

Elephant Trunk Hill, Moon Hill, Crescent Hill, Wave-Subduing Hill, Yangshuo, the Great Bunyan . . . Guilin lived up to its fame and didn't disappoint. During the day, we walked around all the scenic spots and sampled the delicious local cuisine; at night, we returned to sleep on the benches at the train station. Despite the noise and inconvenience of the station, our tiring walk during the day guaranteed us a sound sleep. On the third night, we parted at the station, he heading north and I south. His face remained vivid in my mind for many years, though I no longer remember his name. I often wonder if he survived the Great Tangshan Earthquake in 1976. I wish him luck: he was a good man.

Although I spent a lot more time in Shaoguan and Guangzhou and met many friends in both cities, my three days' stay in Guilin was the most memorable part of that trip. Many years later I would return to Guilin, but I failed to recapture the emotions of my first visit.

My third home visit

Myth has it that "Those who cross the sea become immortals." To more than one hundred thousand *zhiqings* on Hainan Island, it was a bit of self-mockery. Wherever your home, if you did not cross the sea, you remained stranded on the wrong side of the Qiongzhou Strait and your home was a remote dream. The narrow Qiongzhou Strait could make you feel utterly helpless.

In July 1979, the ninth year of my rustication, I was granted my third home leave. Owing to the poor communications typical of those days, it was not until I had traveled a whole day and got as far as Haikou City that I found I couldn't have chosen a worse day for my journey. Due to the imminent threat of a typhoon, all forms of water transport had been suspended the day before and, as a consequence, all accommodation was packed with stranded passengers. Like many others, I ended up sleeping without bedding on a straw mat on the floor of a hostel.

During the following five days, our chances of boarding a home-bound vessel were dashed again and again by fresh reports of where the typhoon was striking. In Haikou, a city overwhelmed with stranded passengers, I could not upgrade to a bed that was free of the nightly bombardments of mosquitos until I had been there for six days. Because of the costs they had incurred during the unexpected and prolonged delay to their journeys, some *zhiqings* had to abandon their plans to go home, check out, and return to their farms. That night at ten o'clock, it was announced that the ferries and ships would resume the next day, which made everybody in the hostel feel elated.

To get on a ferry as soon as possible, I rose early to catch the first train to the Xiuying Pier. Although it was nearly two hours before the first boat was due to depart, the pier was already packed with thousands of passengers. There must have been nearly ten thousand stranded travelers! However, when it was time to depart, no boarding information was given. The crowd started to get agitated. It was only then that we were informed that the sea was getting rough again and the boat was still waiting for the authorities to decide whether they would allow passengers aboard. Despite the mass frustration and anger, nothing could be done.

Ten o'clock brought two explosive pieces of news: the ferry would allow passengers on board, but the long-hulled Red Guard ship would stay put. The crowd was immediately divided into two camps: those overjoyed and cheering and those who were utterly disappointed.

With little luggage and a strong physique, I was able to get hold of a ticket. The ferry immediately filled up and became overloaded. When we reached the middle of the Strait, the sea, which had been whipped up by the rough wind, looked more like ink than its usual blue. Waves washed over the deck, adding to the sufferings of those who were already severely seasick. I was tested as well, and a number of times was on the verge of throwing up. It was another three hours before we landed on the other side of the Qiongzhou Strait and became "immortals," and only then could we relax a bit and appreciate the magical power of the sea.

It was said that on that day mine was the only vessel that the bad weather had not confined to port.

UNDER THE BELL TOWER
Zhang Cheng

When I was watching the televised opening ceremony of the Asian Games, which were being hosted by Guangzhou, the Guangzhou Customs House, fondly known as "the big bell tower,", suddenly appeared and loomed large on the screen. Nearly a century old and situated by the Pearl River, the building is a witness of the social, political, and economic upheavals of southern China. For me, it is also a reminder of a sour personal experience I suffered nearly four decades ago.

In the summer of 1973, after spending a couple of weeks home in Meixian on furlough, six of us *zhiqings* decided to travel back to Hainan together. Taking an early bus before dawn, we arrived at Guangzhou that evening, nearly twelve hours later. Having a cousin who lived in the city, I could have stayed with him during my stopover, but since there were six of us we didn't want to impose ourselves on him. Leaving our luggage behind, we set out with our basic toiletries to find a hostel to stay at for the night.

During the Cultural Revolution, Guangzhou was in a state of turmoil. To check into any public accommodation, a traveler first had to obtain a pass issued by his *danwei*, or unit. On producing the pass to the Guangzhou Tourism Agency, he would then be considered for accommodation and referred to an approved service provider. When we arrived at the nearest agency, we saw on the windows signs saying "Accommodations full," and in the hall dozens of people who seemed to have resigned themselves to their bad luck and were lying on the floor for a night's rest. Further down the road, we were told, there was another agency: we swiftly acted on the tip and took a bus to get there. It was after eleven o'clock by the time we arrived, and once we entered the agency, we became despondent: the benches and floor were filled with those who had failed to find a place to stay. In desperation, we were about to leave. At that moment, however, I spotted a ticket window still open and when we got close, we saw on the glass a sign that said: "Preferential service window for military personnel & overseas Chinese." We again became disheartened. Suddenly one of us said: 'We are from the Guangzhou Army.' It was true that the farms to which we were rusticated on Hainan Island were under the military control of the Guangzhou Army Production and Construction Corps: however, we *zhiqings* were mere "sham soldiers," not real servicemen, and therefore ineligible for the preferential treatment specified on the sign. But it was also plain to us that if we didn't even try our luck, there would be no option for us but to sleep rough. We collected our passes and decided to give it a try.

When we approached the window, we saw a man in his fifties reading a newspaper with the help of glasses. After we handed over our passes, he took a look at them, stared at us coldly, and then berated us in a harsh voice: "How dare you!" "We just want to find a place to sleep for the night," we replied. The old man was obviously taken aback: he tossed our passes under the window and snapped: "Take a good look at the sign on the window!" His rude manner not only didn't frighten or deter us, it amused us. We tossed our passes back and said with good-humor: "We are from the Guangzhou Army, please take a good look at our passes!" With that, he pulled out of his pocket an armband containing the words "Guangzhou Workers' Picket", promptly put it on his arm, and said, with quiet menace: "You *farmhands*, you want to make trouble. I will send you to the public security bureau!" Considering that there were no better options for the night, we quipped: "Great, let's go. We're looking for somewhere to spend the night anyway; that sounds like a safe place." The old man's face turned red at our defiance: he started to curse us in all the rude and foul language he could muster. At that moment, an officer came downstairs to check what all the noise and quarreling was about. He explained that due to its popularity with the tourists, there was a severe shortage of accommodation in Guangzhou, and we must excuse them for not being able to offer any help. To appease us, he rebuked the clerk for his disgraceful behavior and asked us to forgive him. It was plain to us that that was the end of the whole matter: after all, the fact that we were managed by a military body didn't turn us into genuine servicemen. Reluctantly, we dragged our leaden bodies out of the agency.

Since none of us could afford to stay in Guangzhou for more than a night, we decided to go straight to the booking office to get tickets for our voyage to Hainan for the next day. As we arrived at the No. I Pier by the People's Bridge, the big bell over the Customs House struck. It was midnight.

The previous night, we had stayed up into the wee hours to discuss the challenges we faced and reflect on our future, or the lack of it.

And now after a long day of traveling, we were all dog-tired. We also discovered that it was too early for the ticket office to open. We were then drawn to the nearby bulletin board at the entrance to the Customs House. The bulletin board stood beneath a wide canopy and below it were two wide steps: ideal for a good rest. We picked up some newspapers from the ground to give the steps a cursory sweep, then lay down to rest. We reminisced for a while about our quarrel with the clerk at the agency and shortly fell asleep.

The cool breeze from the river soon woke me up. I had never before slept in the rough, and with much on my mind, couldn't get back to sleep again. So as not to disturb my friends, I got up and took a walk along the river toward the iconic Haizhu Bridge.

Strolling along the river, I came across the neon lights of the Nanfang Department Store, the Aiqun Plaza, and the Guangzhou Hotel. Occasionally, the siren from a passing barge or boat would catch my attention. And every now and then, a squad of Workers' Pickets marched past, their red and white canes in their hands. All this gave life to a city otherwise sound asleep. I didn't want to return to Hainan and work again under such harsh conditions: I longed for life in a big city. And yet the arrogance, rudeness, and discrimination against us at the travel agency made me feel despondent. Whenever I think about that incident I still feel sad.

THE SWEETEST OF MANGOES
Chen Hongbo

In May and June, when the mango season hits the streets of Guangzhou, the fragrance of the golden mango drifts in the air to every corner of the city. Haunting me at this time are memories of the mangoes of Daling, the extreme hardship of our rusticated years, and the unbreakable bonds of family.

My unshakable attachment to Daling mangoes has everything to do with the solace they brought to my family during my rustication on the then remote island of Hainan. Previously known as the Nada Propagation Center, Daling Farm, where I was based, had been breeding and propagating many top quality tropical plants for over a decade before the influx of the *zhiqings*. The mango trees in the "fruit company," i.e., No. 7 Company, were said to have been brought back from overseas by our beloved premier, Zhou Enlai. Ivory mango, egg mango, Indian mango—you name it, they were all there. Such mangoes are now common: in those years of our youth, they were incredibly rare and valuable. Every year when they were about to ripen, a militia troop would be dispatched to guard the orchard round the clock, with farm officials making inspections. Once harvested, they would be transported straight to Haikou City and then loaded on to a plane to Beijing. Farm workers outside the fruit company seldom got the chance to even taste them. In 1972, the Pearl River Studio filmed many scenes at No. 7 Company for a popular documentary entitled *Great Fruits on Treasure Island*.

One year during the mango season, I happened to be visiting No. 7 Company to make a report. After a meeting with the captain, I went to the mango orchard to take photographs. The farm workers were carefully picking green mangoes which had just a trace of orange, wrapping them in paper, and placing them in small wooden containers. Once the nearby truck was fully loaded, it was driven to Haikou for a flight bound for Beijing. During the whole process, a militia troop was standing by.

As I was taking photographs, the captain suddenly asked me when my home leave was due. I told him it would be in the next day or two, and he offered to sell me a few to take home. "Can I really do that?" I was caught by surprise. They were, after all, designated as gifts for important people. The captain confirmed that as long as I picked only those of lesser quality, no rules would be broken. He picked a few ivory mangoes, weighed and wrapped them for me, and I paid for them with profuse expressions of gratitude. One of the agricultural pioneers on the island, the captain had always been kind to *zhiqings* and considerate of our welfare.

I handled the mangoes with great care and set out for my home leave the very next day. During the tiring journey from the farm to Haikou City and the following twenty-six hour sea voyage, I cherished them like a treasure. Once the ship landed at Guangzhou, I went straight home. My family was delighted to see me: it was our first reunion since I was involuntarily rusticated nearly two years before. I choked up when I found my grandmother looking even more elderly and my parents' hair grayer. To disguise my sadness and bring some joy to the reunion, I took the mangoes out of my sack. The room was immediately filled with their sweet aroma, and their unusually large size sent my family into ecstasy: they had never laid eyes on such exotic fruit. My younger brothers and sisters were eager to taste them then and there. I told them that since they were grown on our farm, we enjoyed them all the time and that they were of such excellence that they were chosen as tributes to the high-ups in Beijing. And they had just been captured on film! My siblings weren't the least interested in such trivia and went ahead to prepare the fruits. Once my grandmother took a piece from me, her sad look changed into a cheerful smile. A seaman's wife, she knew a bit about tropical fruit. And typical of a Cantonese, she didn't forget to nag that we shouldn't eat too much of it at one go, because mangoes were rather "damp and hot" in nature—bad for the body.

The Liberation Cinema was just round the corner, and so the next day, I bought tickets for the whole family to go and watch *Great Fruits on Treasure Island*. Accompanied by the melodious song, "Determined to Stay on Treasure Island for a New Career," were scenes of our lush orchard and rubber plantations and my fellow *zhiqings* harvesting mangoes in an idyllic setting. After that, my grandmother and parents became a bit less anxious about my life on the farm, and began to smile a bit more. And to this day, whenever I find mangoes on the street, I am reminded that those of Daling are the sweetest and bear the most exquisite fragrance.

Although our home visits were a rarity and lasted only twelve days, they were never just a matter of reunion, recuperation, and a change of scene from the farm. What was also important was to call on the families of our fellow *zhiqings*, report on their well-being, and take back to the farm whatever their families could spare them. In those lean years, everything was rationed: our families were also stretched to the limit and could barely save anything for us. But because each of us was obliged to visit a large number of *zhiqing* families, we always ended up with a heavy load, sometimes well above fifty kilos, to carry back to the farm. I was once given five kilos of biscuits by just one elderly parent: because of the amount of food and supplies I was already due to take back, I hesitated. He pleaded that since work was hard and food was scarce on the farm, this was the only thing he could do for his son. I gave in. At the end of her home leave, He Qinghua, the girl I would later marry, once brought to the departure pier a huge load of supplies on a shoulder-pole, and was stopped at the entrance for carrying excess baggage. It was then that she realized that her load weighed fifty-five kilos, well above her own body weight of less than forty kilos! When the load was lifted from her shoulders, she was unable to straighten up, and it was only with the help of some other *zhiqings* that she was able to accomplish her all-important mission.

As a ritual, we would phone our fellow *zhiqings* when we arrived at Haikou City. It was a walk of several kilometres from the bus stop at Daxi Bridge to the regimental headquarters where I was living, but for those in the remote companies, it could be a walk of more than ten kilometres, a good two hours' hike even without carrying a heavy load on a pole. Once our friends learned that we were returning to the farm, they would wait at the bus stop and help carry our luggage. It was a happy occasion: even the smallest of items from home would remind them of their loved ones. That day, as I was opening my luggage, I was hit by the aroma of *doubanroujiang*, fermented soya-bean paste cooked in deep-fried lard. During my leave, my grandmother had bought some lard using the family's precious meat coupon and prepared two jars of homemade paste for me. A humble yet versatile food, it was a great treat, used as sauce on good days or, when times were hard, a dish on its own. During the long and arduous journey, one jar had been broken and now the fresh smell of the paste filled the dormitory. Staring at the bits of lard and paste sparkling with pieces of broken glass, we fell silent with regret. The paste could have lasted us a long while, not to mention the fact that it was lovingly made by my own aged grandmother.

Pastimes and Leisure

BOOKWORMS

Liang Yongkang

At sixteen or seventeen, one's education is starting to bear fruit. Yet at that age we were opening up the jungle wilderness, our schooling interrupted for an indefinite period. With radio and television both rarities, reading became the staple leisure activity of our *zhiqing* life.

Bedbug in a book

Before rustication, I attended a boarding school in Guangzhou. That experience must have prepared me for living away, for I was never, as some of my contemporaries were, overwhelmed by the sadness of leaving home. Though far short of maturity, I was not so young as to be infatuated with lofty sentiments and high aspirations. What I found hard to cope with was that owing to the power shortage on the farm, we city folk had to resort to oil lamps in the thatched huts—and besides, there were hardly any newspapers or books around. To my good fortune, the boredom of a life without books was soon alleviated by the arrival of Harman.

Harman and I had been in the same year at the elite Guangya Secondary School. Thanks to his remarkable eloquence, he was nicknamed Harman after some noted American diplomat. As a prefect, he stood out for his unusual talents and aspirations. Such was his reputation that years later, many of his peers would still remember him by his nickname.

Harman's journey to our company was rather unusual: deviating from the organized school route, he went to another farm on Hainan before turning up on his own at Daling. When he finally made it to our company, there was a heavy load of books in his sack of bedding and bucket, distinguishing him in yet another way from his contemporaries. Several years into the Cultural Revolution, most of us had subscribed to the prevailing theory that education was useless and unimportant. When I had packed for Hainan, the only books in my sack were a copy of *The Mao Zedong Anthology* and *Quotations from Chairman Mao*, nicknamed "The Little Red Book." Seldom did one come across somebody like Harman who had stuffed so many books into his sack.

In our thatched hut, there were several rough double beds. Measuring three meters wide and two meters long, each was usually shared by two *zhiqings*. Mine happened to be half empty, and on his arrival Harman took up the empty side. Without a bookshelf or desk, we used the middle of our large bed as a storage space, and in it Harman's books were piled up like a sand dune. They occupied not only the physical space between us but, during many a quiet night, our minds. We would sit by the oil lamps on our homemade stools, with the bed doubling as our desk. I can barely remember the titles we devoured during those nights, except for a former Soviet novel, *Brothers Yershov*. It wasn't so much the themes of these works that touched me—themes we were expected to digest and absorb—as the fine descriptions of the emotional lives of the young worker-protagonists.

One night as I was reading, my eye fell on an insect that was crawling across my book: when I tried to squeeze it, I found it was a bedbug. We began a frantic attempt to catch it, but the crafty hemipteran managed to dodge us by moving between the pages. When we turned to our assistant nurse for help to spray our dormitory, she blamed us for our poor personal hygiene and teased us with the remark that, unlike us, the bedbug was a genuine bookworm.

Gunshots on a journey to deliver the highest instructions

The "red treasure book," *The Mao Zedong Anthology*, was, without doubt, the most popular book of the time, compulsory reading at the one-hour "daily study session." Though the normal working day was eight hours, there were all kinds of after-hours' "voluntary work" that were actually compulsory. But the study session that took place after lunch and within normal working hours was a most welcome relief from the toil that the *zhiqings* performed day in, day out.

We didn't just keep the treasure book to ourselves: we regularly communicated "the highest instructions" to the Li people. One night, the regimental cable radio station announced in the high-pitched and agitated tones typical of the time that there would be some important news in the forthcoming *National News* program, which would be re-layed from the Central People's Broadcasting Station two hours later than usual. Following this announcement, our political instructor and his clerk leapt into action: they got the gas lamps set up to turn the ground into a dazzlingly bright space, as if to mark a festive occa-sion. The repeated announcement from the station brought the *zhiqings* out from their dimly lit dormitories. Our clerk, who normally looked rather ill, called lustily for everybody to join the assembly. One of the earliest *zhiqings* to arrive at Daling for re-education, he was our men-tor of sorts. When we arrived, I and another *zhiqing* were charged with turning the company into "a red sea": painting all the walls in red either with Mao's quotations or his portrait. While painting the quota-tions was straightforward, painting his portrait was a challenge. The clerk came up with a solution: first, copy the portrait on to a piece of glass from a wood carving, then project the glass image on to the wall with a flashlight at night and trace the projected image with a pencil. We could then finish the portrait in the daytime with red paint. This project of turning the company into a red sea took us a month and was considered to be an "enviable job" because it exempted us from having to toil in the wilderness.

At ten o' clock, "the highest instructions" were relayed live from Central Broadcasting, followed by our routine "nightly reports." When we were making our way back to the dormitory with leaden eyelids, the political instructor asked me to note down "the highest instructions" we had just learned from the relay and copy them on to some pieces of red paper. While I was doing that, the clerk and a few activists pumped up the gas lamp, prepared the rifles, and brought out a drum. The political instructor wished to deliver Mao's latest instructions to the Li without any delay. Four of us formed a line. The political instructor led the way, a rifle on his shoulder; he was followed by the clerk with the gas lamp; I was third in the line, carrying the red papers; and the captain brought up the rear with another rifle. It was my first midnight hike, and I felt as though I was part of a political mission. Yet it baffled me that the gas lamp and torches were not trained on the path ahead of us, but to the sides: it felt as if we were seeking to forestall an ambush. As I was trying to figure out what was happening, there were three sharp shots from behind me, at which the two people ahead rushed back to where the captain's torch was casting its light. An argument broke out among them about when was the best time to shoot. What eventually dawned on me was that this was not primarily a political mission but a nocturnal hunting trip. Drawn by light, wild animals usually freeze in its beam, which then makes them an easy target for hunters. Before taking aim, the captain should evidently have waited until his quarry was much closer: he had failed to live up to his reputation as a good marksman.

I cannot remember how we made it to the Li village or the rituals that ensued. But what I learned that night was that no matter how tough life gets, and no matter how sacred and serious their mission to deliver vital messages, human beings will always find ways to amuse themselves.

Absurd incidents at the entrance examinations

The third anniversary marking the partial reopening of higher education was 1973. Mao had instructed that colleges and universities should recruit solely from the workers, peasants and soldiers, who after two or three years of study must then return to where they worked. But going to college was an ambition I dared not harbor. Official policy subordinated one's academic achievements to such political criteria as family background. In the previous three years, none of those who, like myself, came from a "politically incorrect" family background had been shortlisted by the regiment. And even if you were shortlisted, there were still rounds of "political assessments" to struggle through. These assessments might take into account the most trivial incidents. My friend Ji was shortlisted and was asked to cut short his home visit in order to complete his application procedure at regimental headquarters. When he was asked to undergo a medical examination, the honest soul told the officials that while he was at home he had already done so at his own expense. That spelled the end of his hopes of entering college. Apparently when this was reported, the official responsible for Ji's political assessment regarded it as a sign that he cared too much about his own health, which ran against the expectation that every one of us should devote ourselves selflessly to the revolutionary cause.

Owing to the poor academic achievements of the first three cohorts, entrance examinations were re-introduced in 1973. I figured that even if I could get through the political assessment, as someone who hadn't opened a textbook since my junior secondary schooling, I would have no chance at all of passing the entrance exams.

The first round of exams was to take place in the regimental school. I was washing my laundry one day when Li Xiaojiang, an old school friend, suggested that I should at least give it a try: if nothing else, those who did would be given time off from their physical labor to prepare for the second round of exams. That was enough to change my mind. A few days later, the results were disclosed: although I scored over 90 percent in Chinese and politics, in gaining marks of between 0 and 30 percent in three science subjects, I thought that that was the end of the matter. But to my surprise, we were both invited to the second round of exams at divisional headquarters. The reason behind it was that there was a quota of applicants for those "redeemable children," and I was among the lucky ones who fell within it. The policy dictated that those in my situation should be given a chance.

There were only ten days left before the second round of exams, which were held at divisional headquarters. The twelve of us who were sitting them began a frantic day and night revision process. Compared to the many who were granted revision leave by their companies, I was short-changed: I had to report for work at the primary school where I was teaching. So during the following ten nights, I had to go through all the senior secondary school textbooks for mathematics, physics and chemistry, subjects that my own education had never included.

When after the last exam I met my friend Li, whom the sleepless nights of intensive preparation had also left with red eyes, we couldn't help but laugh. It was a sign that we both felt we had done well in the exams, but it also meant something that perhaps not so many would be able to decipher. On the eve of the Cultural Revolution, and along with eight other eighth-grade students in our elite school, we had spent a few nights composing a letter lambasting the education system and demanding that entrance examinations should be scrapped. We did so in the conviction that the "feudalist, capitalist and revisionist" system was due for an overhaul. The letter became headline news in the official newspaper and, as a result, some senior members of the Guangzhou municipal government gave us an audience. From spending a night composing a complaint about the exam system to spending ten nights preparing for the exams, we thus became the victims of an historical joke.

The joke didn't end there

Thanks to our hard work, Li and I both did well: I achieved the highest marks in the division and Li came in second. While we were expecting an offer letter, the "Zhang Tiesheng incident" occurred: this entrant scored near zero in the examinations, and yet was lauded as a national hero after he had used the provincial newspaper to excuse his poor performance and attack those who, unlike him, had shirked hard labor in order to prepare for the exams. In our case, I received an offer letter but Li didn't. It turned out that since that incident, there had been a decision that exam results could not be used as the sole criterion of admission to college or university. In the course of one of the exams, a ray of sunlight shone on Li's spectacles and he had shifted his desk and chair slightly to avoid being dazzled. This action was interpreted by the supervisor as an act of arrogance and was used against him when the Zhang Tiesheng incident was at its feverish height.

Fortunately, after the Cultural Revolution, Li got what he deserved: a place in the college and much success in his career as a journalist.

GOING TO THE MOVIES
Hu Zhimin

The list of films that survived the censors during the Cultural Revolution was extremely short. Besides the film versions of the eight revolutionary model plays, the film projection squad of the regiment was allowed only to show a handful of the old revolutionary films, among them, *Landmine Warfare*, *Tunnel Warfare*, and *Warfare across the Country*. All made before the Cultural Revolution, they were far less didactic than the revolutionary model plays: they displayed a sense of humor and were true to life—and they were a joy to watch. Though often repeated, they remained crowd pleasers: thanks to their titles, the projection squad was known as the "triple warfare squad."

Despite our familiarity with the limited stock of approved films, every visit from the squad still triggered much excitement among the audiences. On the day of the screening, as the *zhiqings* went to work with tools on their shoulders, they would be praying for the early arrival of the evening. Not only were there endless discussions about the plots and scenarios of these films but spontaneous imitations of some of the popular scenes. These would continue until sunset eventually sent us back to our dormitories.

After supper, a cinema would be improvised on the patch of ground outside. A large sheet of white cloth was hung up as a screen. Girls, boys, and elders would bring their own stools or chairs, and if a slightly higher chair was placed among the generally low seating, its owner would be booed and he would have to move it to the back. While waiting for the show to start, the audience chatted in groups, whether loudly or furtively; excited youngsters would be scampering about or noisily fooling around. Mothers sat in the shade to breastfeed their babies while gossiping with friends and acquaintances.

At the back of the patch of ground, there would be a desk where the projector was set up. While the projectionist was taking his time adjusting the lens or the lighting, youngsters would be gathering round him curiously, and some naughty boys would even venture to put their hands in front of the illuminated lens to throw on to the screen the silhouette of a big wolf, a rabbit, a bird, or a snake. Some *zhiqings* would join in, pulling faces and sticking out their tongues and prompting outbursts of laughter.

Just before the film was due to start, the captain made a routine speech, announcing the film title and thanking the projection squad for crossing the hills and valleys to promote Maoism and serve the people. While he was droning on, the audience would continue to chat, wishing that, if only on this occasion, he might keep it short.

In fact, those who crossed the hills and valleys for the film also included the local Li folk. However, "local" still involved a trek of several hours through the hills to reach this makeshift open-air cinema. In the darkness, the trail of their flashlights and torches snaked across the landscape. The Li had their own ethnic attire: a blue or black collarless blouse and a close-fitting skirt. Whatever the season, they were usually barefoot. The first encounter with a Li woman who was over thirty could be startling: geometric patterns and dots ran from her eyes to her chin and along her nose to her cheeks. These blue tattoos gave her a sinister air, and with scarlet lips and her teeth blackened by the constant chewing of betel nuts, she could look terrifying.

This age-old custom of tattooing their faces came with a story. To prevent the beautiful Li girls from being kidnapped by foreign tribes, they were subjected from their early teens to this painstaking and painful procedure. Gradually, the different patterns of tattoos became a way of distinguishing between the various Li clans and were also adopted as a fashion-statement by the girls' relatives. Since the Liberation of China in 1949, the young Li girls no longer followed the practice, and by this time it was fast dying out. We were on good terms with the kindhearted Li. During the screening, they would either stand around or just squat on the ground.

One evening in late autumn, *Tunnel Warfare* was scheduled. This was the season when the temperatures on Hainan could fluctuate drastically within a single day. While a sweater might be needed at dawn, by lunchtime most of us would have stripped to short-sleeved shirts, but by nightfall a warm jacket might be required.

Soon the film started. As the "ghosts"—the Japanese invaders—marched into the village and the tense soundtrack began, the *zhiqings* would sing along to the familiar "Ghosts' March." When Gao Quanbao was studying Chairman Mao's *On Long-Term Strategy*, the audience would sing along with its beautiful tune, "The Sun Is Shining." And when the invaders got lost in the tunnels that the villagers had dug in order to confuse them, everybody would burst out laughing as if they were watching the film for the very first time in their lives.

Coping with Scarcity

MOTHERS OF INVENTION

Zhang Huixin

These days our television screens are bombarded with commercials for sanitary napkins: shop shelves are laden with a vast array of them. In our *zhiqing* days it was a rather different story.

Before November 1968, when I was due to leave Guangzhou for rustication to Hainan, I took my household registration booklet to a department store to purchase my monthly ration of sanitary paper. I asked the shop assistant to sell me a pack for my mother, but she asked me for a doctor's prescription to verify that although over the age of fifty, she was still having her periods. Since I didn't have the prescription, I could only get a pack for myself. In those lean years, everything was rationed, and one had to produce a coupon or voucher issued by the state even for one's basic daily needs. One of the many bizarre rules and regulations was that women who were aged fifty and over were not allocated a ration for sanitary paper unless there was a doctor's prescription to prove the need for it. Lin, a close friend of mine from a worker's family who was exempt from rustication, came to my rescue. Before I left for Hainan, she gave me her ration of sanitary paper.

Soon after my arrival, I described to Lin in vivid detail how idyllic and thrilling life was on Hainan Island: the sea, the gulls, the azure sky, the beautiful sunrises and splendid sunsets; the track of clean, fine sand we were driven through on my first night at the farm; my excitement on spotting yet another village hidden in the jungle; our thatched hut which, it was claimed, would stay warm in winter and cool in summer, and so on. In other words, everything in my new rustic home seemed just perfect to me!

For a whole month after the letter was posted, I heard no word from her. By the end of December, just as I was getting anxious about what might have happened, Lin, to my happy surprise, appeared right in front of me. It turned out that after receiving my letter, she was so hypnotized by my rosy description of the island that she went right out to apply to join the quota for rustication to Hainan. And it so happened that she had been assigned to my company. To waive the entitlement to stay at home and study in the city—a most sought-after privilege among *zhiqings*—and to join us within a month, was just incredible. I was deeply touched by her effort to join me but also apologetic for the fact that she had given me her month's supply of sanitary paper.

Within no time, problems arose. None of the shops on the farm stocked sanitary paper. Meanwhile, the supply we had brought with us from home was running out, no matter how thrifty we were with it. Although I had prepared a few small towels for the purpose, they had proved too inconvenient to use and difficult to wash by hand. Despite the urgency of the matter, we were embarrassed to raise it. What were we to do? We were utterly desperate. I must say that I don't expect any of today's young women to understand our anxiety. Just as we were reaching the end of our tether, the company officials somehow learned about this pressing problem of ours and sent people out to find a source of sanitary paper. One day, the supply chief came back with an ox-cart load of white paper, and we girls were told to collect our ration that night! This happy relief came in the nick of time and really solved our number-one difficulty.

However, the "sanitary paper" brought back by our supply chief was around one square meter in size and no different from the crepe paper we had used back in Guangzhou for decorating classrooms during festive seasons. The difference was only that it was white rather than colored. It also came in flat sheets rather than a roll, which were rather thick and hard. Without processing, they were, in fact, useless. Whether they were disinfected or hygienic was entirely beyond our concern. Somehow we managed to overcome our shyness and we were, indeed, jubilant when we took our rations back to the dormitories. Once we returned to our rooms, the thatched hut was turned into a workshop. We cut the sheets, softened them by squeezing them into small balls, flattened and folded them. We exchanged views on how to fold them to make the maximum use of this precious commodity. Again, that combination of fastidiousness and hilarity must seem rather alien to the young women of today.

From then on, the company would purchase such paper regularly. We would go and collect it and painstakingly prepare it. Then in order, so we believed, to sterilize them, we would hang the items out in the sun in discreet cotton bags. It was our good fortune that the supply of sunshine on Hainan Island was not rationed or in short supply. Later on, the regimental shop began to stock a compact size of sanitary paper, and it was only then that the company officials could stop acquiring it. But by this time we had become so virtuously frugal that we remained thrifty with sanitary paper.

Warm thanks to our company officials, especially our supply chief, to our technician and the clerk. Without their concerted efforts, we wouldn't have had a clue how to solve such a pressing yet embarrassing problem. Thanks also to my friend Lin. Although what she surrendered was just a month's ration of sanitary paper, what I found in her act of generosity was the most valuable friendship and love.

These things might sound incredible, but they did happen.

CATCHING GRASSHOPPERS
Feng Xingkai

Soon after the start of the Battle of the Paracel Islands in January 1974, the shortage of supplies to Daling Farm worsened—most probably because the transport system was overwhelmed. The shop had run out of what was my second staple: cigarettes. At first, smokers like myself could easily "catch grasshoppers" on the company premises. Among the older generation of smokers, "Grasshopper" was a euphemism for a dog-end, the butt of an unfiltered cigarette. It was so called because from a distance it looked like a grasshopper. "Catching grasshoppers" was a pleasant way to describe the practice of picking up cigarette butts from the ground. The company's premises were limited: within no time, there were no more grasshoppers to catch. We widened our search to regimental headquarters. But these too were soon exhausted. We were then reduced to catching grasshoppers in the latrines! When they, too, had all been caught, we had to look elsewhere. We gathered leaves of papaya and other trees, and even couch grass, and rolled them up for a smoke. But they were no match for a proper cigarette.

Our troop resided by the Daxi River near a Li village. Every now and then, when there was an opportunity, some audacious *zhiqings* would creep into the tobacco field in the village and pick some of the leaves. Once we got back to our dormitory, we would sharpen a cleaver and chop the tobacco leaves finely. Then we would light up a portable oil stove, put on a rice bowl, turn the fire down and bake the leaves till they were dry. Although the fire was low, one had to remain vigilant at all times and stir the leaves constantly because they could easily catch fire and turn to ashes—ruining our efforts and filling us with utter despair. When the chopped leaves were dry enough, we would use cigarette paper to roll some cone-shaped cigarettes. They looked like a pin, so we called them "pins." The cigarette made in this way had a pungent smell and was far superior to any of today's top brands.

One day, we spotted a *zhiqing* behaving furtively. When we caught him at it again, we used every kind of manipulation to make him confess what he was up to.

Our captain had five children. His eldest daughter and twin sons were all students in our regimental school. His third son, Jiawen, was of pre-school age and it was Jiawen who had been brainwashed by our *zhiqing* friend. It escaped me how he did it, but he managed to talk Jiawen into bringing some cigarettes from his home and handing them over as a "tribute." This transaction hinged on the mere promise that our *zhiqing* friend would never tell anyone about it! Once our friend owned up to his underhand deal, the few of us who were in the know were able to claim a delightful share of the tributes surrendered by our captain's son!

Our job was mainly to dig holes, build terraces, and eradicate couch grass from the hills. By then, some of us had already developed a way of lessening the rigours of our work—by securing a relatively shady spot where the soil was also a bit looser. We would spread out on the hills and normally work at a slow pace. During our captain's daily tour of inspection, some of the desperate smokers would ask him for a drag of his cigarette. He would generously oblige and didn't at all begrudge sharing this most coveted item. Soon this became public knowledge, and more and more *zhiqing* smokers would ask for a smoke. For a time during his tour, we would gather round him under a tree and pass round our captain's cigarette. After ten minutes or so, he would announce: "OK, back to work," and we would all happily oblige and toil away. There were items even money couldn't buy for us. Although at normal times we could get rationed cigarettes, the supply was rather small. Soon the stock at the captain's home was running low, and even the promise of a sweet failed to coax Jiawen to bring out some of his father's cigarettes for us: once again, we were left high and dry.

GIVING OUR STAMPS A FACE-LIFT
Rao Ruiguang

I am a philatelist. My collection benefits from my supportive friends and their families around the world who have been assiduously collecting stamps on my behalf. Whenever I receive a new batch of used stamps from them, I soak them in a basin of clean water for about an hour, carefully remove the scraps of envelope, gently clean away the glue, and then leave them to dry on a towel. Once they are fully dry, I catalog them and add them to my album. Whenever I fancy, I bring them out and admire their designs.

In my *zhiqing* days I handled stamps frequently: I used to give them a "facial mask." In those days life was harsh and work was hard. Two years before I was moved to the Daling state farm in 1968, I had been rusticated in a village in Yacha Commune in Baisha County, drawing a wage of just sixteen *yuan* a month. After the deduction of ten *yuan* for food, there was barely anything left for one's other basic daily needs. With no leisure life whatsoever in this isolated village, we *zhiqings* were consumed by homesickness. To write to our friends and families living far away became essential to our sanity. And like many of my peers, once I got started I could easily end up writing several letters. The ordinary postage rate was eight *fen*: when we felt desperate or there was something urgent to discuss with our friends or families, we might want to send our letter by airmail, which cost one *jiao*. When we were sending food or cloth coupons, a certificate or anything important by registered mail, the postage started at two *jiao*.

To send more letters at the lowest possible cost, I picked up a trick common among *zhiqings*: it was to give the stamp a "facial mask." First, you apply a light touch of glue to its surface and gently blow it dry; then you apply two more layers of glue. It is a balancing act: on the one hand, the glue must be sufficiently thick; on the other, it must remain transparent to avoid arousing the suspicion of the postman. After the glue is fully dry, the stamp can be re-used as if it were a new one. I wrote to all my friends and asked them to do the same thing. When I received a letter with a stamp that bore a facial mask, I would cut it out and soak it in water till the glue was dissolved. When the glue was gone, so too was the postmark. The cleansed stamp was then ready to be used again. Of course, such stamps could only be recycled a couple of times, after which they would become a bit too fragile to handle. In addition, such a trick could only be applied to the ordinary stamps, such as that with the Great Wall design: I never applied a mask to any collector's items. Among the full sets of commemorative stamps I have collected over the years are such rarities as those quoting Chairman

Mao's poems; those depicting the eight revolutionary model plays; and those of national heroes and great leaders. I have also collected special editions of natural scenery, flowers and birds, and so on.

My cunning recycling of stamps eventually came to my father's attention, and he wrote to point out that I was engaged in an illegal act. As a result of his criticism, I stopped, but the practice remained popular among the *zhiqings*.

BIRTHDAY PRESENT

Zhang Huixin

It was no secret that life on the state farm was hard. Although in comparison to those rusticated in rural villages we at least had the good fortune of a rice ration of twenty kilos a month, our hunger pangs never really left us, even after a meal. Can you imagine that at each mealtime less than half a liter of cooking oil was used for the meals of more than two hundred regimental soldiers? Each dish contained barely a hint of any oil. Festive seasons, when a pig or an ox was slaughtered to improve our diet, were really the highlight of our *zhiqing* life, and each person would be allocated nearly half a kilo of meat. While some boys would still find it insufficient and hang around the cookhouse hoping for an extra portion, the girls were thrifty. They would pick out the fatty meat from their portions, fry it for lard and keep it in a jar for later meals. When the festive season was over, they would take a teaspoonful of lard from the jar and add it to those meals that contained hardly any oil.

One day, as I finished washing up in the cookhouse and was about to have my supper, a girl in our dormitory cried out: "It's my birthday today!" At first, none of us replied. But later on, we thought we should really help her to celebrate the occasion. After some discussion, we agreed to give her an extra spoonful of the lard we had saved. She more than deserved it and our act of generosity made us genuinely happy.

Friendship and Love

A BELATED "THANK YOU"

Peng Lijia

August 30, 1971, marked my first home visit after being rusticated on Hainan Island for more than a year. It was also going to be the first long trip I would take alone. I was both thrilled and apprehensive.

From Daling Farm to my hometown of Meixian was a long and tortuous journey. To begin with, it took a day and a half merely to get to Haikou City before I could leave Hainan Island for the mainland. To reach Haikou City, I first had to walk more than an hour from my own company—No. 7 Company—to No. 1 Company and spend a night there. Early next morning, it was another walk to Daxi Bridge to wait for a bus to Haikou City. After a bumpy and dusty ride, which reeked of gasoline, I would not reach Haikou until late afternoon.

That morning, when I was waiting at Daxi Bridge, a dashing young *zhiqing* turned up with a shoulder bag. When he introduced himself in just a few words, I learned that he, Huang Mingqiang, was a Guangzhou *zhiqing* who was working in the transport company. With such an "elder brother" to accompany me, I was elated and felt a lot safer. He, however, seemed aloof and wasn't anxious to chat. On the farm, the transport company and the militia were two of the troops that many aspired to join, and their fortunate members tended to look down on the rest of us. They were usually from a politically correct family background and were political progressives: they were deemed the elite *zhiqings*. As for me, I was the daughter of those who were in one of the "seven black categories,"[11] and whether I was "redeemable" depended on the political assessment of my performance. I could never be assigned to either of those two troops: all that awaited me was physical labor in a run-of-the-mill troop.

Fortunately, once we arrived at Haikou City, Huang assumed an elder brother role and looked after me. He took me to queue for tickets and looked for accommodation. After we filled in the register at a hostel, he took me out to grab something to eat. Soon after we left the hostel, he turned and remarked, to my surprise, "You have fine handwriting." I was thrilled: despite his mind-your-own-business air, he had observed such a minor detail! I couldn't help but notice that he was even smiling at me!

After reaching Haikou, one of the dilemmas which confronted those *zhiqings* who were on a journey home was whether they should go straight to the ticket office and buy a ticket or secure accommodations. If they went straight for a ticket, it was quite likely that by the time they found a hostel, there would be no more room. But if they hunted for accommodation first, it was likely that by the time they reached the ticket office, not a single ticket would be left—and that was worse. As a *zhiqing*, each of us was entitled to twenty-one days' home leave per year, but so circuitous was the journey, and so poor were the road conditions and transport, that no less than nine of those days were allowed for travel. Nevertheless, it was a waste of time and money and a form of torment if we had to stay in Haikou for as much as half a day. As to accommodation, if luck was with us, we might be able to come across a single bed in a row of beds

11. During the Cultural Revolution, the population was broadly divided into "good" ("red") and "bad" ("black") elements, and initially there were five black categories: ex-landlords, rich farmers, counterrevolutionaries, bad elements and rightists. These soon became seven black categories when 'capitalist-roaders' and reactionary academics were added to the list. All were deemed to be class enemies of the proletariat, and if an individual fell into any of these categories, every member of his or her family would bear the same stigma.

crammed into a large dormitory. Failing that, we might have to rent a foldable travel bed for ten *jiao* a night and sleep in an even more crowded, dirty, and noisy corridor; or, when neither of these options was available, to spend five *fen* on a straw mat and sleep wherever there was a meter-wide space in the hostel compound. When even this last option had disappeared, we would have to go from one hostel to another until we could finally find a spot on a floor. This ordeal was part of the collective memory of the Hainan *zhiqings*.

That day, when we found a hostel, there were no more beds in the dormitory but a foldable travel bed for the corridor. Huang let me have it and even helped to find a relatively safe corner to set it up. As for him, he could only make do with a straw mat and sleep on the floor without bedding. Before turning in, he removed his new watch and asked me to take care of it for him: it would be a lot safer to keep it under my pillow than for him to wear it on his wrist in the overcrowded corridor. A watch was a luxury item: I was worried that it might be crushed under my head. Although he reassured me that this would never happen, my instinct when I woke up in the middle of the night was to reach under the pillow to feel if it was still there, and pull it out to check under the dim light that it was not smashed. It was not until the next morning, when I returned it to him, that I felt a heavy burden had been lifted from me.

Next morning, we didn't manage to get tickets and had to spend a second restless night in Haikou. On 1 September, when we eventually boarded the Red Guard No. 7 ship after a smelly train journey to Xiuying Pier early in the morning, I felt tremendously relieved. I can't remember how I survived seasickness and how Huang looked after me throughout the crossing. What I can remember is that as the ship was reaching Guangzhou, Huang asked if I had anywhere to stay during my stopover. When I told him no, he straightaway offered to put me up at his home. During the three days of travel, I had got used to being very well looked after and didn't hesitate to accept his offer. The youngest of five siblings, I had always been apt to depend on others before my rustication. This old habit of mine returned to me at the first opportunity.

It was not until we arrived at his home that I realized how tiny it was. In a two-bedroomed apartment in an old-fashioned shophouse in the ancient western district of the city, three generations were squeezed in under the same roof. I shared a room with his grandmother. I couldn't sleep that night and while lying wide awake in bed, eavesdropped on a murmured conversation between Huang and his mother on their balcony. After Huang explained why we had traveled together, his mother made him promise that he would never take advantage of me, and that he would look after me properly and help me the next day to buy a ticket home. He listened to his mother's unending instructions good-humouredly and with only a slowly growing hint of impatience.

This was the first time I learned that a boy could take advantage of a girl when they were alone together. But as to what sort of advantage it could be, I hadn't the faintest idea. Holding her hand or accidentally rubbing against her when walking past? My hyperactive imagination could only be stretched that far! That was how muddled and ignorant we youngsters were.

The following night was warm and a typhoon was forecast. I went to the balcony for the lovely breeze, and Huang came out to sit opposite me. For the first time in five days, he talked to me in a serious tone. He warned me that I must learn to protect myself and never jump at an invitation to stay at a boy's place. I talked back to him in my head: "I'm not such a simpleton. I only followed you home because after three days of traveling together, I felt you could be trusted." But of course he couldn't hear me.

When I told my mother about my experience of the previous six days, she made me realize how fortunate I had been to meet Huang at the outset, and that I must thank him and his family for their kindness and help. After going back to the farm, I went to his company to return a pen that had mysteriously found its way into my bag. When we met, he seemed to have resumed his arrogance: it felt as if we had never encountered each other before, let alone spent so much recent time together. I forgot all my promises to my mother to thank him: I thought I could put on a haughtier air than he could.

Friendship and Love

In 2010, when I paid a visit to Daling Farm during a business trip to Hainan Island, I went past where his troop had been based but could find no trace of it. I felt a sudden loss. It was in front of his dormitory that I had returned his pen. But now that everything had disappeared, it felt as if I had been dreaming all along. Then and there, I made up my mind to tell Huang how honored I had been that, having known me for no more than twenty-four hours, he had entrusted me with his most valuable property, his watch. For someone from a "politically incorrect" family background, being trusted so readily was a novel experience. I also had to thank him for praising my neat handwriting, a rare compliment which had encouraged me to find and develop my individual strengths. I needed to tell him that over the years I had never forgotten his gallant conduct during the first long journey I had taken alone.

After that trip, I became somewhat obsessive about my mission. I made inquiries about him on all possible occasions. Although I could only remember his surname, Huang, some ex-*zhiqings* from Guangzhou took it upon themselves to ask around whenever they could. Thanks to their dogged determination, they tracked him down eventually and got hold of his contact information! Ten minutes after I sent my text message to him, he texted back: "Am I dreaming? Years gone by, yet you still remember. Hope you are fine. Let's catch up when you are free."

As I was writing this account, I took my diary out to check dates and other details. When I reached the page dated 28 August 1971, I read, "Saturday: As I was returning to the dormitory from a shower, the political instructor told me that my application for a home visit has been approved. I am thrilled to bits. But when I learned that I was the only one of the whole company who had been given approval, I became worried. I have never made such a long journey on my own. Will everything be OK? But then I think this will be a great opportunity for me to learn to become independent. I must treat this home visit as a drill to step up my combat readiness: whatever happens, I will be at once audacious and extremely cautious."

As I read the entry, a wry smile crossed my face.

MORE THAN MERE MEDICINE
He Qinghua

I was rather unlucky, yet also extremely lucky. Unlucky because in March 1969, barely four months into my rustication, there was an outbreak of acute hepatitis on the farm, and I was the first of the three infected *zhiqings* in my company; lucky because I was able to make a speedy recovery thanks to the tender love and care of my workmates.

When I was struck down by the illness, I hadn't the faintest idea that what I had caught was acute hepatogenous jaundice. Neither had the assistant nurse and the barefoot doctors. I threw up repeatedly, and soon my stomach, which contained little even on a good day, became so empty that I suffered unbearably painful spasms. I was rushed to the county hospital twice but was misdiagnosed and treated as a patient with acute gastro-enteritis. The medicine prescribed for me didn't work and merely triggered more vomiting. For nearly a week, I could not take any food or drink: even a sip of plain water would make me throw up. I was so feeble I could barely get out of bed.

Before I left for Hainan, my father had been denounced, wrongly, as a rightist and thrown into prison. My mother was confined to "study class" and not allowed to return home. I was left to fend for myself: when I was preparing for my rustication in Hainan, I had no one to turn to for help. An old lady next door took pity on me and gave me a bowl of stir-fried rice on the day of my departure, and that was the only food I had that day. Nevertheless, I was able to hold back my tears on the ship when many of my fellow *zhiqings* were crying their eyes out as their families saw them off at the pier. But now, while I was lying in the thatched hut, I was suddenly seized with a sense of loss and help-lessness: I feared that the illness would take my life and that I would never see my parents and family again. My room-mates tried their very best to help and comfort me. When they heard that honey might help put a stop to the vomiting, they went all the way to the county town to get a bottle for me in the shop. But it didn't do the trick. They were pushed to their wits' end. An old hand in my squad, whom we called Auntie Li, had come by some fish and insisted on bringing me to her place to eat it. A hot pot of freshly cooked fish was a rare delicacy in those days! Despite the fact that she had three mouths to feed, she picked the biggest piece and put it into my bowl. Devoid of appetite, I was nevertheless eager to please her and show my gratitude, but after two bites I could take no more of it. Even though, at the promptings of common sense, I warned her vehemently that she risked being infected, Auntie Li didn't throw away my leftovers but ate them herself. When I was correctly diagnosed later as having caught the highly infectious jaundice, I was very worried for her health. To my great relief, neither she nor her family were infected during the outbreak; otherwise I would have been guilt-stricken for the rest of my life!

When I was admitted to the hospital for the third time, a doctor from a major hospital was doing the rounds there, and he was able to diagnose my disease accurately. I was immediately put on a ward. During the time I was there, the company officials, veterans, and *zhiqings* from my squad would take turns visiting me and keeping me company. A patient in the same ward played the dulcimer, and thanks to his coaching, I was able to play a few tunes by the time I left. The other two patients in my ward were *zhiqings* from No. 7 Company, also my former schoolmates, though two years younger than I. No. 7 Company was known for having the most resourceful cooks and the best-run canteen on the farm. Every time they came by a pig or two, they would keep some lean pork and liver for those who were unwell. Although I was not part of their troop, I got a taste of their gentle care, and in ten days I was on the mend and my appetite started to return. Whenever the nurses asked me what I fancied to eat, I would say vegetable congee. During the next few days, the nurses went to the vegetable field to pick some young shoots of bok choy. All the Hainan *zhiqings* knew fairly well that quite apart from its young shoots, bok choy of any kind was a rarity in our lives: when we could get it, our staple vegetable was water spinach. When I had bok choy congee, it simply tasted like the most delectable dish ever, and indeed its fresh taste still lingers in my memory after all these years. After three weeks in the ward, I was released on the condition that I take two weeks' rest before returning to work. But when we saw how hard our fellow *zhiqings* were toiling during the major joint campaign, we few convalescing patients ignored the strong objections of the officials and returned to work after just a week.

It so happened that during the outbreak that year, scores of *zhiqings* in my company—No 3—fell ill, along with several dozen local children. The children were quarantined in a big thatched hut and were tended by a few *zhiqing* teachers from Guangzhou. For nearly a month they nursed the children back to health. Not one of them asked to leave their job for fear of being infected.

In the lean years when everybody was suffering from malnutrition, an outbreak could easily have claimed many victims. I made a speedy recovery, which I believe was thanks not just to the medical treatment I received but to something else: the simple love and devoted care of the old hands and my fellow *zhiqings*. Their selflessness, love, and dedication to my well-being were the best one could hope for. More than anything else, these qualities have inspired me throughout the rest of my life.

LOVE IN A FEVERISH CLIMATE

Huang Ronger

While working in the political division of the regiment, I was temporarily reassigned to No. 9 Company, where I had worked as a clerk before being moved to regimental headquarters. My task was to gain firsthand experience of the grassroots before writing a report on my former company.

On my arrival, I began to look around for Li, the secretary of the Communist Youth League and the company's assistant nurse. I was disappointed and a bit lost when I couldn't spot her in the familiar crowd. When I was a clerk, the two of us had once recited a poem of mine at a party. It was a poem about my grand revolutionary ambition to liberate the whole world: it recounted revolutionary history from the Socialist Revolution in Russia in October 1917 to those that had taken place in China, and how, by the twenty-first century, the whole world would have turned as red as communist China.

I joined the Communist Party in 1972. The hot issue then was whether we *zhiqings* should be "rooted in Hainan." For me there was only one answer: to abide by what I had sworn when joining the Party and to remain on Hainan for the rest of my life. So many revolutionaries had lost their lives to establish communist China that to devote myself to the development of Hainan was the least I could do to pay my dues. A firm guarantee of one's intention to stay put was to get married there and start a family. I was twenty-four years old: it was high time to look for a marriage partner. Soon after I was promoted to work in the regimental headquarters, I was attracted to a *zhiqing* who had an "immaculate" background: she came from a family of workers! But she soon enrolled in a polytechnic back in the city. On the day she left Daling, I helped her with her luggage, and after the bus had long gone, ran into a rubber plantation and sobbed under a tree because I had lost my chance with her.

If the child of a senior government official decided to go steady with a fellow *zhiqing* and put down roots in the regiment, the impact on the other *zhiqings* would be enormous. The deputy political commissar of the regiment encouraged me to set such a conspicuous example: he even offered to arrange a date for me. However, I felt nothing for the *zhiqing* he had in mind. The precepts of Marx and Lenin came to my rescue, "The only moral marriage is that which is founded on love." I quoted it to justify my rejection of his kind offer. But the pressing challenge was this: many *zhiqings* were starting to find any old excuse to leave the farm: if I were to show my determination to stay behind permanently, I would need to find a date pretty quickly.

A few days after my temporary relocation back to No. 9 Company, Li showed up on the farm. Her absence, it turned out, was because she had been on home leave. Her return enlivened the Communist Youth League and provided much material for my report. When working with her, I felt motivated and happy. She was pretty and graceful in my eyes; I loved her charming smile.

One day, Li made an evening appointment to talk to me about work. The office was our normal meeting place, but on this occasion, she asked if we could meet up in the kitchen of one of the old timers. In the middle of the little thatched shed was a small round table and on it a small oil lamp. We sat face to face at the table. After we finished discussing work, she asked all of a sudden: "If someone wished to discuss a personal matter with you, what would you say?" "Personal matter" was the euphemism for a romantic relationship which was conducted with a view to marriage.

"I am twenty-four years old. I would consider it."

"What if that someone was me?"

Never had I expected her to be so blunt: I was speechless.

She looked sincerely at me.

"Let me think about it." I finally murmured.

"It is a matter entirely between you and me. I hope you won't tell anyone, let alone consult any of your friends in the company," she responded.

Those to whom she was referring were the best friends I had made while working in No. 9 Company. They were like blood brothers to me. We worked hard together, and after work we would prepare the wall bulletin, play basketball, organize parties, and conduct night classes. We tried our very best to make life on the farm a bit less monotonous. I had no idea why she wouldn't want me to consult them on what for me was such an important issue.

Before rustication, Li was a seventh-grade student at Guangzhou No. 30 Secondary School. Since most of its students came from lower-middle class families in the neighborhood, it was known as a school for philistines. As for me, I was a student at the elite Guangya Secondary School whose pupils were the children of high-ranking government officials and intellectuals. We had a sense of superiority. Moreover, my father had by then been reinstated to the position of deputy director of the Guangdong Provincial Propaganda Department: as his son, I felt as if I had been crowned as a prince. Subconsciously, I looked down upon the students of the humbler schools. Putting aside the difference in our status, would she be able to accept me now that I had decided to stay put on Hainan while everybody else was trying to find a way out?

When I was a clerk in the company, my room in the thatched shed was right next to the clinic she worked at, and the partition between us was less than two meters high. Every day after Li finished seeing her last patient, she would stay behind until late and chat with me over the low wall. One day, our simple and honest captain remarked: "You and the assistant nurse have been staying late alone together. Mind what it says about you." He meant well: after all, the last thing anyone wished to be accused of was being "depraved," one of the most disgraceful and irremovable stains on one's character. Since then, I had tried to stay away from Li and was soon reassigned to the regimental headquarters as a propaganda officer.

The day after our conversation in the kitchen of the thatched shed, I returned to regimental headquarters for ten days of drill, which gave me ample time to ponder Li's proposal. On my return to the company, I asked to meet her by the river. We sat side by side, each wearing a wide-brimmed straw hat—a rule that Li imposed so that we would stay physically apart from each other. I wished to talk to her about my revolutionary ambitions and the challenges ahead for me, but I didn't know where to start. I told her instead that I would like to go steady with her and asked her for a photograph before I consulted my parents. She readily obliged.

A few days later, my close friends asked me to meet them at the vegetable field. They questioned me about my relationship with Li and issued an ultimatum: I had to choose between them and her. This was a bolt from the blue, but I confirmed my allegiance to them: I never wanted to lose their friendship. To this day, I haven't the faintest idea why they had taken such a dislike to her.

After that crucial decision, I met her on the hill one night and asked that we stop seeing each other. She wished to know if this was because my parents had objected. I denied it. I tried to comfort her by pointing out that for her there was no shortage of better prospects in the company. She said she fancied no one but me. I then revealed that I had decided to stay put on Hainan and that I wasn't in good health, having been diagnosed with hepatitis the year before. She assured me that since she was an assistant nurse, my poor health was not a problem and that she could look after me. She started to weep and after a long while, she asked if we could become sworn siblings. As soon as I agreed, she calmly urged me to return to my dormitory immediately to avoid undesirable gossip. I was taken aback by her sudden composure.

When my job at the company came to an end, I returned to the regimental headquarters. Encouraged by my friends, I wrote to a childhood sweetheart, and in the hope of going steady with her, invited her to visit me at the farm. Although the encounter didn't work out, Li was ill for more than ten days after she learned about it. I felt as if I was hurting her deliberately.

In the days that followed, not only did the old timers try to act as my matchmakers but some female *zhiqings* used a third party to reveal their romantic interest in me. For a while, it became public knowledge that I was looking for a wife. During all this, I came to realize that my heart was still with Li: I told my friends that I wouldn't go out with anyone but her. This must have prompted fate: soon, I was dispatched to a remote company to lead an intensive political campaign. We were kept apart both by the demands of my work and the insurmountable physical distance between us. Then came an order for me to return to Guangzhou to work for the Municipal Cultural Bureau as a creative writer. It was a chance not to be missed.

The night before my departure, I walked all the way to Li's company and asked to meet her in the old timer's kitchen, the same thatched shed where we had met when she proposed that we go steady. And just as on that previous night, we sat face to face at the small table with a small oil lamp between us. I told her about my new job. Li remained taciturn and looked a bit aloof. After I finished, she said, with a hint of a smile: "We have both made new choices; my only wish is for you never to forget this sworn younger sister of yours." When I asked what her plan was, she told me she didn't have one yet but we could surely keep in touch. She asked me to send her my postal address once I was settled back home and then urged me to return to regimental headquarters without further ado. Throughout our brief rendezvous, she kept her own counsel; I felt that I was being pushed away by her silence and aloofness. Couldn't she tell that this was our last chance to resolve our "personal matters" and that I wanted to rekindle our brief relationship?

On my lonely walk back to the dormitory, I felt desolate and bereft.

Several decades have passed, and yet what happened between us is as vivid as yesterday. Life is a patchwork of hope and hopelessness, happy success and painful failure. Of all the ups and downs in our lives, what touches the heart is usually the most lyrical and memorable. At times I wonder whether, if I could re-live my youth, I would make the same decisions.

THE GIRL IN THE SONG

Chen Hongguang

Following Chairman Mao's remark that "The countryside is a vast expanse where one can flourish," millions of secondary school students left home during the "Up to the Mountains, Down to the Countryside" campaign for the most remote and deprived areas of the country. At the campaign's feverish height, I signed up in November 1968 to help develop rubber plantations on Daling Farm, Hainan Island.

Soon after my arrival, the farm was converted into a regiment of an army production and construction corps, and within the regiment a number of new companies were set up. I threw myself into my new life, and probably also because I was "a good seed and a red seedling"—from a politically correct family—I was soon picked by the regiment to attend a six-week medical training program. On completing the program, but without any assessment of my medical knowledge or skills, I was reassigned to the militia to work as an assistant nurse.

The militia was one of those newly established companies that took only the cream from the regiment. There were three squads that consisted entirely of men, and one of what were known as "iron girls." Apart from two ex-servicemen—our captain and the political instructor—and a few laborers, the rest of the militia were athletic-looking youngsters aged seventeen to twenty-two. We were armed with rifles, machine guns, sub-machine guns, and some light artillery. As an assistant nurse, I was equipped with a German revolver. Once a week, we were assembled to learn the military basics of defense and to practice handling weapons to prepare ourselves for a war and guard our treasure island, Hainan. That was our duty—because we were both regimental soldiers and members of the militia.

After Daling Farm was turned into a regiment, eight new companies were added to its seven existing ones. In an attempt to hasten the opening up of the wilderness in vast and hilly Baisha County, we rose for work before dawn and would not return to our dormitories until dusk. Taming the wilderness—chopping down bushes, felling trees, digging holes for planting, building terraces—was our routine. In addition, we participated in a series of major joint campaigns in which several troops would join forces to tackle one specific area for rubber planting. The role of assistant nurse was then only part-time: the rest of the day I spent in regular physical labor. A year and a half later, I was so exhausted that I could no longer shoulder the double workload. In most companies, there were at least two assistant nurses: in the militia, there was only me, a single part-time medic. I started to ask for an assistant for the clinic, and even whether I could simply resign my medical role and become a full-time militiaman.

Eventually, an assistant was assigned to me. The daughter of an old timer, she had undergone six months' medical training in the regimental hospital. Of medium height, she was pretty and had a bubbly personality. We worked seamlessly as a team. When I was called to join the main troops to work in the major joint campaigns to chop down bushes and fell trees on the hillsides, she would stay behind in the militia, attending to the sick and the injured in the clinic: and when it was her turn to dig holes for planting and to build terraces, I would take care of the clinic. Although I was her senior in rank, she had been through much more extensive training and was highly competent, better qualified, and with a greater medical aptitude. While I tended to rush things in the clinic, she was patient and meticulous. When the regiment was promoting the use of traditional Chinese medicine, she was able to show her experience and expertise in identifying, gathering and applying medicinal herbs for common ailments, skills she had acquired by growing up in the jungle. Outside the clinic, she was the equal of any man in such heavy physical labor as chopping bushes, digging holes, and building terraces. Kind, warm-hearted and with an ever-cheerful outlook, she was popular in the troop. Through her, I learned how to identify Chinese medicines and picked up other medical skills.

Since being rusticated, we *zhiqings* had routinely chanted, "Be rooted in Hainan" in order to show that we were so dedicated to the development of the island that we would stay there for the rest of our lives. To serve the revolutionary cause I was determined to stay put on the farm. After working with my assistant for a while, I was attracted to and fell in love with her. I wanted to reveal my feelings but didn't have the courage to do so. In those days, "class struggle" was high on the daily agenda, and any false step in our behavior could make us instantly vulnerable. "Capitalist," "promiscuous," and "depraved" were just some of the labels that could be slapped on us. I didn't dare to disclose my feelings for her and had to keep them to myself.

Half a year later, she was reassigned to work in the regimental hospital and I was again left to staff the clinic on my own. Without her around, I felt sad and lonely, and whenever I visited the regimental hospital for meetings or to acquire more medicine, I would find an excuse to be near her and talk to her. I still couldn't find the courage to confess my love, but I was pretty sure that she was aware of how I felt toward her. The militia was a long way from regimental headquarters. After the regiment was converted back to a state farm in late 1974, we did eventually go steady for a short while, but the influence of the class struggle loomed large in our daily lives and took its toll on me. For the sake of my future, I felt I had to sacrifice my feelings for her. Gradually, we stopped seeing each other.

Soon, the *zhiqings* began to find various excuses to leave the farm: they were going to college or had been recruited for a job back home or were taking over a parent's post—whatever did the trick. In March 1979, I too returned to Guangzhou. Without any papers or qualifications, I could no longer work in a medical capacity: I was given a job in a factory.

In the 1990s, the song "Xiao Fang" swept the country, and it rekindled my memories of her. She was my "Xiao Fang" who had helped me to survive that tough time. Whenever the ex-*zhiqing*s got together for karaoke, I would choose that song:

> Xiao Fang lived in a rural place,
> So kind of heart and fair of face.
> . . . While still I breathe, I shan't lose sight
> Of all you gave that lit my night;
> Bestowed a gentle love sublime
> And helped me through the hardest time.
> . . . May your good fortune never cease,
> Your kindness generate increase.
> Through all the years in my mind's eye
> I re-create our last good-bye:
> You watch until my path will bend,
> Still standing at the hamlet's end.

In October 2009, I heard about her, and at a get-together of old *zhiqing*s even got hold of her address. Then, during a holiday in her adopted city, I paid a surprise visit to her. She was thrilled to see me. Though age had caught up with us, her smile, her warmheartedness, the way she carried herself, and her mannerisms all reminded me of the tough yet happy days she had helped me get through. To me, she cast a stylish, energetic figure: I felt as if I had returned to my younger days and I could still see what had once attracted me to her.

We had a great reunion: I learned what had happened to her since I left Hainan. She married an ex-*zhiqing* from the farm and subsequently followed him back to his home city. The hospital where she worked as a nurse was situated in an outer suburb, and owing to the poor transport system, she had to commute for at least three hours every day. In the late 1980s, this working mother overcame many tough challenges and obtained the necessary medical qualifications. She was then transferred to a major hospital in the city. Now a contented grandmother, she has retired and is living in the spacious apartment allocated to her by the hospital. Life has treated her and her family kindly. And, indeed, my "Xiao Fang" has fared much better than her ex-*zhiqing* admirer.

PUTTING DOWN ROOTS IN DALING

Fang Jinqi

I was rusticated to Hainan Island in the fall of 1968, while my three younger brothers were rusticated to Zhanjiang. In those days, my schoolteacher parents had to attend daily "study sessions" to undergo thought-reform and had no time for us. All the necessary procedures, such as transferring our household registration and packing, we had to do ourselves. On 8 November, the second batch of rusticated youth from Guangzhou was transported to Taigu Pier. I didn't feel excited: none of my family could come to see me off. I didn't feel sad either: it was the right thing for me to do to follow Chairman Mao's instructions to go down to the countryside. As the ship sailed into the open sea, I experienced a sense of freedom: in the southernmost part of China I was about to devote my whole life to the revolutionary cause.

On arriving at Daling, I was assigned to the Red Guard Company along with more than thirty new *zhiqings* like myself. After half an hour's walk from regimental headquarters, we came upon five or six rows of thatched huts, which had recently been built especially for us by the old hands. Ten girls shared a long rough bed in a room. This was my first home on Hainan. Soon after we built tiled houses, we moved in but we were still ten to a room. Though we were stretched in terms of resources, we lived like a large family: we read, played musical instruments and to improve our nutrition sometimes cooked for ourselves. In July of 1971, I was reassigned to work in the rubber factory. I moved into a tiled house and shared a room with three others.

When we first arrived in Hainan, we constantly chanted the slogan "Be rooted in the farm for the revolutionary cause." Three or four years later, "Be rooted" in Hainan acquired a slightly new meaning: to get married and start a family there. By then, many female *zhiqings* who arrived at the same time as me had found sweethearts: my mother wrote to urge me to find someone to marry. A *zhiqing* friend introduced me to Ah Hai in her company. It so happened that we had gone to the same secondary school in Guangzhou, though we were never in the same class. With that much in common, we started to see each other. Where to go for a date was always a headache. If we met in our rooms, that would inconvenience the roommates. We could go to an old hand's kitchen, but we couldn't resort to that too often. Going to a movie was a good idea, but that could only happen when there was a film being shown in one of the companies within walking distance. When we ran out of options, we would just walk along the paths near my company's headquarters and find a place to sit down when we wished to rest our feet. But we couldn't sit in the open air for long: the mosquitoes were too ferocious. Eventually we came upon an ideal place: the top of the water tower. Not only were we away from the crowds but the mosquitoes were far fewer as well. In the moonlight, we were attuned to the sound of the insects and breathed in the fresh smell of rubber trees and grass. It was the most romantic time and place for us.

Three years after we started dating, we decided to get married. In September 1976, when we were on our home leave, we registered. No photographs were required on the wedding certificate, and the fee was just five *jiao*.

On our return to Daling we spent our first two nights at a hostel. The farm allocated us a room in a unused hospital. After spring-cleaning it, we moved in, invited our friends over to our new home, and served them with sweets and biscuits. Our home was bare. The bed was supported by two wooden benches given to us by an old hand: on top, we put on a straw mat, bedding, and a mosquito net recently brought back from Guangzhou. The quilt was a gift hand-made by my mother. On the desk were a vase and a thermos, a few mugs, and a teapot from our relatives and friends. We bought our own basic kitchenware and tableware. Soon we were upgraded to a room in a bungalow closer to the canteen. The room was about twenty square meters, the same as the old one. Like the other families living on the same floor, we had the use of less than two square metres in the corridor to serve as our kitchen. As time went by, we gathered more and more stuff: we spent thirty *yuan* on a wooden trunk for our clothing, and soon some *zhiqing* friends made us a chest of drawers, a small dining table, and four folding chairs. We also built a thatched shed in front of the bungalow, as our dining room doubled as a storage room for our work tools and firewood. In the kitchen, we built a small sink. In early 1977, after a "study session" in a Party school near Guangzhou, I paid a visit to Guangzhou and brought back with me a sewing machine given by my relatives. We were planning to stay there for the rest of our lives.

I was pregnant half a year into our marriage. Without a clue about how to look after myself, I continued my work as usual, participating in the militia drills in Baisha County, attending meetings nearly two hundred kilometres away in Haikou City by bus, participating in the building of the hydro-electric station, and so on, and soon I suffered a miscarriage. When I became pregnant for the second time, I was more cautious since I was at risk of a second miscarriage. My mother-in-law came all the way from Guangzhou to Daling to look after me. At first, she stayed in the same room with us and we simply put up a cloth curtain between us at night. Finding this rather inconvenient, she then had her bed moved to the thatched shed. Luckily for us, the thatched shed was big enough. She soon got used to life on Hainan and got on exceedingly well with our neighbors. In early 1978, after seven months' pregnancy, I took my mother's advice and returned to Guangzhou to wait for the delivery. In March 1978, I gave birth to a healthy boy, weighing 3.2 kilograms. When I was nursing him at my mother's place, my mother-in-law moved into my mother's apartment to help me out. It was not until our son was one month old that his father was able to take time off to come to Guangzhou and meet him for the first time.

When our son was seven weeks old, the four of us returned to Daling together.

I returned to work right after my eight-week maternity leave. Probably because of the long-term malnutrition that everybody suffered in those days, I couldn't provide my son with enough milk, and we had to feed him with milk powder and congee. Conditions on the farm were gradually improving, thanks in large measure to the implementation of various national reforms in the late 1970s. Every ten or fifteen days, the farm would allocate an equal share of pork and fish to everyone, with a half-quota for the children. Many people started to keep chickens and some even raised pigs at home. We routinely kept three or four hens for eggs. After it rained, Ah Hai would carry a torch and trace the sounds in the fields to catch frogs in the fields and water. Within two hours, he could usually fill up a lunch box with them, big or small, sufficient to last my son and me for a few days. I made all the clothes for my son. Under the tender care of my mother-in-law, he grew fast; he looked clean and cute and was adored by our neighbors. The son of Doctor Liu was fondly called Da Bao, meaning "Big Treasure," and so our son became Xiao Bao, "Little Treasure." Every now and then some friends would turn up with vegetables freshly picked from the fields, or a portion of pig's liver or lean pork, all with the aim of improving my nutrition. A group of little boys who liked fishing would also give Xiao Bao the biggest catch of the day from their net. As our son grew, a worker passed on his child's cradle and homemade bamboo baby-walker. Some *zhiqing* friends gave us three chairs. The affection and love showered on us made us very grateful: in return, we worked even harder for the farm.

By the spring of 1979, most *zhiqings* in Daling had managed to find a way to return home. Those who could wait no longer for a job would resort to the pretext of being sick or an invalid in order to get themselves moved back. Soon, most of the *zhiqings* were gone.

I returned to Guangzhou in September 1979. Five months later, Ah Hai was offered a job in Guangzhou, and our ten-year life in Daling came to an end. Our home was taken over by an ex-*zhiqing* from Guangzhou, Engineer Wu, who after he had finished college returned to Daling to help build the hydro-electric station. After the completion of the station, he lived there till December 1981. In 2007, I paid a visit to Daling and saw that the few rows of bungalows were still there, though greatly improved: each family, for example, had at last two and a half rooms to themselves.

A WORLD WELL LOST FOR LOVE
Luo Tiansheng, noted down by Liang Yongkang

I followed the zhiqings to Daling
When the *zhiqings* arrived at Daling, they appeared in droves, and their arrival was usually marked by a great fanfare of drums and cymbals. I, however, turned up on my own, and nobody noticed. I graduated in 1967 from a secondary school which was affiliated to the South China Institute of Tropical Crops on Hainan. Since my father was working in Daling, it seemed an obvious choice to join him there. At the time, Daling was enmeshed in fierce battles between factions: as a rubber specialist, my father was implicated and condemned by default as a member of the "techie faction." Once I reached Daling, I went straight to visit my father, who was hospitalized. Before I could head for home, however, I was caught by the radical rebel faction and expelled from Daling at the Daxi Bridge. With nowhere else to go, all I could do was hike the long distance from Daling in Baisha County back to Nada town in Danxian. When I was thirsty I drank from the fields, but had nothing to ease my hunger pangs. I walked for twelve hours—from three in the afternoon till three in the morning—before I reached my home in Nada. I was downcast. What I had wanted was simple: to be reunited with my father and dedicate myself to the development of the rubber plantation, a cause my father had devoted half his life to. My simple wish had been denied, and the experience cut deeply into my young heart.

In November 1968, my elder brother cycled all the way from Daling to tell me that the farm was expecting a huge number of *zhiqings* from Guangzhou. The news re-ignited my hope of returning. On 12 November, the second day after their arrival, I made a quick visit there. I went straight to see the chairman of the revolutionary committee and expressed my goal. My request was granted: after a whole year's delay, I was about to settle in the Lowland Company, a remote unit near the west coast of Hainan Island.

Like father, like son
Before returning to Daling, I had worked in a group which was affiliated with the institute and knew fairly well how harsh the conditions in the company were. My insistence on going there was wholly attributable to the influence my father had over me.

A well-known figure in Daling, my father was fondly nicknamed "Uncle Luo" by the locals. Back in the early 1950s, he had been instrumental in setting up the propagation center in Daling. A respected specialist in growing rubber, he could identify more than one hundred species of rubber tree, and the seedlings he had propagated had been planted all over Hainan Island. He was also a visiting technical supervisor of the institute. But this was just his public profile: there were aspects of his life that remained largely unknown on Hainan. While working in the rubber plantations of Malaysia, he was a member of the Communist Party there. When the Chinese community was expelled from the country in 1951, he was sent to China. When he turned up in Guangzhou, he was forty-nine years old. Before leaving Malaysia, he hadn't the faintest idea what life held in store for him. Seized by his passion for rubber cultivation, he risked his life by packing twenty rubber seeds of fine species and a dozen seedlings in his luggage. He was assigned to the South China Agricultural and Cultivation Bureau headed by the first mayor of Guangzhou, Marshal Ye Jianying.[12] Soon,

---

12. Ye Jianying (1897-1986) was a Communist general named as one of the ten marshals who helped build a 'new China' in 1949. He was credited with removing the 'Gang of Four' from power soon after Mao's death in 1976. This helped to bring the Cultural Revolution to an end and swiftly change the face of modern China.

my two brothers and I followed him to Guangzhou, leaving my mother and sisters behind in Malaysia. The bureau was located on the former concessionary island of Shamian,[13] and we were allocated an apartment on the island. My father reminisced that due to the shortage of drivers he used to double up as Marshal Ye's chauffeur. In 1954, following a strategic decision by the state, a plan was made to develop rubber plantations on Hainan. Director Ye called upon everybody with relevant experience to join the plant cultivation center, and my father was among the first to sign up. He was also among the first experts to set foot on Hainan in order to help build the propagation center at the institute, the first of its kind in Asia.

Owing to the harsh conditions there, my father left his three sons behind, in the care of a cook at the bureau, but in 1955 he sent for us. Since there was no school in the area, my education was held up for two years. After I had spent less than a year at my father's side, the institute relocated the cultivation center to Daling, and he left me behind once again. That was my father—a man who had always put work before his family. Years later, we would blame him for not helping us to return to Guangzhou, for never giving us the fatherly love we so craved. It was not until much later that we started to understand why he had treated us this way: he was consumed by his passion for rubber cultivation. We grew up like orphans: he had never given us an affectionate home. I finally reconciled myself to it when I realized, through growing up in the tough conditions that were forced on me, how much I took after him: I was focused and assiduous. Now I wished to join my father so that he would no longer have to live alone. This was why I had wanted to go to Daling.

A life intertwined with a zhiqing's

Despite all the hardship in Daling, I fell in love with Xiao Chan, a Guangzhou *zhiqing*. I was then working in the militia, an elite company to which only those with a "politically correct" family background

---

13. Shamian Island is on the Pearl River in Guangdong and was a concession which was granted jointly to the British and the French in the nineteenth century. It is close to the pier where the *zhiqings* embarked for Hainan.

were admitted. I was also a probationary member of the Party. When it became known that I was going out with Xiao Chan, the officials tried to talk me out of it. They reiterated that since Xiao Chan had a "politically incorrect" family background—her father was a rightist—my future would be compromised if we got married. But I didn't want to renounce my love for the sake of Party membership: besides, it was not she who was the rightist but her father. In addition, weren't we supposed to offer such people help because of their "bad" family background? That was the Party policy, wasn't it? I ignored the officials' advice, but they didn't give up so easily. They talked to an old friend of my father and asked him to intervene on my behalf. My father told this friend that it was for his son to make his own choice. And thus I failed to fulfill my "great potential": I was never sworn into the Party; I was also demoted from the militia. I have never had any regrets about my decision. Xiao Chan and I got married and started a family in Daling. And we are still happy together.

Escapes, Scrapes, and Tight Spots

WE PLOTTED TO RUN AWAY
Song Xiaoqi

One night at the end of 1969, a secret order was delivered to me outside a thatched hut in Ledong County, Hainan Island. The third group to escape Hainan and return home to Hunan Province was planned for the next night. We would be allowed to take nothing with us except a change of clothing. There were four of us: two boys, two girls.

I had just turned seventeen: it was hardly a year since, on my own initiative, I had followed my older schoolmates to Hainan. I was the squad leader of No. 5 Squad in No. 9 Company, No. 15 Regiment of No. 3 Division.

Though I couldn't be more desperate to return home, I was seized by a sudden sentimental attachment to this place: the coconut trees that grow into the blue sky, a scene so unique to this land; the sound of waves crashing against the rocks; the rows of rubber plants we cultivated on the mountain terrace we built; the clear and bubbling stream; the ex-servicemen—"old workers" who were in fact just ten years older than us; their families; the fellow *zhiqings* from Guangdong and the several dozen of us from Hunan, including my sister. Overwhelmed by such an unexpected attachment, tears welled in my eyes.

On my last day I tried my best to disguise both my excitement and my sadness: I worked even harder than usual at digging the holes for planting, sat, as usual, on the handle of my pickaxe during breaks, and chatted heartily with the other "regimental soldiers" (that was the way we *zhiqings* addressed one another). To be labeled a "deserter" —to run away from the army corps—was disastrous: it was nothing less than a betrayal. If we were caught, heavy penalties awaited us. Yet somehow we justified our plan as merely an attempt to get back to school in our home province and wait for a new assignment.

On 22 December 1968, a "highest command" from Chairman Mao was broadcast on the radio: "Educated youth, go to the countryside to receive re-education from the poor and lower-middle peasants: it is a must." We had no option but to obey. Prior to this directive, though, Changsha City had decreed during the ongoing "Up to the Mountains, Down to the Countryside" campaign that those students born before 31 December 1952 were to be dispatched to the local farms and villages. Though Hunan Province had no quota to send its educated youth to such borderlands as Xinjiang, there were simply not enough farms to accommodate so many of us. If rusticated, we were bound to be dispatched not to the state farms but to rural villages to earn our living like the deprived peasants who were to host and mentor us. For us in the school propaganda troupe, which was in great demand, this came as a double blow: the end of our two years' living under the same roof as a close troupe and of our busy touring schedule. For a while, we could talk about nothing but how to stick together.

Our senior members soon found out that down south in Guang-zhou, thousands of secondary school students were being rusticated to Hainan Island to develop farming. It was said that very soon, the state farm would be handed over to the People's Liberation Army, and those who signed up would be joining a semi-military army production and construction corps like that in Xinjiang, with dormitories, salary, and canteen meals as part of the package. We were seduced, not least by the tropical scenery—blue waves and coconut trees shimmering in the breeze.

At that time, a documentary was being shown that was extremely popular: *Ode to the Army Farm*. It featured the lives of young people who had been recruited from major cities such as Beijing and Shanghai and were now living and working in the Xinjiang Army Production and Construction Corps. They were filmed guarding the borderlands, digging water channels, and cultivating cotton plants, fruit, and vegetables. Under grape-laden trellises, they sang and danced gaily with the Uighur people. Expressing our lofty ideals and ambition to throw ourselves into a great cause, its theme song, *The Borderlands Are Overtaking Jiangnan* (widely thought to be the most idyllic region in China), in particular kindled the enthusiasm of many a young heart. The lyrics express it: "The lake reflects the bright sunrise, / The snow-capped mountains, azure skies / As the sun in glory sets, / The soldiers land their teeming nets . . ." How idyllic! I would have done anything to join the Xinjiang Army Corps. However, one of our leaders, Elder Brother San, had a relative out there and knew a bit about the actual living conditions and customs. He warned us that Hainan Island would offer us something much closer to what we were accustomed to, which I discovered decades later to be the plain truth.

Since we were loath to separate from each other and live with peasants in the villages of Hunan, Hainan Island sounded like a godsend. We entrusted Elder Brother San to go down to Guangzhou to find out how we could be recruited to Hainan. It turned out that owing to the severe shortage of manpower, each farm had placed an officer in Guangzhou to hasten the recruitment process. Of all the new arrivals, those with artistic talents were in particularly high demand: life on the farms was monotonous, and although there was a Maoist propaganda troupe in each, fresh blood was badly needed to improve their performances.

With the photographs of our troupe in his pocket, Elder Brother San was able to show the recruitment officer from Baoshi State Farm how attractive we looked; furthermore, the officer was from Changsha and prepared to speed up the process so that we could go to Hainan Island before the "Up to the Mountains, Down to the Countryside" campaign reached its boiling point in Hunan. We were warned that for our own sake we must be secretive about the scheme. We were instructed to have our all-important household registration transferred surreptitiously, and to pack our bags discreetly: we were to depart quietly on the night of 12 January 1969.

Once I had left Changsha, there would only be my mother and a five-year-old brother at home. My father had met his sudden death four years before on a business trip, my nanny was dismissed two years later on the orders of the "revolutionary rebel faction" at my mother's company, my elder brother worked in a factory in Changde City, and my elder sister was rusticated to Jiangyong in 1965. I didn't want to leave my mother and little brother behind, but neither could my mother harbor any thought of keeping her headstrong and fanciful teenage girl by her side. She also gathered that it might be a lot safer for me to stay with those kindhearted senior members of my troupe than to be sent to live in isolation with peasants in the villages of Hunan. As I was taking leave, all she managed to say was that I should listen to the Party, work hard, take care of myself, and never, ever, go out alone with a boy at night.

It was a cold, snowy night, and the streets were covered in slush. Although my heart ached at having to leave my mother, I also looked forward to a new life, a life dedicated to the exciting and glorious revolutionary cause. When my mother saw me off at the train station, my sixteen-year old brain was a clean slate.

The night train took us to Guangzhou, and while we stayed there we slept on the floor of an acquaintance's apartment. Guangzhou was not new to me. Two years before, when the schools were closed during the revolutionary networking movement, students traveled freely across the country to meet other Red Guard activists and propagate Maoism. So I had decided with a classmate to follow the mob to Beijing for a mass reception by Chairman Mao. Due to our "politically incorrect" family backgrounds, it wasn't until long after the networking movement had peaked that we could timidly claim our right to join the masses. Despite our delay, we learned that Beijing had been so overburdened by those who were waiting for a glimpse of Chairman Mao that nobody was allowed to board the northbound trains. So we chose instead to go to one of the "red holy places," Chongqing City, and pay our respects to Elder Sister Jiang,[14] who had sacrificed her life to liberate China from the ruling Nationalist Party. But the platforms were chaotic and all the westbound trains were overwhelmed: the crowds behaved like refugees stampeding from a disaster in a movie. In the confusion, we ended up boarding a southbound train to Guangzhou.

While in Guangzhou, a Red Guard reception station had accommodated us free of charge and we visited all the "red" spots, the commemorative places of revolutionary history. We were excited—infatuated with the idea of inheriting the revolutionary spirit and turning the whole world into a huge communist state.

Two years after this first visit to Guangzhou, I had changed a little: though I was still consumed with revolutionary ideals, deep down I felt uneasy and during our five days' stopover wanted desperately to board a ship to Hainan. My excitement on catching my first glimpse of the sea, though, was ruined because I got seasick in a fifth-class cabin during our one-day journey. We saw little of Haikou City because a Liberation truck picked us up at Xiuying Pier, and after a ten-hour drive of more than 250 kilometres, we arrived at our farm headquarters in Ledong County. As I looked giddily through the bars of the truck, I was struck by how shabby the whole place was: scattered around the hills were a few rows of tiled bungalows with strangers staring at us curiously. Although we were exhausted and dusty, our youthful vivacity must have shone through, and we learned later that our arrival had caused quite a stir at the farm.

But the truck didn't stop there. Our destination, a newly set up company, was twenty kilometers farther on, where the main road turned into a rough and twisting mountain track. Along this track, we came across a Li village: here and there in the coconut jungle were low and small thatched huts which looked filthy inside. Women with dark skin and blue facial tattoos walked about barefooted and bare-breasted. I was dumbstruck. It felt like being among an aboriginal tribe we had read about in books.

---

14. Jiang Zhuyun was a revolutionary martyr from Sichuan whose feats inspired a novel, an opera (first staged in 1964), and the film *Living Forever in the Burning Fire* (1965).

The twenty kilometers' ride seemed endless. Someone started to sob, prompting the rest of the girls to cry. Even the boys had red eyes and wet noses. By the time we arrived at our company—several rows of new thatched huts located halfway up the hill—it was already dusk. It was a week since we had started the journey from Changsha, our hometown in Hunan Province.

In the tough new environment, we missed our homes. We toured as a troupe as far as Sanya City in the southernmost part of the island, and we endured backbreaking manual labor in the elements. As time went by, we received regular new recruits from Hunan, who were mainly friends or relatives of our troupe. One such newcomer was my elder sister. Rusticated in a Hunan village since 1965, she had had to fend for herself, and every now and then my family had been forced to subsidize her living costs. The news that she could earn a salary on our farm was music to her ears. Despite my warnings and objections, she insisted on joining me on Hainan and after some string-pulling on my part, was accepted by our farm.

By then, there must have been about a hundred *zhiqings* from Changsha who had turned up on Hainan on their own initiative—many in our troop, at least initially. But we were unsettled there: the hardship of our everyday lives, the unending toil, the warm and humid climate, our differences of dialect, custom, and habits from the Guangdong *zhiqings*—all these took their toll on us, making us feel disoriented and homesick. What disheartened us even more was that, in the interest of improving our re-education, not only my school troupe but the whole Changsha contingent, a minority among the *zhiqings*, who were for the most part recruited from Guangdong Province, were being reassigned among different companies so that we did not remain together. The promise of a pay rise to twenty-eight *yuan* per month one year after our stay, twenty kilos of rice per month, and an unrationed supply of cane sugar no longer appealed to us. When our unhappiness got back to our parents, they talked to each other and submitted a letter to the Hunan Provincial Revolutionary Committee (HPRC). They suggested that, first, we should admit the error of making our own way to Hainan without our parents' knowledge, an action which jeopardized the "Up to the Mountains, Down to the Countryside" campaign in Hunan; and, second, that we should offer to make amends by returning to Changsha City so that we could be rusticated to villages in Hunan Province. They pleaded with the HPRC to act on our behalf and request our release from the regiment, so called since our farm was taken over by Guangzhou Army.

The HPRC could not afford to compromise the "Up to the Mountains, Down to the Countryside" campaign. It sent a letter to the political division of the Guangzhou Army Production and Construction Corps, requesting our release to Hunan for reassignment. We were overjoyed and started counting the days to our anticipated reunion with our families: our early fears of living isolated lives in the villages of Hunan had evaporated. Yet during the following days all remained quiet. The People's Liberation Army on Hainan Island wasn't intimidated by the HPRC, and since most of the *zhiqings* from Guangdong were also homesick, the army corps decided to ignore the request. To appease us, though, many hard-working, capable and artistic Hunan *zhiqings* got promoted. Our hopes were thus dashed with hardly a fuss.

Our plot to run away in groups started at about this time. After the first two groups made it home successfully, though not without some close scrapes, it was now our turn. That day, I went to work as usual, and when night fell, I sat down in tears to write a long farewell letter to my troop. In order not to attract attention, we acted in pairs and arranged to meet up at the Ledong Bus Terminal the next morning.

From our company to Ledong County, there was only one trail, which was about twenty kilometres. After meeting at midnight, we two girls began our first night trek. With green canvas bags on our shoulders, we traveled light and walked hand-in-hand to relieve our fear and anxiety. It was a starry yet moonless night. Every time a truck drove by, we would turn our backs to bury our faces in the darkness. But as night drew on, it grew quieter, and soon there were only our footsteps echoing in the dark. Along the path were fields, coconut trees, and betel nut palms, with occasional villages, mainly Li ones. Among trees, these villages loomed large in the darkness, silently threatening us. Whenever we passed a village, the dogs, renowned for their slight build and unusual alertness, would bark at us one after the other, breaking the deep silence of the night. At times like this, I would walk faster and even closer to my companion until we were well out of their territory.

When we started, our pace was brisk. But as weariness and hunger struck us, we slowed down a bit and our steps became mechanical. When I felt exhausted, I silently chanted, as we often did then, a quotation from Mao to boost my morale: "Be resolute, conquer all difficulties, fear no sacrifice, strike for success." However, when dawn broke and we reached Ledong County, we were scared that every one of the few passers-by in its shabby single street might guess our plot and drag us back to our regiment. When we saw the other half of our team, the two boys, at the bus terminal, one of them signed to me to remain discreet and disguise my excitement: we acted like undercover communists in those revolutionary films we had watched so many times. After getting some buns for breakfast, we boarded the bus separately, and it was not until the bus left the county that I could relax a little.

Once the fear of being caught subsided, I was seized by another anxiety: I no longer knew exactly where my home was in Changsha. In a letter from my mother, I was told that she had been removed from her post and sent to a cadre school outside Changsha, and since no one could look after my little brother, she had been allowed, as a special favor, to take him with her. She had been denounced as a rightist back in 1958, and every time a new campaign was launched, no matter how prudently she behaved and how hard she worked, she would become a fresh target for public condemnation. Even though she was a widow with a young child whose three older children had all been sent away, she herself was not spared the punishment of being sent away. Without any of my family in Changsha, I no longer had a home there. Luckily, my fellow runaways were older than me and were able to cheer me up with their sense of humor and optimism. One of them offered to put me up in his shoebox apartment.

After ten hours of painfully slow traveling, we arrived in the late afternoon at the biggest city on Hainan, Haikou City, then just the size of a big county town. Figuring that our absence would have been discovered by our companies, we decided to maintain a low profile: we didn't stretch our legs and explore the city, but once we got our ship tickets for the next day, took immediate refuge in a hostel. The next morning we arrived early at Xiuying Pier to catch our ship. Yet just as I was offering a last prayer to Chairman Mao to bless our chances of escape, we were spotted on our way to the waiting room by an eagle-eyed army officer of our regiment. "Don't run away!" he shouted from his truck. "You can't escape!" Within a moment our dream had been shattered and we were caught just like that. We then used our plan of last resort, arguing that we had done nothing wrong and asking to be sent to the headquarters of the army corps to which the letter from the HPRC, requesting our release, had been sent. There, we were told that since we were already regimental soldiers, we had to obey military orders: the HPRC letter was only a request, it did not have the force of an order.

After we were driven back to our regiment, we were kept in isolation in single rooms, and that night I was able to enjoy my first sound sleep in three days.

The next morning, we were interviewed separately, something we had failed to anticipate. When it was my turn, the official started by commending my consistently good behaviour and also noted my artistic talents and strong stage performances. He then swiftly changed the subject by commenting on my youth and naïvety, and asked who was behind the plan. He also wanted to know who else was plotting to run away.

I told him that it was for the sake of my widowed mother, who was in poor health, and my little brother that I had wanted to return home. I wanted to be closer to them, to look after them. When asked how it happened that four of us were running away together, I said it was because we were close friends and shared everything in our lives. Since the HPRC was not happy with our rustication on Hainan, which had occurred without its approval, we thought we should redeem ourselves by returning to Hunan for reassignment. I also pointed out that since none of those who applied to leave the army corps had been granted permission, there had been no point in informing its leaders of our desire to return home. Having failed to get anything out of me, he sent me back to my room to reflect on my behavior.

For three days we were ordered to attend study sessions: we were not permitted to leave our rooms or visit anyone. But with ready meals, and freed from the daily manual labor of the company, that didn't seem very bad. The news of our aborted escape traveled fast, and many Hunan *zhiqings* in the regiment came by quietly to console us. Through our window bars, they whispered that it was only a minor offence and told us not worry too much.

Our company was twenty kilometers away, too far for anyone to walk to the regiment. But from there it was soon suggested that the real blame for our unsuccessful escape lay with the letter I had left behind on my trunk, minutes before I ran away!

In our company, three soldiers shared a single room in a small thatched hut. When my two roommates didn't see me in the morning, they assumed that I had got up early to water the vegetables. But when they caught no sight of me at lunchtime, they became concerned and reported me missing. Although two groups of Hunan *zhiqings* had already escaped by then, my consistently good behavior didn't suggest to my captain that I would follow suit. He didn't want to raise a false alarm in the regiment and decided to wait two hours for me to show up, meanwhile asking to check if my personal belongings were still in my room. Eventually, though, he asked to have my things searched thoroughly for any clue of my whereabouts.

Once my roommates found and read my farewell letter, they started to cry, which was eventually reported to our captain. He put the letter aside so that it wouldn't weaken any *zhiqing*'s dedication to the Hainan development. The news of our escape was promptly reported to the regimental headquarters and after a quick head count, two Hunan boys were also reported missing. A truck was immediately dispatched to Haikou City to catch us.

After three days' intensive study sessions, we were sent back to our companies with the promise that we would not suffer for our error as long as we did our usual best in all areas. As to the official promise to look into the case of the Hunan *zhiqings*, nothing ever seemed to come of it.

Back in my dormitory and behind closed doors, I was rebuked for having left the letter behind. As my roommates suggested, I should have posted it after arriving at Changsha.

Fate played a joke on us. I returned to my normal routine back at the farm and even resumed my position as a squad leader in the company. I rose early and finished late every day to help to open up the wilderness. My youth and the optimistic streak I had inherited from my father kept me going. A month later, I was ordered to report to the regiment in order to become a member of the Maoist propaganda troupe. Tasked with putting on a show very quickly, some of us joined the divisional troupe two months later. This soon led to a career in the troupe of the army corps and, later, an eight-year spell with the state farm bureau before I followed my husband to his home city, Guangzhou.

No matter how tough life sometimes got, I never tried to escape again.

NO COUNTRY FOR DESERTERS
Chen Zufu

In August 1971, seventeen months after my rustication to Hainan, my application for home leave was granted.

I was the first *zhiqing* from Meixian in the whole No. 7 Company to enjoy such a privilege. In theory, we were entitled to twenty-one days' annual leave, yet it was entirely up to the company officials to decide how to implement this policy—or, indeed, whether to implement it at all. My good fortune turned me not only into an instant object of envy but a postman: fellow *zhiqings* from both my hometown and Guangzhou asked me to deliver letters and packets of dried fish and suchlike to their families. Some insisted that I pay a visit to their parents to see how they were doing.

Of all the "parcels" I was entrusted with, the biggest one was no doubt Lin, a *zhiqing* from Chenghai who had been diagnosed with a fractured hand. No longer fit to perform hard labor on the farm, he had just been granted permission to withdraw from the rustication program. I was to escort him to Guangzhou and help him get on a homebound long-haul bus. When we bade farewell at Guangzhou, I was lost for words: should I congratulate him on such an early escape from the rustication or just tell him to take good care of himself? Whenever I paid a visit on behalf of my fellow *zhiqings*, I also remember the happy faces of their parents: they seemed genuinely pleased to hear, at last, a first-hand account of how their children were living in such a remote place. At that point, I couldn't tell if any of them realized that, instinctively, I was only recounting what they really wished to hear.

When I finally made it home, the warm welcome I received from my family made me feel as if I had returned from another world.

The trip was in fact not a simple home visit, but also sickleave to allow me to seek treatment for a chronic gastric disease which was first diagnosed when I was a mere sixth grade student. It was a stubborn illness, but by the time I was rusticated I had made a full recovery. However, six months into the regime of strenuous manual labour, it struck again, reducing me from a stout fellow to a weakling. I had seen many doctors, but to no avail, and when I began my leave, I weighed less than forty-five kilos. On arrival at home, I tried both Western and Chinese medicine, but neither seemed to be really effective. A returned Indonesian Chinese, the father of a fellow *zhiqing*, then introduced me to a "folk prescription," a unique recipe of betel nut, pig trotter, and pork tripe. It worked, and I quickly put on over forty kilos! In retrospect, I realize that the recipe offers a high dose of fat and protein, two of the substances most lacking in our poor diet on the farm. This might well explain the high number of *zhiqings* who are prone to gastric complaints and illnesses caused by malnutrition.

Time flies. Soon a letter arrived from Hainan urging me to get back to the farm: my two months' extended leave was up, and if I failed to report back in time I would no long remain on the payroll. My parents, however, fearing that my illness might soon strike again and turn me into a lifelong invalid, would not let me go. In fact, they had never wanted me to go to Hainan in the first place—it was I who had insisted on signing up. Knowing how appalling our diet was and how hard the labor, their concern was justified. Yet if I stayed behind, I would be denounced as a "deserter" by the army corps, a serious offence for a regimental soldier. In addition, I would lose my legal status and become a "ghost"—an unregistered resident—in my hometown, because in accordance with procedure my household registration had been transferred to the place to which I was rusticated. Thanks to the tight control kept over the urban populace and their jobs, I would not only lose my food ration and other basic necessities but become unemployable because none of the state companies could hire anyone who was not registered locally.

It was a huge dilemma. When I had defied my parents' greater wisdom and jumped on the rustication bandwagon, I saw it as my own way of changing my fortune by escaping poverty at home. Yet when I arrived at the farm, I was confronted by the harsh realities: the hard labor in all kinds of weather, the harsh environment and living conditions, and the poor diet, let alone my recurrent bouts of gastric illness—I became disillusioned. Our designated mentors, the veterans, who in their twenties and thirties were called "old workers" by us teenage *zhiqings*, looked like living fossils. The cause of their premature ageing was no secret, and I dreaded joining them. So despite the uncertainties and the foreseeable challenges that lay ahead of me, I took my parents' advice this time and risked remaining with my family.

At first, luck seemed to be on my side: a new water pipe factory was looking for a welder, and I landed a temporary contract to maintain its pipes. Yet just a few days into the job, the management learned about my status as a deserter and annulled the contract with immediate effect: they simply dared not risk undermining the national rustication campaign. With my illegitimate status now exposed, it became almost impossible for the factory to pay me. It took me a good six months and the use of a contact who dared to take a risk on my behalf to get through the thicket of bureaucracy and claw back my few days' wages from the factory.

While I was struggling to make ends meet, a friend came to my rescue. In my hometown, which is inhabited by Hakka people, there was a group of farmers from the Chaoshan area, the descendants of those who, decades before, had migrated there to escape the Japanese invaders. On the far bank of the river beside which my family lived, they cultivated lands and were the main suppliers of vegetables for the townsfolk. While most local residents were still reliant on oil lamps, these people not only had the use of electricity in their homes but adopted modern technologies such as tractors and presses in their farming and processing of produce. They needed a mechanic to maintain their machines and various other devices. I was referred to them and became an ad hoc member of their group. Though my wage was meagre, I was compensated with a fair share of meat and other produce at festive seasons.

From the early 1970s, the number of deserters like myself seemed to be on the rise. Since private enterprise, which was dismissed as downright "profiteering" or "capitalism", was strictly forbidden, and the state companies were not allowed to employ any ex-*zhiqings* who returned "illegally," we were reduced to being nomads in our home towns and could only scrape along by doing odd jobs. There was an emerging demand for things like cement making, carpentry, painting and tailoring, so these were our usual trades.

I was in a sense fortunate, because—much thanks to my father—I was a handyman, and even before rustication had equipped myself with some useful skills such as watch-mending, clock and camera repair, photograph enlargement, machine maintenance, and carpentry. It was these minor crafts that gave me a living outside the overwhelming monopoly of the state system. However, I was also very unfortunate because I lacked resources and personal connections, and so my application to the local rustication office to withdraw from the rustication program because of illness was turned down repeatedly on the grounds that I didn't meet the criteria. At a time when nothing could really escape the state's radar, we deserters were at the mercy of capricious and corrupt local officials—we were reduced to living at the lowest stratum of society.

With no foreseeable future, I became despondent. For a time, I considered throwing in the towel and becoming a monk. But when I looked round and found that even the temples had been badly damaged in the "revolutionary furnace," I wondered how they could lift me out of my plight. Influenced by an old neighbor who handed me a copy of the bible, I frequented an underground church for a while, but since its gatherings were periodically raided, it was no haven.

In 1975, a sympathetic officer at the rustication office tipped me off: the state was beginning to relax its policy and allow *zhiqings* to return home to take up the job of a parent who was about to retire. If I got back to Hainan, I could become eligible to take advantage of this new scheme—get my household registration transferred back to my parents' home and resume my residential status in my hometown! The effect of being an unregistered resident was so demoralizing that my parents needed little persuasion: a return to Hainan would be the only way to get the hell out of the predicament I had been stuck in for over four years. And so at the end of 1975, with a letter of self-criticism in my sack and without waiting for a response to the request I had submitted to the farm, I went back to Daling.

With no inkling of whether I was still on the roll or of how I would be treated, I didn't have the guts to go straight back to my troop. I spent a night in the neighboring company with a fellow Meixian *zhiqing*, and it was not until the next afternoon, when the troop was supposed to be slaving away in the elements, that I crept down that secluded lane. At night, I paid a visit to the political instructor's place with my letter of self-criticism. Earlier on, when I suddenly encountered him in that narrow lane, he had merely acknowledged me with a stern "So you're back!" That night, though, he was a lot more accommodating, and after receiving my letter, told me that I must first cover for a substitute teacher who was on leave, after which I would be given a further assignment.

Was that it? I couldn't have been more baffled.

In a shabby building between No. 7 and No. 15 companies were two classrooms that accommodated four classes. I taught primary grades three and four students in one room, while the only other substitute teacher taught primary five and six. My two groups sat back to back and I took turns teaching them in the same room.

Despite the unexpectedly fair treatment, I suffered a guilty conscience. When I walked past my students after school, I would feel as if they were pointing their fingers at me and calling me a "shameless deserter." Perhaps this was because, as far as I was aware, I was the only deserter who had come back to the farm. I worried whether my plan to return home and take up my parent's job would materialize and, if not, whether I would be trapped on this remote and isolated farm for the rest of my life.

Fortunately, the company officials seemed quite satisfied with my performance, and to my great surprise I was not only reimbursed for my travel but given the pay rise I was owed. In my first Spring Festival since my return, I was even entrusted with organizing a party to mark the occasion. What was more surprising was that even after the substitute teacher reported back to work, I was still spared from physical labor and was assigned to work as the company clerk and propaganda officer. I have never figured out why. Was it because of my recurrent illness a few years back, or was I now considered a rare "talent" that should never be wasted on mundane hard labor? In any event, the psychological pressure of being a "deserter" gradually eased off and I felt a lot more settled on the farm.

The sympathetic officer in the local rustication office had kept his word: soon after, a letter arrived requesting my return to take up my parent's post. Another happy surprise was how helpful our political instructor was throughout—he went out of his way to brave the bureaucracy and get me released from the farm. On 27 March 1976, exactly six years after my rustication, I boarded a homebound Red Guard ship. Like the day I landed on Hainan six years ago, it was overcast, and when I looked back from the deck at the receding island, I was seized by nostalgia for the very place I had paid such a high price to escape.

When I retired several decades later, I found in my personal dossier the letter of self-criticism.

THE ROCKY ROAD TO REHABILITATION
Chen Hongbo

It is more than three decades since I returned home, and yet the bitter-sweet memories of the days before my rehabilitation are still vivid.

By 1977, many resourceful *zhiqings* had, in one way or another, managed to leave the farm: they were going to college, had an offer of employment, were taking up their parent's job, and so on. My wife and I had an offer from the Guangzhou Chicken Farm, and the Guangzhou *Zhiqing* Office had sent a letter of transfer to our farm to enable us to accept the offer. Since we had been promoted as cadres on our farm, approval was required from the cadre department of the state farm bureau so that we could be relieved of our cadre status before the transfer could be processed. Two weeks after the letter was sent to the authorities, I became worried. With the consent of the officials of our farm, I decided to call on the state farm bureau to find out what had happened to our request. After more than an hour's walk from our home to Daxi Bridge, I boarded a bus for a journey of several hundred kilometers to Tongshi, the headquarters of the state farm bureau.

We had been in the first wave of *zhiqings* to arrive at Daling Farm in winter, 1968. Thanks to the trust and care of our farm officials, we were promoted to work in the regimental headquarters less than two years after our rustication. We got married in 1976, and six months later my wife became pregnant. It was typhoon season and, apart from pickled Chinese radish, there was nothing to eat. My wife had always been rather weak,[15] and after a spell of violent morning sickness came signs of a miscarriage. When I sent for a doctor from the farm hospital, it was a typical day in the monsoon season: the sky had opened up and the bucketing rain was being blown about in a high

---

15. See her piece *More than Mere Medicine*.

wind. This, however, didn't stop Doctor Li from picking up his bag of medicine and braving the weather to visit my wife. After a second visit the following day, I was greatly relieved but I remained desperate over the food crisis. We had made several attempts to raise chickens, but due to our inexperience none survived the chicken pest. While I was racking my brains, Lao Zhang, our director, called in with a bunch of fresh and tender bok choy. We were deeply touched. During the rainy season, nothing grew in the fields, and he himself had many mouths to feed. And typical of those simple and honest veterans on the farm, Lao Zhang was taciturn, and after offering just a few words of comfort to my wife, he left. At that moment of crisis, the freshly picked bok choy was more invaluable to us than ginseng.

Four or five months into the pregnancy, we started to get ourselves prepared for the birth of our first (and, as it would turn out, our only) child. A medical incident at the hospital sent a shiver through my bones: after losing a great deal of blood when giving birth to her child, a farm worker had lost her life. When I looked at my thin and sickly wife, I desperately wondered how to safeguard her wellbeing. A month later, I submitted a request that my wife be allowed to visit her home for better care and nutrition. Thanks to the understanding of the farm officials, I was able to return her to Guangzhou to await the birth under the care of our families. This proved to be a most sensible precaution: when the baby was due, my wife suffered from dystocia. Thanks greatly to the better resources in Guangzhou, both mother and newborn child were safe. Under the tender care of our families, my wife made a speedy recovery, and our adorable daughter brought much joy to all. Unfortunately, once her eight-week maternal leave was up, my wife had to return to the farm. Our families, of course, tried to resist it, and since more and more *zhiqings* were steadily making their way home, they resorted to the rustication office of their companies to find all kinds of ways to get us a job offer from the Guangzhou Chicken Farm I mentioned earlier.

The ride from Daling to Tongshi passed through Nada, Wushi, Pingkou, and the Five Fingers Mountains. When I arrived seven or eight hours later, it was early evening. The next day, I went straight to the director of the cadre department. He must have been in his forties, and when he saw me, he made a sour face. Without hearing me out, he remarked in a disdainful voice: "I know, a couple want to return home together. What a bad impact that would have! If you want to leave, only one of you can do so: your farm has been notified of the decision." I pleaded with him, explained my circumstances, and begged him to grant us a great favor. He simply turned his back on me.

By then the central government was relaxing its rustication policy and our farm officials had already approved our request. Had he simply released both of us, no government policies or regulations would have been violated. And yet this callous official had refused to take our circumstances into consideration, which presented us with a dilemma: either we stayed behind as a family or would be obliged to live hundreds of miles apart. That was how arrogant and cold-blooded power could be. But what else could I do but drag myself back to Daling and get the household registration of my wife and baby girl transferred to Guangzhou? After my wife was rehabilitated, she had to juggle single-handedly between caring for a newborn child and doing a job in a remote suburb far away from our relatives. As for me, I had to stay put on the farm, which triggered a renewed, lengthy, and exhausting effort by my family to use their contacts and connections to get me back home. Thankfully, they finally succeeded. In November 1978 I was reunited with my wife and daughter.

When I reflect on this episode, how I wish that our love will ensure that we are never separated again.

THE STAMP OF SUCCESS
Huang Xiaowei

When an old school pal was co-editing a book about the *zhiqings'* experiences on the army farms of Hainan Island, one of the proposed titles was "The Stamps of Daling." I, too, was rusticated to Hainan Island, and stamps—not the sticky postal kind but those that are used to imprint a design on paper—feature distinctively in my memories.

It was at home that I learned how to engrave the devices that are used to make the stamp. My tools were a set of three engraving knives one could come by cheaply in shops, and my first material was a piece of bone tablet from a neighbor. There was an engraving workshop in town, and after school, I would gaze at the engravers across the counter and then try to imitate them at home.

My father had a book called *Diary of Fine Arts*. A collection of documents of those in high office, such as mobilization speeches, presentations of government policy, outpourings to the Party, tracts of self-criticism and confession, exposés and criticisms, it bizarrely contained some inserts in the form of impressions by the revered painter Qi Baishi. In order to rescue the master from these tidal waves of class struggle and political rhetoric, I removed the inserts with a pair of scissors and pasted them into a plain notebook—and there it was, my first collection of impressions by renowned engravers. In the workshop, the stock materials for stamps were wood, horn, bone and rubber, and the tools were skew-chisels. That was why they were the only type I used. Years later, I would learn from a book that to cut stone, a flat chisel is preferable.

Before rustication, I had acquired a few soapstones and a thread-bound copy of a Ming dynasty work on the Chinese language, from which I learned about a poised and decorative form of writing that is known as engraving script. Also known as seal script, since seals and stamps can serve similar purposes, it was illegible to the untrained eye, and yet this refined script is the apogee of Chinese calligraphy and painting. When I packed for Hainan Island, these items, which were officially condemned as "feudal, capitalist and revisionist," were tucked away in my sack and would make a journey across an ocean before settling in a hilly nook. Located at the foot of a hill, my company consisted of two or three rows of thatched huts scattered around a path, together with our cookhouse and a shallow stream by a vegetable field. The fashion item of the day was a white vest. On its front was some large, eye-catching Mao-style calligraphy that read "Guangzhou Army," and underneath was "Production and Construction Corps" in small, regular print. The way to display this vest was to wear an unbuttoned shirt over it. The claim was that, from a distance, this look would give us an air of true mettle and add a spring to our step.

Less than two weeks after our arrival at the farm, it became known that my elder brother and I had artistic and literary gifts. But I kept a lid on my stamp-cutting hobby. To this very day, engraving is regarded as a specialist trade, and professional engravers must register with the public security bureau of the municipal government. During the upheavals of the Cultural Revolution, my brother and I had the good fortune to be labeled "redeemable children," which, unfortunately, also meant that we could easily be considered as *irredeemable*. When walking a tightrope, politically speaking, you must ensure that you do not get blown down by the winds, so discretion is essential.

I kept my little secret for a long time. In our company, we had to put our stamp on the payroll when our meager salary was handed out. The pair of stamps I had cut for my brother and me when we lived at home looked rather out of place here: they were too sophisticated and grandiose for the wretched little space on the payroll that was allotted to them. We didn't mind our stamps outshining everybody else's, but the supply chief wasn't particularly thrilled about the way in which they made his payroll column misaligned. Eventually, he prepared a separate sheet for just the two of us. Aesthetically, it was immensely satisfying for our stamps to be given the room to breathe: psychologically, with our names appearing each month on a separate sheet, we felt as if we were being singled out from the team—something that was usually a prelude to public condemnation. We felt exposed, and this intensified our sense that we were vulnerable. To reintegrate us into the team, I cut a pair of new stamps, one for my brother and one for myself, on the very tiny Qingtian stones that I had buried in my sack. The modest, docile impressions they made blended nicely into the main payroll: it was reassuring to be accepted back into the revolutionary fold.

From then on, requests steadily came my way to carve personal stamps, and one was from an old hand named Lao Zhang. Of medium build, lean and with a dark tan, Lao Zhang was illiterate, but astute, efficient, and full of energy. When we were building terraces and digging holes during the major joint campaigns, he was usually the first to finish his quota. It emerged that as soon as he arrived at the ground we were to tackle, he would take a quick look round, identify where the soil was loose and proceed to dig in that particular part! Hence while we were struggling to remove stubborn tree roots on the rocky slopes—in political terms, to bury "imperialists, revisionists and counterrevolutionaries"—he would have finished his patch, helped some Chaozhou female *zhiqings* with their quotas (they were regarded as the prettiest), and then gone off to collect firewood for his kitchen.

I came to know him better during a fire. After we had finished clearing the bushes and saplings for rubber plantation, we set fire to the area as usual. However, the wind suddenly changed direction, and in no time the flames had spread across the bamboo forest to the windbreak and reached a nearby Li village. On the edge of the village, there was an isolated thatched hut in which a leper was quarantined. In all sorts of dialects, we shouted to alert him but to no avail. At the critical moment, Lao Zhang pulled a towel from his waist, charged into the hut, and carried the leper out on his back just before the roof fell in. He spent the rest of the day as if no such life-and-death drama had occurred and went home, as usual, with a bundle of firewood on his back.

At the evening assembly, he was commended by both the captain and the political instructor. Yet to my disbelief, he was never declared the role model that such extraordinary bravery deserved. When he approached me for a personal stamp, I did not hesitate for a second, and when I delivered it he treated me to a dish of stewed chicken. This was quite a surprise because I had always given my services free of charge. The chicken presented a small dilemma: anything privately reared was outlawed, and without doubt the chicken had been privately reared. Yet its aroma was so heavenly, and our stomachs had for so long encountered nothing better than plain rice with soy sauce or pickled Chinese radishes, that just this once we allowed our primal instincts to get the better of our ideological principles. I shared the feast with my brother. How we wished that the chicken was meatier and the pot of stew larger!

To my surprise, there was a shop in Haikou City that stocked Qingtian stones at a dirt-cheap price. We *zhiqings* were treated with disdain, yet the stones could be touched and examined freely. On the way back from my first home leave, I bought quite a few and later received more requests to make stamps. As well as the ones I made for individuals, I was asked by our supply chief to cut a stamp that he could use to mark our meal coupons. Since meal coupons were the one currency on the farm that had any value, the only stamps they were meant to bear were official. To cut an unauthorized one for our company canteen might therefore land me up to my neck in the class struggle. Who was to say? I dared not take the risk.

For a time, I was assigned to the political division of the regiment in order to draw up an educational chart about the class struggle which could be used for touring purposes. The propaganda officer also asked me to cut a tool to stamp the collection of books in the library—another request that could land me in trouble because the books were meant to carry only an official stamp. But it was harder to refuse a propaganda officer of the regiment than a supply chief of a company. I took my time to think it through and, in the end, agreed on the one condition that my other duties would be suspended for a whole week. The reason I gave was that it would take time to acquire the right materials, but in reality I had surreptitiously borrowed some banned, "politically incorrect" books and would spend a good three days devouring them. The material I chose for the library stamping tool was taken from the branch of a guava tree. It was my first attempt to carve a stamp from wood and my engraving knives were only cheap ones, so I had to abandon it. This was the only occasion I engraved on wood or, for that matter, engraved an official stamping tool.

Because of my hobby, I would become a surrogate parent for many *zhiqings*. In the late 1970s, after the end of the Cultural Revolution but before the national rehabilitation campaign, there was a surge of *zhiqings* who were desperate to return home. Some took the lofty route: they got themselves out by having family or friends in high places. For the majority, the usual trick was to get hold of a job offer back in their home city or secure the offer of a place at college. If neither of these things materialized, the fallback was to feign illness. To wangle a doctor's diagnosis was a lot easier than forging the offer of a job or a college place. Once a diagnosis had been obtained, we had to produce a signed and stamped letter from our parents in order to get the farm officials to consider our release on medical grounds. Snail-mail, even when registered, could easily go astray or be delayed by typhoons and other unforeseen circumstances. The mail service couldn't be entrusted with vital documents that concerned our future. But the major problem was our parents: most of them were illiterate and had never owned a stamp.

The first to entrust to me the cutting of a stamping tool for his parents was a Guangzhou *zhiqing* whose name and features I have long forgotten. Normally, I would use one of my Qingtian stones as a stamping tool, engrave the stamp into it, give the tool to my "client" and my job was done. To make an impression on a document, you applied paste to the tool and then stamped it on to the document. The tool can be kept for generations. But engraving a stamp into it was a strenuous and lengthy process. It seemed such a waste of my time and energy to engrave a tool for the single object that my fellow *zhiqing* had in mind. I therefore decided to ditch the hard work and draw an impression straight on to his parents' letter. After years of practice, I knew very well what an impression looked like, and I could easily create it on paper in a way that looked identical to the impression made by a stamping tool. I found the right size matchstick and after trimming it slightly, applied some stamp paste on to it before drawing an impression of his parents' imaginary stamp on the letter. The whole process took no more than fifteen minutes and, to the untrained eye at least, the impression was almost indistinguishable from a genuine one.

The story of my achievement spread, and soon a fellow Meixian *zhiqing* also asked me to forge the letter of appeal from his parents. Since the early 1960s, we had been instructed to take as our role model the young soldier Lei Feng, who was said to have dedicated his whole life to helping others and studying Chairman Mao's works before he lost his life in an accident. His diary had recently been re-published in a newspaper and one of the best-known excerpts was "Youth, Oh

Youth." To differentiate the handwriting from my own, I copied the style of our revered role model as it appeared in this extract. To tell the truth, I was prompted not by hero-worship but sordid pragmatism: his handwriting was easy to copy. For the subsequent letters I forged, I couldn't continue to adopt Lei Feng's distinctive italic style, so I resorted to imitating the handwriting of the parent of whoever my next "client" was. To my utter relief and amazement, my skill paid off, and all my clients made a successful return home. When plotting my own escape on medical grounds, I was sufficiently emboldened by my success to counterfeit the sharp and vigorous strokes of my mother's cursive script! Regrettably, it left much to be desired but still did the trick, landing me safely back home in 1979 after ten years of rustication.

Since then, engraving has gradually recovered its artistic status, and these days, a refined stamp once again adds the indispensable finishing touch to Chinese calligraphy and painting. With a fine engraving knife made by an old school pal, I have returned of late to my long forsaken passion and have pleasurably explored the different scripts and styles. I engrave my observations and cut personal stamps for friends and acquaintances. When I look at the surviving efforts of my youth, I realize how rough they really were. The paper has turned yellow, brittle and fragile, yet to me they are more precious than any expensive or elaborate collection.

MY LUCKY ESCAPES

Huang Ronger

Protected by a helmet

In 1970, I was reassigned to work as a clerk in No. 9 Company. It was a new company: apart from a few old hands and a few *zhiqings* like myself who had been rusticated for over a year, the troops were mostly teenage girls from Chaoan and Meixian who were more comfortable doing embroidery or singing folk songs in the mountains. During a major joint campaign, I led a team of over sixty *zhiqings*. Since most of my young troops were delicate girls in colorful attire, I—in a plastic helmet—was nicknamed Hong Changqing, the name of the Party representative who is disguised as an overseas Chinese merchant in *The Red Detachment of Women*, one of the eight revolutionary model plays.

During the campaign, it so happened that the troop working right next to us was the militia, which was composed largely of mighty young men. They worked ferociously hard, swiftly tackling one area after another, and as their singing faded into the distance, our troop was still struggling with a single area. I knew well that despite their relatively sluggish progress, my troops had tried their best, and in an attempt to catch up, I suggested that the few men in the troop should focus on the heavier task: felling trees with an axe. One day I was knocked unconscious by a vine as thick as my arm. Entangled in a few nearby trees, including the one I had just felled, the vine landed right on my head. After regaining consciousness with the help of the girls, I found that my plastic helmet had not only been split in half but had landed several meters away!

Spared by a bandit

There were two instances when a supply chief was killed on his way back from regimental headquarters where he had been collecting his troop's pay. One day, when our supply chief asked me to collect the company's salary on his behalf, he asked if I wanted armed protection. I declined the offer because I never thought such bad luck would befall me.

On the shortcut from headquarters to my company, I suddenly recalled the two fatal robberies and as I entered a particularly dark area of the woods, grew apprehensive. I became as alert as a rabbit, my eyes wide open and my ears attuned to the rustling of the wind. The further into the darkness I penetrated, the more frightened I became. To calm my nerves, I resorted to singing aloud.

Then all of a sudden, I sensed danger: somewhere ahead, I caught sight of a shadowy figure! With no weapons to hand, I quickly rolled up the dozen copies of the *Regimental Soldier's Paper* I had also collected from headquarters. Then a stranger suddenly appeared right in front of me waving a machete! We stared at each other for a few seconds: but just as he seemed to have materialized from nowhere, he just as suddenly disappeared. I had no idea what had gone through his mind: had he been fooled by my baby face and small build and assumed I wouldn't be the bearer of three thousand *yuan* of workers' salaries, or had he simply confused my roll of paper with an unusual cudgel? All I can remember was that the moment he disappeared, I raced wildly toward my company as if the bandit had been right behind me.

My saviour

In our battles against nature and our work on construction projects, we made ready use of explosives for such tasks as extirpating stubborn tree roots or extracting rocks from a quarry. The inexperienced *zhiqings* barely out of their teens were put at great risk when they first handled explosives, and I too had a life-and-death moment. It happened when we were digging a new well and resorting to explosives to break the rocks under the topsoil.

As the clerk and also a Party member, it fell to me to ignite the explosives on this project. At the beginning, it was no problem at all: once I lit the fuse, I jumped up and off I ran out of the danger zone. As we dug deeper, three explosives were required, and before lighting the fuses I cleared the site as usual. After lighting them, I suddenly found that this time I couldn't reach up to the ground to heave myself out of shaft! I yelled for a rope to be dropped down but was told that none was available.

As the burning fuses were getting shorter and shorter and I was wondering, panic stricken, how the hell I was going to get out, I heard a shout: 'Here! Quick!' It was Hou Jingjie, a Meixian *zhiqing*. When I looked up, he already had one foot perched firmly on a rock protruding from the shaft and a hand clinging to the edge of the shaft. He held his other hand out to me, and once I seized it he gave me a pull. When we had run barely ten meters away from the shaft, there were loud explosions followed by myriads of shattered rocks flying up into the air and then falling on the ground around us. Xiao Hou stuck out his tongue and made a funny face, and then burst out laughing as if we had just won a game. But I failed to see anything funny about it: had my weight pulled him into the shaft with me, we would have joined the flying bits of rock! From then on, I called him my savior.

Rescued by Chinese silver-grass

In the summer, Hainan Island is visited by typhoons, and one of our priorities was to take precautions during the typhoon season. While working in the political division of the regiment, I was once dispatched with Lao He to inspect the precautionary measures in No. 5 Company. I had once worked there, so after the inspection I stayed behind to catch up with friends, and it was not until a typhoon struck that I took my leave.

On the way back, I had to cross a small bridge over a stream. But by the time I got there, not only had the bridge been swept away, but the stream had grown into a roaring monster of dense rapids. Darkness fell quickly and when my face was pelted with raindrops as big as beans, it was painful. I stripped down to my underpants, tied my raincoat and rain shoes to my waist, jumped into the water, and was ready to swim across to the far bank. But the rapids were so powerful that I was swept downstream, and no matter how hard I paddled I just couldn't reach the far bank barely a few meters away. Soon it dawned on me that there was a cliff nearby. Then some two meters away from the cliff, I caught sight of some Chinese silver-grass. This grass was normally the last thing we would touch for fear of being cut by its sharp edges. But that day, I swam toward it with all my might, grabbed it, and was eventually able to make it to the far bank, my hands covered in blood.

When I reflect on my *zhiqing* life on the island, some of the things I recall are: the warm-hearted name the Chaoan girls gave me—"Elder Brother Dongbin" (I was then known as Dongbin rather than by my birth name); the delectable snacks they made for the Guangzhou *zhiqings*; a chair which was made for me by a Hainan *zhiqing*; and my saviour, Xiao Hou, whose strong hand yanked me out of the shaft. Whenever I reminisce about them, I feel I am blessed.

MY BRUSH WITH A SHARK'S FIN

Deng Xiaodan

I was moved to No. 11 Company in November 1969. Soon afterward, our clerk was promoted to work at regimental headquarters and I became the acting clerk. When our supply chief was on home leave, I was asked to cover for him. The thing I remember best about that stint was handling the salaries. In those days, salaries were paid in cash. It was more than an hour's walk through the hills to collect it from headquarters.

One day, I set off early for headquarters, carrying a machete with a blade of sixty to seventy centimeters long, the kind we used for chopping medium-sized trees. I couldn't understand how, by the time I had packed the salaries into my shoulder bag, it was already dusk. For safety's sake, I decided to spend the night at headquarters with a close former schoolmate who was working in the transport company. Living in a thatched hut, she had the unusual privilege of occupying a single room of her own. The problem was, the mud partition was only about the height of a man: it didn't provide the solid sense of safety that we two girls so desperately wanted that night.

Our average salary was around twenty *yuan*, and there were about a hundred of us in the company. The amount of cash I was carrying that night was only about two thousand *yuan*. However, they were all in one *yuan* notes, and my shoulder bag was so filled with them that there was no room for the letters I had also collected from headquarters on behalf of the whole troop.

What to do with my bulky shoulder bag so that we could have a peaceful night's sleep? We racked our brains. Hold it tightly in my arms? It just didn't feel secure enough. Then we recalled the scene from a film in which the undercover revolutionary makes a lucky escape from a police search by hiding a piece of confidential information under the quilt-cum-mattress. That seemed ingenious to us, and we decided to follow suit. Emptying the cash from my shoulder bag, we laid it neatly on the bed at the end where our pillows were. Then we returned the straw mat to its place and put our pillows on top. After covering ourselves with a sheet, we felt perfectly safe and slept soundly that night, our heads resting on the cash.

Years later, while I was working in Hong Kong during its miraculous economic boom, one of the catchphrases to describe a man of wealth was to say that he "has a shark fin in his dish." As a deprived new immigrant, the only thing I could boast was that as an acting supply chief I had once slept on a mattress of cash.

The next morning, I rose early and had some breakfast. Then, with a bag stuffed with one *yuan* notes on my back, some letters in my left hand and a newly sharpened machete in my right, I set off for my company. The huge trees with dense canopies and the new rubber trees along the hill trail provided some much-needed shelter from the tropical sun, and it was usually quite pleasant to walk in the shade. But that day all I could feel was a chilly eeriness. During my walk of more than an hour, I stayed as alert as a small rabbit—with a firm grip on my machete, I was ready for a fight at the first whiff of danger. In the end I arrived home safe and sound, and the only people I came across on that journey were a mother and son, the son walking in front with a set of scales on his back, the mother following with two heavy buckets on a shoulder pole.

After my return to my home city, I once recounted this experience to a friend. But instead of praising my courage and resourcefulness, he criticized the company officials for being so callous, saying that it was unfair both to me and to every one of those whose survival depended on such a meager salary. I was rather deflated by his response, but when I think of it now I can see his point. But this episode typified how we tried to behave at that time: to do well, to act bravely and responsibly, to remain ignorant of what didn't concern us, and to be generally likeable.

BEING DEER TO SOMEONE

Liu Jingan

In the spring of 2012, I paid a visit to Daling Farm with a group of ex-*zhiqing* friends. The next morning, I went straight to where No. 2 Company used to be based. In the nearly forty years since I had left, things had changed drastically, but fortunately I was still able to track down in the wilderness an old well which has remained vivid in my memory.

That well was our "paradise." Without running water, we gathered here every evening after a hard day's work to cleanse our sweaty and soiled bodies and wash our laundry. There were two rough thatched "shower sheds", and while the girls would carry a bucket of water to take a shower inside, we boys would simply strip down to our underpants *in situ* and pour buckets of cool water over ourselves. How refreshing! But winters on Hainan Island could be a bit chilly. A big crude stove was built, and on wintry days a large wok was brought over to provide warm water for our showers. Although we were all so exhausted by the end of the day, we had such boisterous fun during those relaxed evening hours that you would have thought we had an endless supply of energy.

I was a cook. Although this job provided a lucky escape from toiling in the elements, our hours were long and we would always wait till the whole troop had finished their showers and laundry before fetching water for the washing up. By the time we could take a shower, it was usually rather late.

One night after finishing my work at the cookhouse, I went back to the well, as usual, for a shower.

Collecting water might sound simple: put a bucket onto a hook fixed to a two-meter-long bamboo stick, lower the bucket down the well with the bamboo stick; then once the bucket reaches the water, tip it over to allow the water in, and once it has filled up, straighten the bucket and pull it up. For new or unsteady hands, it was easy to spill the water while raising the heavy bucket and end up with one that was half empty. But what was even worse was that at times the bucket became unhooked when it was tipped and sank to the bottom of the well. However, as a cook, collecting water for the cookhouse was part of my daily routine, and I couldn't have been more skillful at it.

That night, though, when I tried to get a third or fourth lot of water for my shower, the bucket came unhooked. This happened quite often, and I didn't hesitate to jump into the well to retrieve it. Taking a deep breath, I dived to the bottom to search for it. It didn't take long to find and I resurfaced. Although the well was two meters deep, I deftly flung the bucket out of the shaft. Then finding my way by the familiar gaps in the brick wall, I climbed up. I am not sure why but the last few bricks near the ground were particularly slippery that night, and every time I reached there, I would lose my grip and fall straight back down the shaft. After several attempts, my hands were sore and the skin on my fingers was torn.

From the well to our dormitory was quite a distance: as it got darker, the chances of anyone walking past were dwindling. If I stayed in the water, my body temperature would drop fast and so would my energy level. Not long before, a *zhiqing* in No. 1 Company was found drowned in the river. Another *zhiqing*, a cook from the same company, went down the well to retrieve a bucket and suffocated—just days before he was to return home. I began to feel scared: I had to find a way to get the hell out of that deep shaft.

To keep my energy level up and gain time to be rescued, I first needed to get my body out of the chilly water. Fortunately, before jumping into the well, I had, as a precaution, lowered the bamboo stick into the well. I now inserted it into gaps in the shaft, and with it, suspended myself so that at least my upper body was no longer submerged.

I then needed to send out a signal for help. Despite the growing danger, I didn't resort to cries of "Help, help!": it would sound too horrendous to my ears and my sense of pride wouldn't allow it! But if I didn't make some kind of noise it might not be until the next morning, when someone came to fetch their first bucket of water for the day, that I would be rescued! After careful thought, I decided to make a high-pitched, single-syllable call: "*woo, woo . . .*" Although I tend to talk quietly, my voice that night was loud—thanks either to the reverberation of the deep shaft or, more significantly, to my primal wish to survive.

I soon lost track of time and became extremely thirsty and apprehensive. I don't know how long I made that *woo-woo* sound before I eventually caught sight of an indistinct flash of light in the scrap of dark sky above me. What's more, it seemed to be getting closer and closer! I continued calling until the ray of light was shining down the well! Then I saw the outline of someone wearing a hunter's helmet with a light built into it. When its owner eventually located my shivering self, he took a quick look round the shaft. He asked me to stay calm, pull the bamboo stick out of the shaft, and pass it up to him. Once he got hold of one end, he asked me to hold on to the other, and as he pulled, I was able to use the gaps in the brickwork to climb steadily up.

It was not until I stood on solid ground again that I could tell who my saviour was: Su Yuanyu, an old timer.

After asking how I had ended up in the shaft and if I was injured, he chuckled: "I thought I'd heard the barking of a muntjac! But the only creature who was drinking at the well was you!' His chuckle seemed to have a magical power that banished all my unease. It happened that Lao Su was on night-duty as a sentry when he heard my call and mistook it for the bark that a muntjac makes to attract a mate! Equipped with a hunter's headgear and gun, he homed in on my unusual cry for help and was ready to bag his trophy.

In the national drive to develop the borderlands, old farmhands like Lao Su had been recruited since the early 1950s from all corners of the country. Some were ex-servicemen, some were townsfolk, and some were peasants from western Guangdong Province. Their lives were even harder than ours: they built from scratch the first roads, bridges, and thatched huts in this wild, uncultivated island. By the late 1960s, and before the influx of *zhiqings*, they had opened up a number of tropical crop plantations in the virgin jungle. The island's real agricultural pioneers, they had laid the groundwork, however rudimentary, for our arrival and survival. Barely literate, many were taciturn, and few could express the lofty revolutionary ambitions that were on the lips of us "educated youth." Assiduous, artless and enthusiastic, they were then mostly in their thirties, but were called "old workers" by us naïve youngsters and generously shared their life experiences with us. In winter, they would set up a rough stove for warm showers to help us ease our stretched and strained muscles: in summer, they gathered herbs from the jungle to make tea, which would dispel the heat from our bodies. When they got lucky with their hunting, they would invite a few of us to share their trophies. And at work, they would pass on to us all the know-how they had mustered over the years. They were our true mentors and friends.

The day after I was mistaken for a barking deer, I was able to scrape together a "feast" for Lao Su as an expression of my gratitude. By the time I made my first return visit to the farm, he had, alas, passed away, and I couldn't tell him just how grateful I was to be able to witness the miraculous transformation that has occurred in Hainan and elsewhere.

Aiming High

THE STUDIOUS SENTRY
Su Haitao

At the end of April 1973, the peanuts we planted near the militia base were ripening. A sentry was needed at night to keep the wild boars at bay. I volunteered and was given the job.

In fact, I had a hidden agenda. After the revelations which followed the death of Chairman Mao's designated successor, Lin Biao, toward the end of 1971, I began to reassess my life and, as a result, became bewildered and couldn't see where my future lay. In 1972, I picked up some textbooks, which had been discarded some five or six years ago, in order to enrich my mind. There weren't many books available, and I soon exhausted them.

Since my maternal aunt lived in Hong Kong, I got my mother to ask her to get me some English books. After they arrived in Guangzhou, I gathered them up while on home leave and took them back to the regiment. Those that made it to the farm included *English 900*, published in the United States, and *An English Grammar Handbook* published in Hong Kong, together with a short-wave radio set. While the grammar book could be read almost openly, *English 900* had to be hidden and read in secret: I would open it only at night while I was in bed, and also took care never to read it aloud. At that time, Voice of America was broadcasting *English 900* at midnight, and on a number of occasions I tuned in to it under a blanket. But we were working day in and day out; if I stayed awake for the program every night, my body might not be able to take it. Besides, because I didn't have earphones, I could be caught in the act. With my "politically incorrect" family background, I might have been required to "stand on the ping-pong table"—be publicly denounced. I woke up from nightmares about this many times. Acting as a sentry against wild boars was a heaven-sent opportunity to learn English in solitude.

Armed with an iron tube and an iron stick, I brought along in my shoulder bag a mosquito net, a blanket, a machete, an oil lamp, an anti-mosquito incense coil, and the books and radio. After supper, I walked to the peanut field. There was a small thatched shed to give shelter from the rain, and inside, a bedstead consisting of two boards and a straw mat which were laid on four crutch-like supports. I put up the mosquito net and spread my blanket on the bed. My nocturnal abode was complete. When night fell, I turned on the radio for music, news, and anything else that was on. I also read a book, and, of course, every now and then I fulfilled my duty as a sentry by striking the iron stick against the iron tube and yelling.

Before midnight, I got my book ready, tuned my radio to Voice of America, and then listened to *English 900*. Before I became a sentry, I had finished the first book of the series without reading the exercises out loud, and it was liberating that I could now read them aloud, despite my residual fear of getting caught.

The next day, two things troubled me. The first was that when I inspected the field in the morning, I found that a small patch of peanuts had been eaten by the boars, probably during the forty minutes that the program was being broadcast. I couldn't neglect my duties for the sake of English, neither could I bang the stick on the tube while I was listening to the program. The second issue was that after midnight I felt too hungry to fall asleep.

To my amazement, all my worries were dispelled that night by a visit from Lao Jiang, our deputy captain. A kind-hearted man, he took the *zhiqings'* welfare seriously. After listening to my complaints, he burst out laughing and said: "You are such an ignoramus, aren't you? Hungry? Help yourself to the peanuts. What you can possibly eat in a month will never amount to those devoured by the boars in merely a few seconds. Bring along a small stove and a pot and boil some for yourself. As for keeping the boars at bay, don't bother with the tube or the yelling. In your guard and messenger squad, there are plenty of fuses for exploding stones for building purposes. Bring along a small roll every evening and chop each fuse down to ten centimetres. Then just before going to bed scatter them round the field, especially in the breezy areas: boars don't like the smell of gunpowder! You're guaranteed a sound sleep every night without having to worry about them stripping the peanuts."

The penny dropped: it was that simple. The next night, with a small stove and a pot from friends and a roll of fuses on my shoulder, I went to my shed. I followed Lao Jiang's instructions: the peanuts were delectable. At the beginning, I was gripped by a sense of guilt, but I soon got over it. Insomnia triggered by hunger was torture, and besides, compared with what the boars devoured during my first night, what I could eat was mere "peanuts" in both senses! Scattering the fuses round the field worked magic as well: there were no more forays from the boars. Years later, when I reminisced about this to Lao Jiang on a visit to the farm, he just chuckled. He might well have forgotten about it, but I hadn't, and I remain grateful to him.

From then on, I scattered the fuses round the field before midnight, listened to the radio and, gradually, even dared to read aloud with the presenters: then I read on my own for an hour or two. Because of the night shift, I was entitled to take a break during the day, but since I slept quite well at night I didn't need much time to catch up with my sleep during the day, and while the others were out toiling in the elements, I could spend a lot of time on my English. At that age I was like a sponge, taking in everything easily. It was a happy time: I felt enriched. But happy times fly by: a month later the peanuts had ripened, and I had to bid farewell to the shed and return to my old job, with some of the more difficult parts of *English 900* still to be learned by listening to the radio.

The stint was brief, and I didn't get to learn much English, but it made a deep impression on me. Due to my family background, I kept a low profile on the farm and was indifferent to many things in the regiment. Over the years since my return from rustication, the memories of those days have grown hazy. The copies of *English 900* became tattered from overuse, but I still have them. After the peanut field episode, I became more confident and realized that even if I could no longer receive a formal education, I could teach myself and work hard to make my dreams, however impracticable, come true. Over the next few decades, the experience must have exerted a subtle influence on me: no matter what I am working on, I always give it my best efforts, and I have thus achieved something I am proud of.

A SERIAL DREAMER

Peng Lijia

I am a dreamer, and always have been.

Like many girls my age, my first dream was colored green: I wanted to join the army and wear its green uniform and shoulder bag—for, you see, being valiant and bold rather than feminine was all the rage at that time. After reading such revolutionary novels as *Daughter of the Army*, I longed to become a heroine, to live a military life, and work in the army production and construction corps. I plotted with three friends to escape from home and join the renowned Xinjiang Army Production and Construction Corps at the far-flung northwestern border. Our plan was aborted: we had neither money nor food coupons at our disposal.

In 1969, the new Guangzhou Army Production and Construction Corps came to Meixian to recruit "regimental soldiers": due to the fierce opposition of my family, I couldn't sign up. I cried my eyes out when seeing off those lucky new "regimental soldiers" amid a fanfare of drums and gongs. When the army corps returned the next year, I got myself a place through dogged determination. After I had signed up, my grandmother ignored me for several days—I didn't dare to look her in the eye. On 24 March, early on the morning of the day I was due to depart for Hainan, I went to say goodbye to her in her bedroom, which doubled as our living room. Frail and confined to the room, she made me a mug of hot tea and said: 'It was not that I didn't want you to join. What upset me so much was that you got outsiders to talk me into it, which indicated to the world that I was backward and conservative." At that point, it really sank in that I was about to leave home: I began to weep, and in the queue of new recruits with big red flowers on their chests, my weeping was the loudest.

I also had a "white" dream at that time—to become a practitioner of traditional Chinese medicine and wear the white uniform. My grandmother was doing poorly: I wished I had the magic touch to clear up all her health problems. Just before my rustication, my elder sister managed to borrow a book on traditional Chinese medicine. Although I was only a seventh grade student, I didn't simply endeavor to master its medical theory: I copied it word for word. My elder brother, who by then had been rusticated, sneered at me: "It's a complete waste of time. In the army corps, you'll be no more than a coolie!" I ignored him. Hadn't our teachers taught us "Where there's a will, there's a way"? It had never crossed my mind that the sacred name "regimental soldier" could have anything to do with me bathed in sweat, with a pickaxe or machete in my hands, hacking away in the elements.

It turned out that my brother was right: once we arrived, we were handed a machete to hack down bushes and creepers, and a pickaxe to dig holes for planting rubber trees. In the after-hours, we participated in the construction of our dormitories. We worked over ten hours a day, all in the name of "learning from Dazhai," once an almost uninhabitable village in Shanxi Province whose people had allegedly done everything by themselves and become self-reliant. But I had a plan. When I saw our assistant nurse carrying a medical box on the way to work, I offered to carry it; when I found some medicinal herbs on the hills, I picked them and handed them in to the clinic. "Who knows?" I thought, "One day I might be noticed, sent for two or three months' medical training in the regimental hospital, and return as a proud assistant nurse." But my self-esteem was severely diminished by the sarcastic remark that I was currying favour with the assistant nurse. Cold water was poured on my hot ambition.

Thanks to my love of music, I soon hatched a new plan. When a *zhiqing* from Haikou City was visiting home, I gave my last month's salary of twenty-eight *yuan* to him and asked him to get me an *erhu*. This canny friend got one at the bargain price of eighteen *yuan*; the neck was slightly damaged but it didn't affect the quality of the sound. He knew because he was an excellent *erhu* player. I handled it like a piece of jewellery: I took out an old pair of army trousers from my trunk, cut off the legs, and made a cover for it. At night, I learned to play such popular folk tunes as "Beaming with Joy," and such paeans to our great leader Chairman Mao as "There Is a Golden Sun in Beijing." I was mesmerized by it, though my roommates never were. I ignored their complaints. I had a conviction that my talent would shine through: soon I would be chosen to join the Maoist propaganda troupe and would no longer waste my youth in backbreaking labor. But after a while, the complaints became irritable and sarcastic: "Such a nuisance! How can we sleep in such a din?" "If she was so damned good, why didn't she enroll in the Guangzhou Music School?" But still, I couldn't care less and put in more hours of practice. The company officials came to talk me out of it. Eventually, though, it was the remark of a fellow Meixian *zhiqing* that put an end to my musical ambitions: "You are such an idiot. You have tarnished everybody's good impression of you!" A few nights later, I quit practicing when my roommates were getting ready for bed. To my surprise and delight, I was eventually given a chance to show off my musical skills in the regiment. But it was a mixed blessing: sitting side by side with those talented players, it dawned on me that I could never play at a professional level. I must look elsewhere for opportunities.

My next dream would eventually make me who I am today. Whenever the supply teacher of the company school was on leave, I was asked to cover for her. I noticed that once I entered the classroom, the youngsters would greet me in their soft and tender voices: "Hello, teacher," and all of a sudden I felt taller and grander. With my seven years' education and feminine touch, I threw myself into the role and, in return, saw admiration in their eyes. When class was over, I would make up stories to tell them and they would become so captivated that the whole class grew extraordinarily quiet. They liked being around and playing with me; I loved to see their unaffected smiles. I delighted in being with them for the simple yet boundless pleasures they afforded.

My fifth dream kept me in a feverish state for quite a few years. In January 1973, Huang Ronger, a propaganda officer in the political division of the regiment, announced that he was printing an anthology of poems by Daling *zhiqings*. Like lighting a torch for a lone walker in pitch darkness, it ignited my enthusiasm for writing poetry. Isn't poetry the echo of our dreams and aspirations? I had an abundance of both. It became an obsession: I worked on my poems while toiling in the open, washing my laundry, even during my naps and dreams. I produced three poems and they all got published in the anthology. In that process, not only did I start to find beauty in conventional subjects such as hills, rivers, sunsets and morning dews, but I also glorified all the symbols of our hardship: the pickaxe, our sweat, the calluses on our hands, our bare feet. Encouraged by our enthusiasm, Huang set up a creative writing group in the regiment on 8 November and in order to publish our work launched an irregular mimeographed periodical called *The Morning Sun*. Naïve and passionate, we aspired to "occupy the literary front," "champion new socialist things," and "pay our dues to revive the cultural life of our troops." Although neither the group nor the periodical outlived the brain-drain which occurred when the army pulled out from the farm a year later, what survived was the sheer passion for literature and the optimism that we maintained amid our adversaries. I continued to pour my revolutionary passion into verse, and with the help of fellow poets on the farm, my work appeared regularly in the *Regimental Soldier's Paper*, and sometimes in *Hainan Daily* and *Hainan Youth*. On one occasion it was included in an anthology published by the Guangdong People's Press. Known only for my sensitivity and melancholy among the *zhiqings*, I acquired some distant fans who saw me as "a notable female poet" residing on Hainan Island. But just as the fan mail appeared, I began to grapple with the recognition that there was little in my work except the outpouring of passion for the revolutionary cause. I wanted to be as fresh, lively, and humorous as my fellow *zhiqing* poet Chen Hua; as witty and profound as Li Xiaojiang, one of the best known poets among us; as mature and eloquent as Huang Ziping, and so on. The more I read their works, the less contented I was with mine. I found that with only seven years' rudimentary education, I had little to fall back on in my writing.

I was blessed. I came upon a devoted teacher in Ping Zhengming, an entomologist from the South China Institute of Tropical Crops who was demoted to No. 9 Company to run the small shop. Despite the long walk over the hills from my own No. 7 Company, I would visit him on Sunday, our only day off, and be his avid audience in a shop permeated with a pungent, mildewy smell that blended with that of the sweet, sour, bitter, and spicy items on the shelves. In addition to free tuition in history, literature and writing, the session would include a lunch of fresh black bean sprouts carefully timed to coincide with my visit. After Ping was reinstated to his institute, he referred me, to my happy surprise, to a colleague of his, a lecturer in Chinese literature: I resumed my studies by corresponding with a heaven-sent lecturer whom I had never met. Years later, when I was on the campus he taught at and studying in the same year as his daughter, I learned what sort of torture and hardship he had endured while he was tutoring me! It made me, a nobody, wonder what good deeds I had accumulated in my previous life in order to deserve such extraordinary kindness.

The more we learn, the more ignorant we find ourselves. My sixth dream was to go to college to expand my horizons. Because of my new passion for reading, I acquired two nicknames, "the deskbound Buddha" and "the nail on the bed."

After I was assigned to work as a correspondent at the end of 1975, I came across my third teacher: Liang Yongkang, an ex-*zhiqing* and at that time newly graduated from Guangdong Normal College, who in accordance with government policy had just returned to work at Daling Farm. His desk was directly opposite mine: as well as Chinese, he taught me mathematics. Thanks to these teachers, in the second year after the portals of higher education were re-opened, I was enrolled in autumn 1978 at South China Normal College to read Chinese, even though I had received only seven years' formal education. My dream of becoming a teacher was finally realized—nearly a decade after it first came to me. But my aspiration to be a caregiver and my interest in music haven't been wholly abandoned, for one of my specialties is music therapy.

A PHOENIX IN THE HEN-HOUSE

Su Zhaoxin

The first hurdle: drafting an application

Going to college was not only a lingering dream for many *zhiqings*, but a realistic way of escaping a life limited to farming. In 1970, higher education was partially reopened to workers, peasants and servicemen, but in Daling the privilege was largely confined to those *zhiqings* who were politically progressive. For the majority, going to college remained a mere dream.

All of a sudden there was a change of fortune. In 1977, just as we were gathering together for a meal to celebrate National Day, rumors sprang up across the country and were widely debated. One of them was that after being closed for eleven years, the portals of higher education were about to reopen. Although we treated this with a certain scepticism, we were also excited. At the end of the month, the official media carried the news that college entrance examinations would indeed be reintroduced.

Those who were eligible to apply that year were workers, peasants, current and ex-*zhiqings*, ex-servicemen, cadres, and current high school graduates. They must be single and about twenty years of age, but under twenty-five. For those with rich practical experience and who had made a significant social contribution in research, or those with a unique expertise, the age limit was thirty years irrespective of matrimonial status.

To the *zhiqings* who were over age, the regulation posed a hurdle that was almost insurmountable. Those who had left secondary school between the years of 1966 and 1968, at the height of the Cultural Revolution, were by this time more than twenty-five years old, and although they could claim, after ten years of manual labor in the countryside, to have "rich practical experience," it was hard to show that they had made "a significant contribution by research." No matter how hard I racked my brain for evidence of such a contribution, I had to leave the relevant space blank when I filled in the application form. As I handed the form in, the meticulous clerk spotted the blank space and suggested that I should put down a "unique expertise" of some sort. When I confessed that I had none, he pointed out that if I left the space blank I would simply be ineligible to apply. Young and arrogant as I was, I joked that my unique expertise was in handling a hoe. He explained with good humor that that wouldn't count and urged me to think again. I replied tartly that it would be wonderful if I could improvise some unique expertise for myself just by thinking about it, and asked that if anything occurred to him he would jot it down on my behalf. He gave me a mirthless laugh. I never found out if he did. I reckoned that since there must be thousands of *zhiqings* in a similar position, the state could hardly ignore the aspirations of those young people who were "over age."

Preparation: the minor campaign by lamp-light
On the day the news was confirmed, the entrance examinations were only slightly more than a month away. The hurdles were high and many, and there was no time to waste. The first hurdle for the army of applicants was to secure copies of secondary school textbooks. To our advantage, there wasn't much content in them, and they were easy to follow. The textbooks used before the Cultural Revolution were more systematic and comprehensive, but they had been lost during the political turbulence. Like soldiers who have been summoned to war at the last minute, we armed ourselves with absolutely anything that might help our performance.

Without any of the fuss that was made in later years, the college entrance examinations that year were treated as a run-of-the-mill event: no allowance was made for the applicants' circumstances. Daily work continued as usual: it was not until night fell that we could resume our study. Power was cut at nine o'clock, and before then, a dormitory of eight people was simply too bustling to allow quiet study. It was not until nine, after my roommates gradually went to sleep, that I could find enough space to read by the dim light of an oil lamp, an old companion of my life as a *zhiqing*. During the major joint campaigns, it often happened that several troops would combine to tackle a major task under glaring lights. Solitary study under a dim oil lamp was a rare sight and was therefore jokingly referred to as the "minor campaign." My energy level was high: when the light died away in my lamp, it was usually time for the rubber cutters to get up for work. My little lamp used over two liters of oil during those forty days of study and I shed nearly two kilos in weight, a tangible cost imposed by the exams.

Unlike today, no supplementary study materials were available: all we could resort to was the secondary education we had received before the Cultural Revolution. Compared to those who were working in production or rubber cutting squads, I was lucky. I was teaching in the primary school of No. 3 Company, and my colleague used to be a student of the elite Guangya Secondary School. During breaks or after hours, we would work at exercises in various subjects on the blackboard. With a solid foundation in all subjects, she gave me useful tips and help, something I will never forget.

The exams: swapping firewood for a permit

As the exam dates approached, the permits to sit them were being distributed to applicants via the local authorities. You'd expect it to be a straightforward process, wouldn't you? But in our case, there was a catch. The farm demanded that in exchange for a permit the applicant must collect sixty kilos of firewood and deliver them to a designated location near its hostel. It turned out that since the many applicants in Baisha County were widely dispersed, two exam venues had to be found: one in the county town, the other in Qifang. Qifang, where we were assigned to sit the exams, was more than thirty kilometers away. With no bus to get us there, we had to spend the nights in Qifang in order not to be late for the exams. The farm in Qifang provided two thatched huts as our dormitory, but the food and water had to come from the one hundred and forty exam candidates. While our rations of oil and rice could be forwarded to Qifang by the state farm, firewood, as usual, had to be found by each of us. In dismay, I spent a good half of my day off collecting wood from two rotten trees and delivering them to the required location.

The exam permit in those days looked no different from a newspaper: it was thirteen centimeters in length and nine centimeters wide. On the front were the name of the exam venue, details about the applicant, with a recent photograph, and the exam schedule. On the back were a set of rules and regulations and a conspicuous reminder: "The exams are open: applicants are allowed to bring secondary school textbooks and the dossier on the Eleventh National Congress. Notebooks or other materials are not allowed." My permit number was Zhou386714, the evidence of a life-forming experience.

Two days before the exams, our farm conveyed to Qifang our firewood and rations of rice, oil and salt, together with a large iron wok. Stoves were built, and boarding facilities set up. The next day, the candidates arrived with their sacks in two trucks. They were then shown the exam venue in a secondary school. The thatched classrooms were neat and tidy, but with their tiny windows and lack of artificial lighting they were rather dark. To the Daling candidates they were good enough—far better than my classroom in the company. While I was wandering about in the dark thatched hut, I couldn't help but wonder whether any of us would be lucky enough to rise like a phoenix from a henhouse.

The exam room: a thatched hut

Exams started at eight on 11 December. Although it was eleven years since I had sat an exam, I wasn't intimidated by the solemn atmosphere, a likely case of the dead mouse which feels no cold. I sat for four subjects: mathematics, politics, Chinese, and combined history and geography. The examiners must have taken into account the absence of teaching and the circumstances of the candidates, for the maths exam was a piece of cake. Neither did I have much difficulty in completing the papers for the other three subjects. I can barely remember any of the questions, apart from the essay topic which was set for the Chinese exam. Because of the country's change of leadership, following Mao's death and the subsequent end of the Cultural Revolution, we were to write, under the title "The new situation in a year of radical reform," about a real life event which would illustrate the importance of the class struggle in running the state. For people like us, with "rich practical experience," this was no big deal.

The offer letter: a long journey to the county

About a month after the exams, a dozen of us *zhiqings* were summoned to Baisha County People's Hospital for a physical check-up: only those who scored 270 and above in four subjects (out of a possible 400) were eligible. After the Spring Festival in 1978, it was said that some *zhiqings* in nearby state farms had been made an offer. All was quiet for the Daling candidates: we were nervous. Eventually, though, the education officer of our farm dropped by my classroom one morning and asked me to set off immediately to collect my offer letter from the county education bureau. From Daling to the Baisha county town, there was only one bus a day: a round trip would therefore take at least two days. Besides, we had to make a trip to headquarters for an ID pass and then to our company to collect a food coupon, which would allow us to buy food outside the state farm. By the time all these things were done, the bus had already left and I had to wait for the next day's. When I eventually made it to the county education bureau, the office was closed for the day. It was not until the third day that I was able to exchange my exam permit and ID pass for the offer letter. I learned that I was the first person to receive an offer in Daling that year. It also transpired years later that of all the college entrance examinations conducted in China, the competition that year was the fiercest. Of the 5.7 million applicants, only 270,000 were made an offer. I had been lucky.

The offer letter looked ordinary enough: its paper quality was just slightly better than that of the exam permit. Half the size of a standard A4 piece of paper, it listed my major subject, the venue and time of registration, and, most important of all, how to transfer my household registration and employment details. It also stated that students without any financial means were entitled to a state disbursement of sixteen *yuan* per month, and those who were employed before enrollment could continue to draw a salary from their last employers. This policy lifted the financial burden from us once and for all. I completed my four-year degree course on a monthly salary from Daling: indeed, it was the blood and sweat of those who had continued to toil there that had provided for us, the white-collar workers. How we could repay such a debt is a matter for another chapter.

DIGGING MY WAY OUT

Yang Yanhui, noted down by Yang Chuanzhi and Peng Lijia

It was October 1971 when I left home in the beautiful and fertile Jieyang County for rustication on Hainan Island. I was seventeen. Assigned to No. 7 Company in Daling Farm, I felt quite contented in my first three years. Though small of stature, I had a healthy appetite and I slept well. I was energetic and didn't in the least mind any of the heavy manual labor. It took time for my urban contemporaries to get used to working in the fields: for me, it was a piece of cake. For example, whenever I saw some *zhiqings* struggling to carry their heavy quota of bricks, I would offer to help, and it made me genuinely happy to be in a position to do so. Many of the *zhiqings* from urban areas liked to chat about everything under the sun. I liked listening to them—for me, it was a way to acquaint myself with things I had never heard of. It was satisfying to be around my educated peers. I also loved seeing them pick up a book to read when they found a moment to spare. Through them, I became aware of the power of knowledge and the fact that one's education did not stop with one's schooling. Because of my diligence and good intentions, I was admitted to the Communist Youth League just three months into my *zhiqing* life. Once this happened, I felt a great sense of belonging and potential: I thought that nothing was too difficult for those who set their minds to it.

From 1974, a few *zhiqings* from the urban areas began to leave the island, doing so on various grounds, such as taking up a parent's job or going to college. Soon the singles' quarters became dominated by *zhiqings* from the rural areas. I started to find it hard to get through the day. At night the place seemed dark, cold and desolate: during the day, the workload that previously had been distributed to a large squad was shouldered by just the few of us who were left behind. Building houses, propagating plants, digging up the fields, cutting rubber, tending vegetables, raising pigs, felling trees for firewood . . . the list seemed endless, and there were never enough hands for it. It was not that I minded the much heavier workload. Rather, it was the feeling of being mediocre and incompetent, and what I found unbearable was that there was no one to hang around with for a good laugh, and no sign of bookworms. What was my future? Was there an end to the tedious repetition of hard labor? Would I be stuck here alone for the rest of my life? I felt despondent.

After many restless days and nights, it dawned on me one day that although I could never compete with the educated *zhiqings*, I was clever with my hands and had an endless supply of energy. Through years of working in the propagation center, I had acquired a knowledge of plants and had mastered the techniques of planting, propagating and transplanting more than a hundred species, such as orange, mango, jackfruit, rubber, and avocado. This was an exceptional asset. Why didn't I make something out of it? Living in a rural area surrounded by uncultivated country with free river water flowing by was another asset. What was the point of my anxiety? Why didn't I take full advantage of my skills and circumstances and see what I could do with such resources?

In 1980, I began to put my ideas into practice. It was a tough start. After I finished my duties for the company, I looked round for a wild, deserted area for my experiments. Eventually, I identified as most suitable a piece of land between the reservoir and No. 16 Company. It was virgin bamboo forest. I chopped down the bamboo, dug up the whole area, and eventually opened up a field of nine *mu*, all by myself. In the following few months, I planted mango trees, rubber trees, coast oaks, eucalyptus, and orange jasmine. It became a routine for me to work there after finishing my quota of labor for the state farm. Weeding, digging the soil, transplanting . . . I threw myself into my private enterprise. I got into the habit of talking to the green shoots: to me they were alive with human emotions. The need to look after one and a half acres of new shoots eased the feeling of loneliness and frustration that had been nagging at me for years.

In due course, I had my first crop of young plants. However, I had been so absorbed in propagating and tending them that it had never crossed my mind that unless I found a buyer, my efforts would be futile. And it was not until I consulted the old timers and technicians in local propagation centers that it struck me what sort of a challenge I was up against in marketing the plants! I threw some clothes into a bag and started to tour all the departments in Dongfang County that were in a position to purchase plants: the forestry bureau, the agricultural bureau, the water conservancy bureau, the tropical crops bureau, the science and technology bureau, and so on. I talked to anyone who would lend me an ear, but I failed to find a single buyer. My eager heart felt as if it had been doused in icy water. When my savings ran out, I returned home and, to my great relief, my plants had been doing well during my absence. I started to think about linking up with a business partner. But communication was painfully slow and difficult: the telephone was still a luxury item in the early 1980s.

The next year I repeated what I had done the year before, except that this time I carried more savings with me and toured almost the whole island. Yet all I got for my enthusiastic sales pitch were cool reactions from all the departments I visited. However, I didn't despair because by then I had already reconciled myself to the fact that without my own propagation center, I had nothing. I knew I had to be patient: I learned from the urban *zhiqings* that it is always calm before a storm: I should keep my spirits up. I also believed that providence never forsakes a man who does his best.

October is the golden month for planting on the island, and that October, the monsoon season was wetter than usual. All of a sudden, the tropical crops bureau in Dongfang County ordered twenty-five thousand mango seedlings at a price of five *jiao* each. I was thrilled and made a handsome profit of thirty-five hundred *yuan*. My first pot of gold! It was as if a ray of light had suddenly been cast on my path, and I had a future and could hope again. With hindsight, I learned the reason that my first attempts to sell the plants had been unsuccessful: there are two seasons on the island—the dry season in the first half of the year, and the wet season in the second half. During the dry season, planting is time-consuming and costly; in the wet season, it is much more straightforward. That was why I had clinched no deals in my sales tours in the first half of the year.

The next month, I received an even larger order: thirty-two thousand young rubber trees. There was a problem: I didn't have enough stock! But then it struck me that I could easily order the balance from other suppliers. That was the first time I got into the business of buying to sell. I asked around to find out who had the best stock of fine young rubber trees. I mixed them with mine, sold them to my client, a county tropical crops bureau, and earned a profit of one thousand *yuan* from the transaction. Though the profit wasn't as high as my first deal and extra legwork was required to make up the stock I lacked, I was thrilled at having stumbled across a way to expand my business.

Through the above transactions, I built up a good reputation for the quality of the young plants and my service, and this proved to be crucial to my future business development. The next year, I absorbed nearly all the business in Dongfang County. And during the process, I found that fruit plants sold far better than rubber trees, and I started to focus my propagation business on these. This strategy reaped a greater profit.

Development on Hainan was still rather sluggish in the early 1980s, and the orders soon stalled. I tried to diversify into sugar cane plantation, sugar making and gold mining, but none of them worked out. After a series of failures, I was forced to return to what I knew best:

soil, and the techniques and expertise gained from working in No. 7 Company. I stopped being so restless and was able to see where my strength lay—in propagation, in which I had gained a sound reputation. In 1989, I expanded my business across to the mainland in Guangdong Province, and the following year, I set up a mango plantation in the neighboring Guangxi Zhuang Autonomous Region. Today, my flowers and plants business spreads across the three urban areas of Guangdong: Guangzhou, Shenzhen and Foshan. I have become a noted figure in my industry.

I regularly remind my two sons how tough it was to start out while I was still working for No. 7 Company in Daling three decades ago. I tell them that without the help of the old hands and the influence of the ex-*zhiqings* from the urban areas, I would never have got to where I am. Without them, I might have been just another elderly peasant in my hometown of Chaoshan. After a hard day in the fields, I would be killing time with a cup of *gongfu* tea at night. Although with my physical strength it might not have been a problem for me to support a family, I could never have afforded to put them through college. I am grateful to No 7 Company for everything its old hands and ex-*zhiqings* have given me.

Twists of Fate

A LIFE LESS ORDINARY
Che Zhiming

It is said that to be a collector of objects is to collect fragments of history, sentiments, unforgettable experiences. I own nothing valuable, but I do possess a unique item which is extremely precious to me. It is a piece of poetry embroidered with scarlet silk thread on a length of white silk. A memento of my *zhiqing* career, it testifies to the extent to which, after the violent baptism of the Cultural Revolution, a generation which was contemporary with the heyday of communism in China remained imbued with lofty ideals.

The poem was written in the spring of 1973, the fifth year of my rustication on Daling Farm.

Early one evening, while I was still driving a bulldozer for No. 12 Company to help clear the wilderness, I received a telephone message from our political instructor: my father had turned up at regimental headquarters and I was granted three days' leave to spend time with him. It was such a bolt from the blue that I just couldn't believe my ears: it was seven years since I had last seen him!

After handing over the bulldozer and my work to a fellow *zhiqing*, I went to company headquarters to check with our political instructor. Indeed, he confirmed, not only was my father waiting for me at regimental headquarters right now, but he had met with the regimental officials and learned about my performance during the past few years.

It was the end of October 1966 when I learned some utterly incredible news about him. By then, the Cultural Revolution had swept the whole country, resulting in great upheavals and chaos in every nook and corner. Schools were closed indefinitely to make way for the emerging Red Guards and their unprecedented and repeated acts of rebellion—all of which took place with the approval of Chairman Mao. I was among the many who jumped on the bandwagon of free travel across the country to "spread revolutionary ideas," meeting up with other Red Guards and venerating all the "red sacred places" of our revolutionary past.

When I returned to Guangzhou from Beijing, I found to my surprise that the walls of our courtyard had been turned, inside and out, into a sea of political slogans and posters. At night, my elder sister and I could not stop wondering why our father hadn't come home for several days. In the past, no matter how busy he was at work, he would always make time to talk to us during our home visits from boarding school.

While we were trying to think of a reason for his prolonged absence, we heard knocking at the front door. As soon as we opened it, two military men from the Guangdong Provincial Public Security Department sent us packing. They also told us that our father had been imprisoned and was being kept in isolation for further investigation.

What the devil had happened to him? Why on earth should our beloved father be prosecuted all of a sudden? A northerner, he had been a primary school teacher before he joined Mao's army to liberate the whole country. A veteran of both the War of Resistance against Japan and then the Civil War, and once a regimental chief commander under the leadership of Liu Bocheng and Deng Xiaoping, he had suffered many wounds and bore several deep scars on his body. The Japanese had once put a huge reward on his head. Father loved to spend time with us, and his revolutionary stories taught us many things. We adored him: he was upright and tough, a hero in our eyes. We loved his sense of humour, his infectious laugh, and the thrilling stories of his many narrow escapes in the two wars.

In my dim memory, he once taught us a poem by the Russian poet Alexander Pushkin, entitled "If Life Has Cheated You." The poem was hugely popular among young people, and he used its simple verse to teach us to look on the bright side, no matter what cards were dealt to us. He was anxious that his high office didn't mean that we would be spoiled. He often reminded us that in wartime his life had been saved by ordinary people, and therefore that we must love them and keep a humble heart at all times. Though at our tender age we couldn't understand everything he taught us, his words made a deep impression on us.

Only fifteen and fourteen years old, and boarders at the elite Guangya Secondary School, neither my sister nor I had any idea how to live on our own when we were swept out of our home. Guangzhou, like everywhere else in the country, was steeped in the violence that resulted from conflicts between the various Red Guard factions. To our great good fortune, the mother of my school friend, Li, courageously took me in, and my sister went to live with a school friend of hers. We lived far apart in Guangzhou, but we were sheltered by those kind people in the street whom my father had taught us to love. During the "Up to the Mountains, Down to the Countryside" campaign at the end of 1968, we were sent to live farther apart on Hainan: my sister was rusticated to the Red China Farm in Lingao County, and I to Daling Farm in Baisha County.

We had never been allowed to visit our imprisoned father, not even before we were rusticated to a place many miles from home. And it was now seven years since I had last seen him.

From No. 12 Company to regimental headquarters was a twisting and hilly track of twelve kilometers. But that night, it was a mere two hours' brisk walk for me! There was no camera to capture that emotional moment when we first met, but so vividly cherished in my heart, it has stayed with me ever since. Now sixty-six, thin and silver-haired, he seemed to be in good shape. I learned from him that since he no longer faced the sweeping charge of "being in conflict with the people" but some lesser "offences in connection with the people," he was confident that he would soon be rehabilitated. He regretted that we had been caught up at such a tender age in his problems, but added: "Keep your chin up. Life is bound to test us through hardship," a sentiment which has remained with me all these years.

It so happened that on his way to my regiment, he had visited my older sister in No. 8 Regiment of No. 5 Division and was very proud of her progress. He encouraged me to learn from her, and not to be dedicated to work alone but to advance politically by becoming a Party member. Later, my sister would be sent by her farm to study medicine back in Guangzhou, becoming the first in our family to benefit from higher education.

Soon after this most unexpected visit, my father was reinstated to the Huiyang Prefectural Party Committee of Guangdong Province, and in April of that year, an order from the Guangzhou Rustication Office arrived for me to return home.

I couldn't wait to be reunited with my father, yet I also couldn't stop thinking of the farm, my regimental soldier friends, the bulldozer that I had been driving for years, the rubber trees we had planted, the jackfruit, the thatched hut . . . In four and a half years, how attached I had grown to my new home in this remote corner of the world! The hardest part was to bid farewell to the old hands who had always treated me like family. It was the farm and its simple souls that had helped me get through the dark hours of my young life.

In the time before my departure, I lost a lot of sleep. One night, under the dim light of my oil lamp, I wrote a long poem entitled "Reluctant to Part," subtitled "To My Old Schoolmates and Comrades-in-Arms at Daling, Who Stuck Together Through Thick and Thin." Then I walked all the way to regimental headquarters and handed it to my old pal Li, whose mother had taken me in unconditionally when I became homeless in Guangzhou. I asked him to edit it for me.

Li, too, became sleepless after reading my poem, which has now been lost. At dawn, he composed a poem which he dedicated to me as "Harla," my nickname at school. Following the strict tonal pattern and rhyme schemes of an ancient structure, the poem reads:

Dielianhua

To Harla on the eve of his return to Guangzhou

The dew on the rubber trees drops like tears,
Four winters, four springs,
My comrade-in-arms on his way home.

Words are scarce equal to the time we shared,
Our parting so sad.

Ten years' weal and woe,
Have bound our red hearts,
Sealed our revolutionary friendship.

Work hard though hills and rivers sever us,
To bring credit to our Chairman Mao.

Two other friends have left their mark on this precious "collector's item." Xiao Wu, a fellow *zhiqing* from Haikou City, was brought up in a traditional scholarly family and had been practicing Chinese calligraphy since he was little. After reading the poem, he copied it on to a length of white silk. Xiao Liao, who was rusticated to Daling at sixteen, was, like many a Chaoshan girl, versatile and dextrous, and had learned to embroider as a little girl. The three of us had been driving a bulldozer to help open up the jungle surrounding the regiment: after spending thousands of days and nights working together, we became the best of friends. Xiao Liao offered to embroider the poem as a farewell present.

While the poem was the expression of my friendship with Li and composed spontaneously, sewing materials were hard to come by in those lean years. Not stocked in any shops on the farm, the white silk was an offcut from the material used in the transport company to filter diesel oil. As for the scarlet silk thread, needle and hook, they could only be obtained in Guangzhou after I had returned home. After receiving these things from me, Xiao Liao spent more then twenty nights embroidering the poem on the silk cloth.

In the letter that accompanied the poem, she wrote: "When we first met, I thought that as a member of the red princelings and a former student of the elite Guangya Secondary School, you would be one of the arrogant crowd who thought themselves a cut above the rest of us. But you turned out to be none other than a diligent worker with a charming personality. Not only were you a good team leader: you have been like a dear elder brother to me."

I don't know about the other "red princelings," but for me, the experience on the farm couldn't have been more precious: it has shaped my character. Snatching me from an enviable and cosy ivory tower at the age of fourteen, it dropped me straight into the workaday world, opened my eyes, and enabled me, with a humble heart, to develop a friendship with my peers from all backgrounds—people I subsequently learned to love and respect. My tough experiences made me into the strong and sanguine man who is described in the Pushkin poem that father had taught us.

After I received the embroidered poem, I framed it and hung it on the east wall of my apartment. Decades later, the white silk has long since faded and turned yellowish, but the dense embroidery is as scarlet as ever.

THE BIG RED UMBRELLA

Su Haitao

Rusticated to Hainan on 10 November 1968, I didn't return to Guangzhou till April 1975. During my six and a half years on Daling Farm, I spent five on the regimental basketball team. The person I remember best is Nie Qixian, our regimental commander. From northeast China and a veteran of the civil war, he was affable and easy to get along with.

My membership on the basketball team had much to do with Nie. In my first Spring Festival on Hainan, the farm organized a tournament. As an active long distance runner and basketball player during my school days, I was a natural choice for our team, the "Lowland Company," and we won the trophy. Soon, the farm set up the "Daling Basketball Team," with *zhiqings* as its backbone, to compete with the nearby farms and the outpost based at Yulin in Sanya City. In 1969, when the state farms were about to be transformed into an army corps, some military officers came to Daling Farm to make an inspection. I was among the group to receive them. Out of the blue, one of them hailed me in a booming voice: "Hey, aren't you Daling's No. 9?" I hadn't the faintest idea who he was, least of all that he was the commanding officer of the outpost at Yulin, whose basketball team had just lost a game to us.

When the army took control of the state farms, Daling Farm was renamed No. 13 Regiment of No. 4 Division of the Guangzhou Army Production and Construction Corps. Apart from production and construction, all the major operations were headed by military personnel. My company, the Lowland Company, was renamed No. 6 Company. But what surprised us most of all was that Nie, the commanding officer from the Yulin outpost, would become our regimental commander.

One day at the end of 1969, our political instructor asked me, to my happy surprise, to report to the guard and messenger squad. True to its name, the squad was responsible for providing security and messenger services to regimental headquarters, but its other function was to be the regimental basketball team. With my "politically incorrect" family background, I had never harbored the thought of being selected to join this elite squad, made up largely of the best basketball players of the regiment. But in the circumstances, I did not doubt that Nie had had a hand in the matter.

Nie wasn't just a devoted basketball fan: he liked to play as well. Whenever we won a game, he would be exhilarated and become extremely talkative: when we lost, he became very quiet. Although we could tell he was unhappy, he would never point his finger or interfere in the training, which was delegated to two servicemen who were equally enthusiastic. When we played away games on the island, he would be our self-appointed leader. Our favorite games were at the Baimajing fish port and the Shilu iron ore mine: the food at these places was simply the best, there usually being fresh seafood and meat—a great treat in those lean years.

Two matches made the biggest impression on me. One was against the team at the Yulin outpost, the one Nie used to lead. It was a tough game because Yulin was stronger, but we put on a brave and unrelenting performance. It goes without saying that, as a past leader of the Yulin team and the present leader of ours, Nie was hugely nervous, tense, and conflicted throughout the game: he wanted us to win, yet he knew how strong his former players were. In the end, we won by a small margin. He was so exhilarated by our hard-earned victory that as we left the court he patted each of us on the shoulder and treated us to a late night dinner at the hostel.

The other memorable match was when we joined forces with Longjiang Farm to play against the junior squad of the Guangdong Provincial Team. I had been an admirer of the latter's two coaches since my secondary school days. Although its players were fairly young then, many would soon become core members of the main provincial team, and two of them would even play nationally. Since the Guangdong juniors had just lost two important games, one to the army corps and one to the divisional team, they were desperate to end their losing streak by beating us. It was a close and fierce match, and in the end even their coaches took turns playing. As a defender, I was forced to use all my skill and craft within the rules to contain and block one of my towering idols! Although we lost by twelve points, we felt that the defeat was an honorable one. And for the first time ever, Nie was actually beaming after we had lost a game!

It was a common perception that basketball players had an easier life in the regiment. How mistaken that was! Besides taking part in all the major joint campaigns, we were responsible for quarrying stones for the construction of a dam. The dam we helped to build is still being used today, a testament to our hard work. When regimental headquarters was building the office buildings, we were charged with supplying all the beams by going into the hills to fell trees and transport them down to the construction site. We also worked with the old hands to build our own tiled houses as dormitories. Moreover, there was a spell when we had to take turns guarding the storage warehouse at night. During the typhoon season, I even joined a member of the telephone operations staff to maintain the telephone lines in extreme weather.

Whenever it was quiet or the eve of a major competition, our task was to focus on training and practice. The training program was arduous and after several years of heavy exercise, my knees were worn out and I could no longer jump and bounce as much as I wanted to. After many failed attempts to see about my knee problems on the island, in 1973 Nie sent me back to Guangzhou for treatment, but to little avail. It was time for me to retire from playing basketball. Nie, however, would not hear of it and insisted on keeping me in the team as a substitute.

In 1974, I was reassigned to teach mathematics and became a class teacher in the regimental secondary school. Although by then I had more time on my hands, I was expected to lead my students in all the major joint campaigns and to play as a substitute whenever there was a basketball match. The students in the regimental school were all local rural kids and were considered unruly. Some of the female teachers found them challenging. My reputation as a former key basketball player served a crucial role in taming them: the naughtier the boys, the more awed they were by my status on the regimental team. I picked two of the well-behaved boys as prefects, and soon the whole class changed for the better. I got on exceedingly well with them. Although I worked in the school for less than a year, twenty of my former students, who had scattered over several provinces, came to Guangzhou in 1992 to see me. I was very touched.

In my six-and-a-half years on the farm, I went through some bad periods, but all-in-all, I have mainly fond memories of my *zhiqing* days. It helped that both the commander and the commissar of the regiment were enthusiastic basketball fans. The commissar was also a huge fan of Beijing opera. Whenever he had time, he would ask the members of the Maoist propaganda troupe to play musical instruments while he sang a few extracts. As for Nie, he always seemed to be smiling, and he cared greatly about the welfare of the *zhiqings*. Whenever he was free, he liked to share his military experiences with us, especially how the unit he was in had liberated Hainan Island in 1950. Nie was like a big red umbrella over me: I was shielded from the prosecution liable to fall on many who shared my "politically incorrect" family background. With him as my protector, I felt more relaxed than many other *zhiqings*. The basketball team was a blissful oasis for me. When I applied to return home just before the army handed back the management of the farm to the local authorities, I was given a green light all the way—something I have appreciated to this day.

In December 2008, I paid a visit to Daling with some ex-*zhiqing* friends, and we met up with Nie for dinner. While we reminisced about our *zhiqing* days, it became clear that despite his seniority and being wheelchair bound, Nie, like me, had a vivid memory of all the highs and lows of the regimental basketball team.

TWO LIFE CHANGING INCIDENTS
Liang Yongkang

In May 2011, some Daling veterans paid a visit to Guangzhou with their families. At the dinner party, I met for the first time in more than three decades my namesake from the same troop.

Over forty years ago, I was one of the thirty Guangzhou *zhiqings* who were assigned to the remote Lowland Company, later known as No. 6 Company. On my first night at the thatched hut I learned that among my dozen or so roommates I had a namesake. The next day, and without my knowledge, he changed the last character in his name from *kang* to *heng*, and from then on, he became fondly known among us as "Hengji."[16] I was rather touched by the prompt action of my namesake, who came from a worker's family.

He turned out to be an affable, no-nonsense sort of guy. A few days after we had settled on the farm, and when the remaining nutrition in our bodies was depleted, we started to experience hunger pangs. When we came across a field of cassava in our company grounds, it was suggested that we should dig some up for a feast. This met with an immediate objection because, as somebody put it, without permission, it would amount to stealing. Hengji asked why we didn't just damage some. Then the company would have to dig them out and use them for food. Without further ado, he went off to fetch an ox-cart and drove it toward

---

16. In the Cantonese speaking areas of China, the character *ji* can be added to the end of a male name as a term of endearment

the cassava field like an heroic soldier charging the enemy lines. Within a few seconds, a heavy crop of cassava was flattened. Over the next few days, cassava became our staple for every single meal: we became so sick of it that we couldn't tell which was the worse evil, hunger pangs or cassava with each meal. A while later, just as we became really fed up with the pickled Chinese radish that had been our only dish for a long spell, the pigs raised by the farm also began to suffer from the severe shortage of food and looked as small as puppies. I am not sure whether the sties were opened on purpose or the pigs themselves, being so thin, squeezed through the gates, but a dozen or so of them were running free. We were called to chase them back to their sties. Hengji and another Guangzhou *zhiqing* charged to the front with a sickle, and during the chaos they quickly slaughtered a pig. That night, we finally tasted pork!

Several years later, a passing comment made me wonder if sharing a dormitory with my namesake could well have played a part in determining my fate. I did not remain at the grassroots level for long: soon after the army took over the state farm, I was promoted to work as a correspondent—the mouthpiece of the regiment. It baffled me at times. How was it that such a crucial and sensitive squad could accept someone like me, who came from an intellectual, or "politically incorrect" family? I was, alas, firmly within one of the "seven black categories" which consisted of ex-landlords, rich farmers, counterrevolutionaries, bad elements, rightists, capitalist-roaders and reactionary academics. At a meeting of regimental bureaucrats, I seemed to chance upon the answer. After the commissar finished reading a long report that we wrote on his behalf, he observed, in his routine comments, that some officials had become rather bureaucratic. He quoted the example of a *zhiqing* from a worker's family who had been confused with his namesake, and the namesake was subsequently promoted to be a clerk at regimental headquarters. The commissar never divulged the name in question, nor have I bothered to confirm if I was the one who profited from the mix-up. Soon after this revelation, I was sent back to work in the company. Whether the two incidents were linked is quite beyond me and remains one of the unresolved mysteries of my life.

Years later, names seemed to play another significant role in determining my fate. By the time the first batch of rubber trees which had been planted by the *zhiqings* had acquired nearly ten tree rings, many of them had left, and those who remained on the state farm were trying all sorts of tricks to get the hell out of there. Though still trapped on the farm, I had swapped the title of *zhiqing* for that of "worker-peasant-soldier-college-graduate," and therefore none of the usual excuses that enabled the *zhiqings* to return home would apply to me. The whimsical nature of government policy had played a trick on me. In the fourth year after higher education was partially re-opened in 1970, and at the mercy of a new government policy to allow some "redeemable children" (those with problematic family backgrounds) to embark on higher education, I was enrolled at a college, having obtained the highest marks in our division. Three years later when I graduated, the government decreed that all "worker-peasant-soldier-college-graduates" should return to their last employers and I was sent straight back to where I had been rusticated years ago as a cadre! When the university my wife worked for sent a letter of negotiation to transfer me, I was matter-of-factly told by the head of the cadre department at the state farm bureau that since Baisha County was the autonomous county of an ethnic minority, no state-assigned bureaucrat was allowed to leave. However, when I met up with an old fellow student who worked in the human resources department of the county, she offered to make a call to the cadre department of the bureau. She didn't know how much it would help, but her department had some dealings with the cadre department. When I went back to the bureau the following day, the head of the cadre department, by whom I had been icily treated the day before, changed his tune completely. He was unusually warm to me, and after a quick check of my name, completed all the paperwork for my transfer! I discovered later that my friend's father was the senior Party secretary of Baisha Li Autonomous County. Since I shared a surname with my friend, the head of the cadre department might well have assumed that I was related to the Party secretary—something that would explain his rapid change of heart. But of course I have never bothered to prove my theory: I have simply let it remain another unanswered question in my life.

The Long Way Home

SET SAIL GUY

He Weixian, noted down by Liang Yongkang

I am called He Weixian, a name which, apart from the middle character, I share with a famous person, the billionaire He Xian. Known as Ho Yin in the Cantonese region, He Xian became a celebrity in Hong Kong and Macau for his business empire: I became a celebrity in Daling because I was rusticated there for over forty years.

Hardly any *zhiqings* know my real name, yet none will be unfamiliar with my nickname. Whether or not they know me in person, they are aware that there was a *zhiqing* from Guangzhou called "Set Sail Guy" who had been left behind in Daling. Whenever they visited, they made a point of dropping in on me "out of admiration." When we ran into each other in the headquarters, one even asked if I knew where "Set Sail Guy" was. Isn't that funny?

An inevitable question from the ex-*zhiqings* was, Why hadn't I left yet? I read little, neither had I ever held high positions in Daling. I could never chant the old *zhiqing* slogans like "Be rooted in Hainan" with any degree of conviction. But over the years, I had always dreamed of returning home and had never stopped trying to do so. It is a long story.

Let me start with my nickname, "Set Sail Guy."

I grew up in the old commercial district of Xiguan in Guangzhou and was known around the neighborhood as a mischievous lad. Thanks to my father's job in a shipping company, my playmates gave me the nickname "Set Sail Guy." I was the second son, so it fell to my elder brother to be rusticated during the "Up to the Mountains, Down to the Countryside" campaign. Yet, due to his poor health and timidity, my parents made me, their fear-nothing son, stand in for him. I went to Hainan Island at the age of fifteen.

During the rush to return home, some *zhiqings* would take their parents' jobs, some go to college, some just leave on health grounds. For reasons unknown to me, I missed all these opportunities. I was asked, "Why not follow the others and fake an illness so that you can apply to leave for health reasons?" But what official who saw such a tall and stout guy would ever believe him?

By then, my mother and younger brother had already emigrated to Hong Kong, and my younger brother was running a fairly successful business there. Through her contacts, my mother obtained a single entry permit to Hong Kong for one of her children. Probably feeling guilty for making me stand in for my elder brother during the rustication to Hainan, or more likely because my circumstances were worse than those of my brothers, my mother insisted on offering me this permit to move to Hong Kong.

When I heard the news, however, I hesitated. There was one person whom I could not leave behind: Ah Jiao, the person who would become my wife.

A *zhiqing* from Chaoan City, Ah Jiao was an assistant nurse in our company, No. 14. Already tall and at an age when I was still growing fast, the food ration could barely keep me from hunger. When I was hospitalized with a leg injury, I found not only that the food there was not rationed but that there was always something tasty in the assistant nurses' cupboards. To stay in the clinic longer, I dirtied the wound to the extent that it became infected and I ended up staying there for a month, during which I ate a staggering sixty kilos of rice! That experience taught me that to avoid hunger one must find an assistant nurse. Ah Jiao, the petite newcomer to the clinic, ate little. I started to frequent the clinic for her endless supply of unfinished food rations, satay sauce, pickles, and snacks from her hometown. Soon we became friends and, believe it or not, some of her secret admirers from Chaoan became so jealous that we fought over her.

One year, my mom visited her hometown and asked me to take some leave to meet her in Guangzhou. This was a daunting task for me. I never had a cent in my pocket. My salary of twenty-two *yuan* was all spent on food to keep me from starving, so a home visit was a luxury beyond my means. That day, Ah Jiao sensed the weight on my mind—when she learned about my dilemma she walked more than five kilometres to No. 9 Company, where she was first rusticated, and borrowed money from her townsfolk. Adding her own savings to it, she scraped together thirty *yuan*, a large sum in those days and one which I had little chance of repaying. Her kindness and faith in me were unforgettable.

When the *zhiqings* returned home, it was not uncommon for couples to go their separate ways. I could not, however, relinquish a love which had been born in hard times. This was the first time I gave up an opportunity to leave Daling, and for the same reason, Ah Jiao gave up her opportunity to return home and take the job of one of her parents.

We got married and started a family. My mom continued her efforts to get me over to Hong Kong but, because of me, to no avail. Not wanting to wait indefinitely, she paid a visit to Daling to discover why. Without informing me, she took a van from Haikou City and went straight to Daling. The driver drove her around Daling several times, but no one knew who He Weixian was. It was not until she ran into an old acquaintance, Lao Yang, our veteran farm manager, that she found my home. That day, Ah Jiao summoned all her arts to prepare some dishes which were normally affordable only on festive seasons. Yet, despite a long day, my mom's appetite was spoiled by the poverty in Daling. In the dim light, she saw for the first time how tough life had been over the years for her son. Were it not for the eight-month-old grandson she was holding, she would have burst into tears.

After dinner and with my children fast asleep, my mom revealed the purpose of her visit: with a single entry permit and an air ticket, she was going to take me back to Hong Kong. The next day, as I followed my mom to the airport, Lao Yang persuaded Ah Jiao to see us off at Haikou. At the airport, I stopped at the yellow line in customs, still undecided if I should follow Mom through. Ahead was my elderly mother and a comfortable life in Hong Kong: behind, my wife with our eight-month-old son and a life of endless poverty in Daling. I was torn. I don't know how long it took, but all I could see was my wife with our son in her arms. I could not cross that yellow line. My mom left with tears in her eyes.

And so Ah Jiao and I stayed in Daling for forty years to wait for a permit to return home. Life was tough but our days together were sweet and we never regretted our decision. Sometimes I would tease Ah Jiao and say that for forty years I had been repaying the thirty *yuan* she had lent me, and that the debt had still not been erased.

When my ex-*zhiqing* friends visited, they would sometimes ask if I felt lonely now that nearly all the others had gone. At the beginning, when I saw them off one by one and waited until their buses had disappeared, I did feel sad. During the five kilometer walk back along the hilly track, pangs of loneliness, despair, and helplessness would strike me in waves. Eventually, though, I grew numb.

I am lucky in having a cheerful outlook, I am loyal to my friends, and I never mind putting myself at risk to help those in need. I make friends easily, and while old ones are gone, new ones keep coming.

Every now and then, the farm organised political campaigns. There were once two Guangzhou *zhiqings* who were held "on suspicion of making counterrevolutionary posters." This was a serious offence, and if convicted, they would be in big trouble. I was then in the militia, and true to its name, it was tasked with military missions to suppress enemies. That day, I was ordered to watch them in their cell.

They were confused and terrified. Though we had not been to the same school in Guangzhou and I didn't know them well, I thought that what they most needed was comfort, care, and love. Besides, the handwriting on the posters was childish and didn't look like theirs. When I approached them, they said they didn't commit the offence and they were afraid of nothing, but they were consumed by boredom while they were in the cell. When no one was watching, I would put a book under their mess tins at mealtimes. It was a big risk: if caught, I would be the one to be prosecuted. More than a month later they were proved innocent, and we became great friends.

There are also friends with whom I have been through some life-and-death moments. One happened while I was still working in the hills. After a day of backbreaking labor, we were dragging our leaden bodies down the slope when we suddenly caught sight of a tree with a trunk as thick as a pillar lying across our track. On getting closer, we noticed its black and white pattern. Then in the twilight, I realized that it was not a tree trunk, but a huge python! Blood rushed to my head, yet my limbs were bathed in cold sweat. I told an old hand named Ah Bing, and when he saw it, he was frightened too: it was the first time in all his years on Hainan that he had come across such an enormous snake. Without further ado, we attacked it.

Once the python heard us, it was ready. With its head high and its tongue darting forward, it whirled toward us. Since we couldn't get too near it, we aimed for its extremities. I don't know where my strength sprang from, but I tore a tree from the ground which was the size of my arm and broke it in two. Ah Bing picked up one piece to hit its head, but the python caught it with its mouth. He then tried to pin its head to the ground with all his might while I was trying to seize its tail. But the tail was too slippery and whipped me hard. Eventually I worked out how best to subdue it, and reached for its genitals. But the python was so strong that it eluded me.

Fortunately, Ah Bing had heard many years ago that pythons cannot stand the smell of sweat and that the Li would use their sweat-soaked clothing to catch them when they saw them in the hills. After a long day, and this struggle with the python, I was soaked. I took off my shirt and hurled it at its head, which was being pinned to the ground by Ah Bing with a thick branch. I wrapped it firmly around the python and strangely enough, having been so violent and powerful a moment ago, it became slack. After smashing its head with our hoes, we too collapsed on the grass. When we surveyed the battlefield, everything had been flattened: it had taken us a good half-hour to win the fight.

We carried the python back to the company and put it on a scale: it weighed over forty kilos and measured nearly four meters! With great delight, we cut it open, cleared its innards, and peeled off its skin.

I chopped a piece off and shared it with my mates. But this was a luxury that Ah Bing could not afford: with four children, he had heavy financial burdens. He sold his share to the farm workers for ten *yuan*. We sold the skin to the collective purchasing station and got fifty *yuan*.

That wasn't the end of the incident. It was reported to headquarters, and for selling the meat Ah Bing was criticized for capitalistic behavior. An investigation was launched. When I was spoken to, I said that if that counted as capitalism, I would accompany Ah Bing to "stand on the ping-pong table" and be publicly denounced. For a time, we were criticized at all the political study sessions as typical capitalists. On those occasions, my hands sweated as much as they did when I was fighting for my life against the python.

A question I am often asked is what was my life like in Daling after nearly all the *zhiqings* had left. While the ex-*zhiqings* are all too familiar with the harsh conditions that existed, it doesn't take much of anybody's imagination to realize how tough it was to raise two children on a combined salary of about one hundred *yuan*. At first, my mother would help out from time to time, but gradually that stopped because she thought that the easier our lives became, the less likely it was that we would leave. How funny and yet how exasperating!

But life had to go on. When nearly all the *zhiqings* had left in 1985, the farm officials took pity on the last *zhiqing* from Guangzhou and I was moved to the rubber factory. Except for the days when rubber was cut, it was quiet and I had some time on my hands. Since there was barely any form of transportation from Daling to the main road, I figured that if I ferried passengers with a motorcycle, I could not only help the farm workers but take home some extra cash. With money from his younger brother for a Honda 125, "Set Sail Guy" began his sideline as a motorcycle taxi driver!

I was honest and straightforward. I never haggled over the fare. Come rain or shine and no matter how bumpy the road, I and my well-maintained motorcycle were only a phone call away. My service was well regarded.

I always offered to help whenever there was a problem on the road. On one occasion, I drove several dozen kilometres into town to get the needed parts for a broken-down jeep and did so without checking if I would be paid. After it was fixed, a person in the jeep who looked like an official learned that I was a Guangzhou *zhiqing* and praised my conduct. He said we shared the same surname, He, and after leaving his name and phone numbers with me, asked me to call him if I should ever need any help.

I did run into trouble once. I can't remember the exact details, but my motorcycle was confiscated, leaving me with no option but to walk all the way home. Daling was several dozen kilometers away, and I would have to walk back again to retrieve my motorcycle. In despair, I recalled the promise of my namesake and phoned him. At that moment, the traffic policeman was yelling: "You can beg to whoever you like, but your motorcycle is going to be confiscated." Yet from then on, things took a turn for the better.

First, the chief of the traffic police arrived. Handing me a cigarette, he rebuked his subordinate. It turned out that my namesake was an official in the county public security bureau, and he wasn't impressed by what he had overheard on the phone. The policeman was frightened and pleaded with me to send his apologies to the official. I readily obliged because, like me, he was only trying to make a living. When I left, with my motorcycle tank filled up by the traffic police, I felt as if I had just won a major battle. Exhilarating!

Afterward, whenever my friends needed help, I would pay a visit to the official in town and whatever he was doing, he would drop everything, settle me down, and get his subordinates to help me. With my new friend in a high place, my "boat" was given a green light everywhere it went, even long after it was due to be scrapped for over-use. It was treated as a special case.

Daling is in Baisha Li Autonomous County. The Li were dirt-poor, and some young delinquents would take a ride without paying. When this happened, the only remedy was to do nothing: otherwise, they would smash the motorcycle, even assault the motorcyclist. For this reason, many motorcyclists avoided them at all costs.

I had my fair share of dealing with such delinquents. Once when I requested the fare at the destination, I was asked if I wanted to stay alive. As we were arguing, a senior Li villager came to my rescue. After finding out what had happened, he had the youth spanked, and then told the crowds: "This big chap, he is a Guangzhou *zhiqing*, a good fellow. We all know him: he grew up in Daling from a young lad to a big man. He is still here, so it isn't easy for him. From now on, no one is to bully him."

At that remark, my eyes filled with tears, and I remember thinking that over the years sincerity had won me many friends, and that it still held true that good people would get their rewards. If you valued the title *zhiqing* you would get the care and respect due you. And indeed, the title of "the last *zhiqing* from Guangzhou" had brought me many favors from those good people.

Time flies, and soon I entered my fifties. In 2010, a good-hearted farm official informed me that there was a new decree: those who had settled down in the areas where they were rusticated were now allowed to return home. While I was working my way through the bureaucracy which was a prerequisite of my return, I chanced upon a paper inside my personal dossier documenting the unfair review of my father by his employer. I feel strongly that the utterly groundless remarks in it had shut all the doors to my return home. That paper had tied me to Daling for a good forty-one years!

To rectify the injustice, I visited the former employer of my father. The person who handled the case used to be a *zhiqing* as well, and he felt immensely sympathetic and apologetic for the distress that this paper had caused me. In the name of the Communist Party Committee, he immediately annulled it.

In 2010, Ah Jiao and I were finally able to have our household registration transferred to my hometown of Guangzhou.

As we grow accustomed to the life of a modern city, we still dream about the clear blue sky and green hills of Daling; those familiar, deeply wrinkled faces; our mouse-catching pet snake; and of course, the terrestrial "boat' which was driven by the "Set Sail Guy" for more than twenty years—my motorbike!

Looking Back

JUST ONE MEMENTO
Ou Nianzhong

These were times of both passion and perplexity. Does that sound a bit self-contradictory? But that was how we felt as *zhiqings*. On the one hand, most of us—the first groups of Red Guards during the Cultural Revolution—were infatuated with the idea of destroying the old establishment and building a brand new "red world." We aspired to follow Chairman Mao's directive to struggle to forge a new life in the vast expanse of the countryside. On the other hand, we urban, educated youngsters were confronted by the crude realities of the remote places we were rusticated to: the hardship of everyday life; the toiling, day in and day out; the obstinate and backward views and practices of the largely illiterate peasants and veterans, our designated mentors. In the thick of these realities, we could not see where our future lay. Bit by bit, our ideals were eroded by our encounters with the countryside. We became perplexed.

By 1972, despite the frequent and resonant chant of slogans such as "Take root in the farm," "No end to rubber importation, no end to our efforts," and "Take root in the borderland—I love my army corps," most *zhiqings* were scheming to find a way out: no one really wanted to put down roots and spend the rest of their lives in a rubber plantation on Hainan Island. It was an open secret that there was a disparity between our public enthusiasm and the private disenchantment that our rustication had brought. Those were the days when you were the only one who knew whether you meant what you said.

I was one of the Guangzhou *zhiqings* in the Lowland Company, so called because of the unusually large area of level terrain that it covered. A remote company in the farm, it opened up the wilderness for rubber plantation, and was a mere twenty kilometres away from a fishing village in the Gulf of Beibu on the west coast. A little further to the west was open sea. When the farm was taken over by the Guangzhou Army, we were proudly proclaimed as "regimental soldiers," and our company was renamed No. 6 Company, No. 13 Regiment.

Several decades after my rustication, I met another *zhiqing* who, just before I was moved elsewhere, had been promoted to my company as a political instructor. As we were recalling old times, he took a photograph out of his pocket and asked if I could remember the event. Sure enough, it was a group of *zhiqings* rehearsing *I Love My Army Corps*, and the director was none other than me.

It was a black and white photograph taken in the grounds of regimental headquarters. At the back were a few rows of the chorus in white shirts; at the front, the band in blue work uniforms. With passion clearly written on their young faces, the chorus were singing at the tops of their voices. Standing in front of the band with hands waving high in the air was I. The camera, which was right behind me, captured a tall, stout figure: it looked exaggerated, surreal.

Photography was a luxury. This picture was said to have been taken by Chen Longsheng, a political officer of the regiment, using a Rolleiflex twin lens reflex camera which belonged to the regiment. As if to preserve its value, the photograph had been laminated. It awakened a host of forgotten memories.

To prepare for the celebration of National Day, I was called up to regimental headquarters that year and tasked with providing a suite of songs which I eventually ended up composing. I was chosen for the job because of a rather absurd experience prior to my rustication. During the Cultural Revolution, the nation's musical and theatrical life was moribund and Guangzhou was no exception. Apart from the eight revolutionary model plays, there was hardly anything to see. I was a secondary school student when, in 1966, the incessant political purges, looting, and violence broke out across the country. In Guangzhou alone, the activities were led by two factions, "The Red Guards Combat Songs" and "Long Live the Red Guards," with members drawn mainly from the universities and secondary schools. Their bands, for example, were composed entirely of secondary school students.

A member of Combat Songs for more than a year, I participated in its rehearsals and more than a hundred performances. The troupe was not disbanded until, for "revolutionary purposes," the schools were instructed to reopen in late 1967. Combat Songs imitated the style of the hugely successful revolutionary musical film, *The East Is Red: A Song and Dance Epic*. The orchestra, for example, was over a hundred strong, with composers and directors coming from the Guangdong Provincial Troupe and including noted musicians such as Qiao Fei. I miss those days: I have not only dreamed about them but about the possibility that their performances might be revived.

In retrospect, I was very fortunate to have become involved with Combat Songs: it kept me occupied and thus, when schooling was suspended across the country, safe from the political purges, looting, and violence that erupted everywhere. Thanks to this involvement, I had at least some exposure to the arts during my formative years.

After we joined the farm on Hainan as *zhiqings*, the artistic talents of some of us from Combat Songs were acknowledged, and this subsequently turned us into key members of the Maoist propaganda troupe of the regiment. My former classmate, Zhu Jianqiang, would even work his way up as composer and director from the regimental troupe to the divisional troupe and then to the army corps troupe.

Leisure activities on the farm were monotonous. Though every now and then the film projection squad would tour the regiment, their stock was limited to just a few antediluvian revolutionary films such as *Landmine Warfare*, *Tunnel Warfare*, *Lenin in 1918* and the eight revolutionary model plays such as *The Legend of the Red Lantern*. Whenever a film was shown in one of the companies, we would trek through the hills for at least an hour in order to catch it. When the North Korean revolutionary film *The Flower Girl* was shown at divisional headquarters, some even hiked over forty kilometres to watch it.

As "class struggle" was the eternal principle which underlay everything, including our everyday life, culture existed merely to subserve it. In January 1970, when I was sent to divisional headquarters to attend a theatrical festival, the political commissar, a military man, announced that cultural activities were never merely entertainment but ideological warfare. If we did not equip everyone with proletarian ideology, the capitalists would win this war. Every regiment or troop must therefore take propaganda—cultural activities—extremely seriously. His speech sent all the regiments and troops into frantic efforts to form their own groups and singing ensembles to use culture to propagate Maoism and win the war of ideas.

The Maoist propaganda group in the regiment recruited its members from both regimental headquarters and the individual troops. When a series of performances was arranged, the members would be called up, and after the tour they would return to their troops. Apart from watching films, the rehearsals and performances constituted their most important leisure activity.

The idea of creating *I Love My Army Corps* was dreamed up by a propaganda officer in the political division of the regiment, Huang Ronger, who, in his attempt to demonstrate his political orientation, changed his name during the Cultural Revolution to Huang Dongbin—"Dongbin" sounds the same in Chinese as "heading toward the [revolutionary] east." Initially a barefoot doctor, he worked his way up from company clerk to head of all the propaganda efforts of the regiment. A passionate activist, he would a year later set up an amateur literary group, and also found *The Morning Sun*, a mimeographed periodical for which I would design the covers and even make some stencils.

Back in November 1969, less than a year after I had joined the farm, Zhu Jianqiang and I were asked to compose a cantata called *Army Farm Song* for a show at regimental headquarters. Since by this time, 1972, the talented Zhu had already been reassigned to the divisional troupe, it was left largely to me to compose for *I Love My Army Corps*.

As a temporary regimental propaganda member, I was put up at the regimental hostel. From my window, I had a view of the dark Keling Hill and its virgin jungle. To the west, a red dirt track ran through a vast rubber plantation. Not far down the track was a dam, and below it a river. The river was tranquil most of the time and we swam and bathed in it. Whenever there was a flash flood, however, it would turn into a roaring monster.

Consumed by revolutionary passion, many *zhiqings* contributed to the writing of *I Love My Army Corps*, such as He Yancheng, Zhu Zhaoyu and Li Xiaojiang. Li's poems were published in the provincial newspaper, *Nanfang Daily*, something that made him a celebrity on the farm. With the lyrics spread out before me, I would sit at the desk and try to come up with some tunes. With no formal training in composition, I had only my natural ability to fall back on. When Combat Songs were rehearsing at the Guangzhou Beijing Opera Troupe, I had once climbed into the library of a nearby music school and stolen some books from its shelves, among them a textbook on composition published in the former Soviet Union. To my dismay, I learned from the preface that it must be read under the supervision of a qualified music teacher.

But luck was on my side: I had a copy of *The Long March*, a suite of songs from *The East Is Red*, a rare vocal work. In both the score and the style of the lyrics, *I Love My Army Corps* was heavily influenced by it.

The suite consisted of five songs: "Setting Sail," "Receiving New Soldiers," "The Opening-up-the-Wilderness Work Song," "A Rubber Plantation Connected to the World," and "I Love My Army Corps." Presentation was varied, involving choirs, mixed duets, female ensembles, and so on. The musical sources were merely what we could gain access to at that time—revolutionary songs and Hainanese folk tunes—and thus were severely limited. We took the whole matter seriously: the *zhiqing* who composed "A Rubber Plantation Connected to the World" had to rise at three thirty every morning to cut rubber.

As was typical of the time, the basic style of the suite was passionate and uplifting. For example, "Receiving New Soldiers" included these lyrics:

With coconuts and fragrant mangos,
we relieve them of their shoulder bags and welcome them to
their rooms.
Roars of laughter and applause resound in the dormitories,
old and new soldiers forge a friendship.
From the five lakes and four seas,
we are here to develop the new southern borderlands together.

Who could deny that it was imbued with heroism and revolutionary romanticism?

The next step was to score and arrange the music for the band, which I had a vague knowledge of through my stint with Combat Songs. In my diaries, there were some basic instructions on how to score: it was a real case of learning on the job, with limited resources and little talent. The Chinese say: "When the tiger is away from the mountains, the monkey proclaims himself king." Well, that monkey was me.

The members of the chorus and band were recruited from various troops. After the toil of opening up the wilderness and cutting rubber, they had to hike hill and dale for rehearsals at regimental headquarters. From no one was there ever a word of complaint.

Eventually, time was up and we were ready to take the stage. On National Day, a large piece of blue cloth was hung up in the otherwise empty grounds of the regimental headquarters, dazzling lights were switched on, loudspeakers were pulled out from the storage room and hung on posts or trees. The audience sat in groups on their own crude stools. The chorus wore white, the band blue. After the band sat down in front of the chorus, I went to the center of the stage to direct: *I Love My Army Corps* was solemnly presented.

I'm not sure if it was because organizing the event exhausted me, but I had a temperature before the show and fell ill right afterward.

When the Maoist propaganda troupe of the army corps toured our regiment, we once again staged *I Love My Army Corps*. It was warmly received.

Despite the lofty ambition and revolutionary passion that found expression in *I Love My Army Corps*, we were increasingly disenchanted by reality, and nobody wanted to put our claims into practice by taking root in Hainan. Although when we signed up for rustication to Hainan—willingly or under coercion—we had all wanted to "liberate the whole world" and end the importation of rubber, by 1973 the extreme hardship, the major joint campaigns following one upon another, the sheer isolation, and the inescapable and continuous political crusades had not only drained us physically but destroyed the last of our ambitions to establish a brave new world on this remote island. Indeed, less than half a year after the celebration of National Day, many *zhiqing*s would, under various pretexts, seek to leave the farm for good: "I suffer from poor health," "I'm going to college," "I'm joining the army." They would "leave through the front door" or slip out of the back, whatever worked. Ironically, the first *zhiqing*s to leave were those whose parents used to hold high offices and who had been prosecuted as "capitalist-roaders" at the start of the Cultural Revolution, but who had been reinstated in the subsequent political campaigns. Once this happened, their priority was usually to get their children out of the poor, remote, and mountainous regions to which they had been rusticated. For most of the latter, the tried and tested way out was to bury themselves, after the daily toil, to study for the partially reopened entrance examinations in order to earn an offer from a college. Those who had yet to leave would employ all sorts of tricks to escape.

In October 1974, the army, too, withdrew from the farm, and its management returned to the local authority. Following this disheartening event, Huang Ronger, the propaganda officer who was the brains behind *I Love My Army Corps*, was one of the first to leave. I went to see him off, and we parted at the Daxi Bridge. Having lived on Hainan Island for over ten years, I was one of the last to go—in 1979.

The other day I read this passage from *Up to the Mountains, Down to the Countryside*, published by the *Guangming Daily Press*:

> The campaign to develop the rubber plantation led by the Guangzhou Army Production and Construction Corps was hindered by various natural conditions and undermined even further by mismanagement. The unrealistically high production

targets were never supported by sufficient manpower, proper machinery, fertilizer, seedlings or young plants: around thirty percent of the plantations were neglected . . . Hard work did not yield sufficient benefits, and the farm's losses increased annually. The central government had to withdraw the army and hand the management of the plantation back to local government.

When I spoke to many of those who in various capacities had been involved in creating *I Love My Army Corps*, I couldn't find anyone who had kept a copy of the suite or who could remember all its titles. And that included me.

All that was left was the black and white photograph of our performance.

BIOGRAPHIES

The Editors

Ou Nianzhong (b. 1949, rusticated from Guangzhou 1969–1979) was a farm worker on Hainan, then a technician. In 1982 he became a broadcaster and was involved in media reforms that were eventually adopted nationally. He is a former vice president of Radio Guangdong and of the Southern Media Institute, and a former president of Southern Television. A prolific author and editor, he is also the deputy executive president of the Guangdong Cultural and Media Research Institute. In 2010, he received the Order of Merit of the Federal Republic of Germany for his lifelong efforts to promote cultural exchanges between China and Germany.

"Some maintain that adversity is the breeding ground for talent. But I believe that it suffocates more than it breeds."

Liang Yongkang (b. 1950, rusticated from Guangzhou 1968–1973) worked mostly as a correspondent on Hainan Island until his "politically incorrect" family background caught up with him and he was demoted. He became a worker-peasant-soldier-student in 1973 and on completing his college courses was obliged to return to the farm in 1976. He left Hainan in 1979 for a lectureship and in 1983 became involved in setting up the Guangdong Higher Education Press, where he served in various senior capacities.

"Some maintain that they have no resentment or regrets about their rustication. I resent every minute of it—the fact that I could not do things of my own free will."

"When feudalism dominates a society, blood lineage rules."

The Contributors

Cao Nancai (b. 1947, rusticated from Zhanjiang 1968–1975) was at first a laborer and then sent to work as a correspondent on the Leizhou Peninsula, on the side of the Qiongzhou Strait opposite Hainan Island. After returning home, he became a factory worker and later read philosophy at Sun Yat-sen University. Since 1982, he has worked in various capacities for the Guangdong provincial government, among them deputy to the standing committee of the Provincial People's Congress.

"My rusticated years were tough yet innocent, rugged yet magical."

Che Zhiming (b. 1951, rusticated from Guangzhou 1968–1973) was a squad leader on Hainan Island before being assigned to drive a bulldozer. After his father was reinstated to high office, he was sent home to manage state factories, companies, and holiday resorts.

"Rustication made an indelible impression on us. I don't think anyone can ever forget the experience."

Chen Guanli (b. 1953, rusticated from Guangzhou 1969-1980) was a farm worker on Hainan Island. His father died in 1971 after being denounced as a "rightist" and imprisoned for fourteen years. In 1983, he went to America to continue his education but for financial reasons was unable to complete his studies. He is a coordinator at an American exhibition center.

"The hardship on Hainan Island tempered me, and in a lifetime of frustrations has given me determination and drive. It's an experience I treasure."

Chen Hongbo (b. 1949, rusticated from Guangzhou 1968-1978) worked on Hainan Island as a cook, farm worker, correspondent, and propaganda officer. On rehabilitation, he administered and taught in schools for a while, and after a spell as deputy head of human resources in a state agency, managed various state enterprises. On numerous occasions he has been made a role model by the municipal government.

"The fate of the individual is inseparably linked to that of the state. Whatever the circumstances, being optimistic and hardworking is the key."

Chen Hongguang (b. 1951, rusticated from Guangzhou 1968–1979) became an assistant nurse on Hainan Island after a six-week training course. On rehabilitation, he became a quality controller in a boiler factory.

Chen Mingguo (b. 1949, rusticated from Guangzhou 1968–1980) spent his time on Hainan Island helping to clear the wilderness. After rehabilitation, he worked in a school library and then completed a teacher's training course.

"Time slipped by and we accomplished nothing. Our rustication was sour, bitter and spicy: anything but sweet."

Chen Yanhua (b. 1951, rusticated from Guangzhou 1968–1974) was involved in a series of experiments on rubber plants on Hainan Island. On being rehabilitated, she completed a number of diploma courses and worked in the state agency responsible for the inspection and quarantining of commodities.

"Assiduity, thrift, and tranquillity are the qualities I pursue."

Chen Zufu (b. 1951, rusticated from Meixian in 1970–76) tried to escape rustication on Hainan Island by overstaying his home leave for more than four years. While working in a state factory after rehabilitation, he rose from manual worker to technician and engineer after completing a degree program by correspondence. The winner of a number of awards for industrial design, he is the owner and chief engineer of a factory.

Chen Sanxing (b. 1955, rusticated from Yangjiang 1970–78) was engaged in clearing the wilderness, planting, and cutting rubber on Hainan Island. Upon returning home on the pretext of ill health, he worked in factories before running his own in 1992.

"Eight years of rustication taught me how to live through adversity. I shall never forget my fellow zhiqings *who lived and struggled alongside me in those hard times."*

Deng Jingxi (b. 1949, rusticated from Guangzhou 1968–1977) cleared the wilderness, planted and cut rubber on Hainan Island before becoming involved in a series of experiments on rubber plants. After returning home, he worked his way up from a worker to an officer in a state knitting mill. He later became a college administrator.

"Dedication, diligence, meticulousness, truthfulness, and inventiveness: these are the qualities I have appreciated wherever I have worked."

Deng Xiaodan (b. 1951, rusticated from Guangzhou 1968–1973) completed a diploma in Chinese medicine and then worked in a pharmacy before migrating to Hong Kong in 1989.

"Infatuated with revolutionary ambitions at the start of our rustication, we gradually became disillusioned. We experienced all sorts of mood swings in those days."

Dong Zhennan (b. 1951, rusticated from Guangzhou 1968–1974) helped to clear the wilderness and cut rubber on Hainan Island while working on a series of experiments on rubber plants. After rehabilitation, he worked in a state factory which made construction machinery. On completing an industrial course, he became involved in mechanical design, and was later a sales manager. In 1994, he set up his own business.

"Worker, peasant, 'soldier,' college student, businessman—I've tried them all. I have no regrets regarding my life."

Fang Jinqi (b. 1948, rusticated from Guangzhou 1968–1979) worked for a few years in a rubber plantation on Hainan Island. In 1972, she was reassigned to the rubber factory and then promoted to be secretary of the Communist Youth League in Daling State Farm. After returning home, she worked in school administration.

"If you are handed a lemon, make it into lemonade. That is what I learned from my eleven years of rustication."

Feng Qiqin (b. 1949, rusticated from Guangzhou 1968–1975) was a farm worker on Hainan Island, then a teacher. After suffering from a high fever for four years, she was eventually diagnosed with rheumatic myocarditis and sent home. She worked as a statistician in state factories, and later as an accountant.

"My youth was lost to Hainan. Yet the stamina which I gained through those years of rustication helped me to pull through later on."

Feng Xingkai (b. 1955, rusticated from Guangzhou 1970–79) never completed his primary education. On rehabilitation, he held a number of administrative jobs before starting his own business. After it folded, he worked as a driver and driving instructor.

"Our rustication was full of hardship and the stains of blood and tears."

He Qinghua (b. 1948, rusticated from Guangzhou 1968–1978) was a farm worker for a spell before being reassigned to work as a correspondent, and later as the secretary of the Party committee of Daling Farm. Soon after returning home, she worked for a state enterprise in various administrative and managerial positions.

"The diligence and stamina that were instilled in me through my rustication proved to be the most valuable assets of my later career."

He Weixian (b. 1954, rusticated from Guangzhou 1969–2010) was a member of the militia and later a farm worker on Hainan Island. From 1985 he was reassigned to the farm's rubber factory as a maintenance worker. He and his wife were not rehabilitated until 2010, when a new government decree allowed all those who were still rusticated to return home without preconditions.

He Yancheng (b. 1949, rusticated from Guangzhou 1968–1977) was a farm worker on Hainan Island, but also toured regularly with the Maoist propaganda troupe and helped school children to put on propaganda shows. After rehabilitation, he worked in a state company and in his spare time published a number of self-help and reference books.

"I was most fortunate and proud to be in a position to help the rural children of Hainan Island."

Hou Jingjie (b. 1954, rusticated from Meixian 1970–79) worked in construction, production, and logistics squads on Hainan Island before being assigned to grow vegetables for the regimental school. After rehabilitation, he worked in a state trading company before setting up his own business in 1998.

"Life was extremely tough on the farm. Yet what I picked up through living and working with so many educated young people from the cities has been most beneficial to me. I am grateful to them: I miss them dearly."

Hu Zhimin (b. 1951, rusticated from Guangzhou 1968–1971) was a laborer, and later a clerk on Hainan Island before being moved to an army factory in northern Guangdong Province to work as a statistician. On returning home in 1978, she worked in the finance departments of various state sectors.

"My life has been permanently marked by rustication, a time when I was lost and deeply repressed."

Huang Jian (b. 1954, rusticated from Yangjiang 1970–1980) had various menial jobs on Hainan Island as well as working as a teacher on the farm. On returning home, he worked for a state enterprise in a number of administrative and managerial positions.

"During our rustication we lost out considerably: yet I value that experience. After all, it was the time of my youth."

Huang Ronger aka Huang Dongbin (b. 1948, rusticated from Guangzhou 1968–1975) was a barefoot doctor, clerk, and propaganda officer before being transferred home to take up a writing post in the municipal cultural bureau. After a spell as a journalist, he migrated to Hong Kong in 1985 to pursue a career in media and real estate, but has retired to Guangdong.

"When I arrived at Hainan Island, my dream was to become an author, to write a masterpiece about the new social experiments of the human race. That masterpiece has yet to appear."

Huang Siqin (b. 1953, rusticated from Meixian 1970–79) was a nursery school teacher, rubber cutter, and assistant nurse on Hainan before returning home to begin a career in a tax office. She remained in the civil service until her retirement.

"My memories of Hainan Island and the rubber plantation might be fading, but not the friendships that were forged in such suffering."

Biographies

Huang Xiaowei (b. 1951, rusticated from Meixian 1969–1979) was a farm worker on Hainan Island. After returning home, he worked in a printing house. Since retiring, he has renewed his interests in calligraphy and stamp engraving.

"The impressions I drew with matchsticks for my fellow zhiqings helped them to return home and start a life and a career. I am still most proud of my role in helping them to get the fresh start we all deserved."

Jia Hongji (b. 1951, rusticated from Guangzhou 1968–1975) was a logistics squad leader on Hainan Island. Since returning home, he has worked his way up in state factories from maintenance worker to manager, and then general manager.

"The zhiqing: as an individual, he or she was an urban school-leaver, the absent child of an ordinary family reduced to primitive conditions. As a generation, the zhiqings provided the irreducibly lively moments in the epic of the People's Republic."

Kong Dexiang (b. 1950, rusticated from Guangzhou 1968–1979) worked on clearing the wilderness before being assigned to set up and run a new company on Hainan Island. On rehabilitation, he worked in the state electric power sector.

"Our experiences of rustication must never be forgotten. Preserve the memories. Make sure that the rusticated youth are remembered in human history."

Li Haiming (b. 1953, rusticated from Guangzhou 1969–1979) was a farm worker and then a cook on Hainan Island before returning home to start a career in the post office.

"My biggest regret is that when I earned a college place in 1978, I couldn't take it up because of the difficulties created by the farm officials. But in my later career, that experience put me one step ahead of the field."

Li Huguang (b. 1953, rusticated from Guangzhou 1969–1979) became a farm worker on Hainan Island after being tainted by the denunciation of his father and denied entry to senior secondary school. When his father was rehabilitated, he was allowed to return home and was assigned to work in a state factory. When the factory closed, he was laid off and resorted to self-employment. In 2010, after the failure of his business, he emigrated to America.

"From the hard, lean times of the Great Leap Forward to those of the Cultural Revolution; from being deprived of an education to enduring rustication; and later on, being made redundant by a state enterprise . . . I have seen it all. My life is typical of those who were born in the 1950s."

Lin Yuhua (b. 1952, rusticated from Meixian 1970–76) spent some time as a farm worker and a member of the propaganda troupe before being reassigned to work as a teacher. She left Hainan to become an accountant and migrated to Hong Kong in 1996, but has returned home to run her own business.

"The six years of toughening on the island gave me the power to face later challenges. I have no regrets whatsoever."

Liu Jingan (b. 1949, rusticated from Guangzhou 1968–1980) held many jobs on the farm and experienced many dangerous moments on Hainan Island. He counts himself lucky to be alive. After rehabilitation, he worked in the commercial sector and when he was made redundant re-trained as an accountant.

"My generation has lived through many as yet untold hardships and dangers. That is what I want later generations to know."

Lu Sui (b. 1952, rusticated from Guangzhou 1968–1976) helped to clear the wilderness, planted rubber, raised pigs, and also worked as a nursery school teacher on Hainan Island. After returning home, she worked as an accountant in a primary school.

Lu Zhongmin (b. 1951, rusticated from Guangzhou 1968–1976) was engaged in propaganda and woodland management on Hainan Island before being assigned to grow vegetables. On rehabilitation, he worked in the state water supply and treatment sector. After completing professional training, he was engaged in the research and development of automatic control systems for industry.

"In my youthful days, times were tough and the obstacles were many. To my relief, I was able to fulfill my dream of returning to school after the eight-year interruption of rustication."

Luo Tiansheng (b. 1947 in Malaysia) followed his brother to Guangzhou in 1953 so that they could be reunited with their father, who was a rubber specialist. He followed his father to the Nada Propagation Center on Hainan Island in 1955 and then to Daling State Farm in 1968 to work briefly as a farm laborer. After teaching on the farm for over a decade, he was transferred to work in government offices.

Ma Guizhen (b. 1953, rusticated from Meixian 1970–78) was a farm worker on Hainan Island. In 1978, she was reassigned to work in a rubber factory in Tongshi and later to a supply and marketing company of the Hainan State Farm Bureau.

Mei Fuming (b. 1949, rusticated from Guangzhou 1968–1977) worked on clearing the wilderness and later in construction on Hainan Island. Since returning home he has worked in a secondary school.

"It still saddens me that it was only because of my father's early death that I was allowed to return home in order to take up his job. If by staying behind on the farm I could have given him another twenty years of life, I would willingly have done so."

Peng Lijia (b. 1952, rusticated from Meixian 1970–78) was first a farm worker and then a correspondent. On completing a college course in 1982, she began teaching and is a professor of Music at Xinghai Conservatory of Music. She has published a number of books and been involved in many multimedia productions which focus on the use and care of the voice.

'With dreams come hope. On its wings, I have turned my passion into my livelihood. I couldn't have been happier."

Rao Ruiguang (b. 1950, rusticated from Shantou 1966–1979) was tainted by the fact that her parents had been placed in one of the "seven black categories." On the farm, she worked as a rubber cutter, cook, member of the propaganda troupe, and teacher. Upon rehabilitation, she was assigned to work in a nursery in Guangzhou. She was made a role model in her profession many times over.

"After what we withstood on Hainan Island, there isn't much we can't overcome."

Ren Jie (b. 1950, rusticated from Guangzhou 1968–1975) worked on clearing the wilderness and rubber cutting on Hainan Island. On returning home, he studied banking and worked in the Industrial and Commercial Bank of China until 1985. Two years later, he set up his own cosmetics company.

Song Xiaoqi (b. 1952, rusticated from Changsha, Hunan Province 1969–1978) was for a year a farm worker, and for eight years a regular member of the propaganda troupe. Soon after rehabilitation to her husband's hometown, Guangzhou, she began a flourishing television career as journalist and producer at Guangdong Television, and has many feature programs, documentaries, and books to her credit.

"My aim is to reflect on what I see and hear and to write about what I've experienced, and this includes the bitter and complicated years of rustication."

Su Haitao (b. 1949, rusticated from Guangzhou 1968–1975) soon became a member of the guard and messenger squad as a basketball player and later a teacher on Hainan Island. On returning home, he was first a cook and later a technician and senior engineer at the Guangdong Forestry Institute, where he led a number of research projects.

"Those tough years of rustication seemed like a waste of our lives. But they could also be seen as valuable training for one's later career."

Su Zhaoxin (b. 1949, rusticated 1968–1978) planted rubber on Hainan Island before being transferred to work in regimental headquarters and later as a teacher. When higher education was officially reopened in China in 1977, he was among the first students to be admitted. He has since become an academic.

Wang Guangzhen (b. 1945, rusticated from Haikou City, Hainan Island, 1968–1977) trained briefly as a barefoot doctor on Daling Farm and then worked as an assistant nurse. On rehabilitation, he trained first as a doctor and then as a teacher and worked at schools in both capacities. In 1988, he became a national role model in the school clinic sector.

"My whole life has been devoted to keeping the promise I made on being sent to train as a barefoot doctor."

Weng Ruiwen (b. 1952, rusticated from Meixian 1970–72) was a farm worker on Hainan Island before joining the People's Liberation Army. On being discharged in 1977, he was assigned to work in the science commission of his hometown.

Wu Xianfang (b. 1952, rusticated from Guangzhou 1968–1975) worked for two years on the rubber plantation and was then assigned to raise pigs. On returning home, she became a worker in a mechanical maintenance factory, and after completing a part-time degree in statistics, worked in administrative and managerial positions in a state enterprise.

"The great hardship of our rustication brought a surprise gift in later life: stamina."

Xiao Peihong (b. 1951, rusticated from Chaozhou 1970–1983) worked, after returning home, in a factory which made painted pottery.

"The tough days of rustication unexpectedly prepared me for the challenge of being made redundant in later life."

Xuan Guangchi (b. 1948, rusticated from Guangzhou 1968–1977) was a farm worker on Hainan Island until diagnosed with a fracture in his right hand and sent home. He worked in the publicity office of Guangzhou Cultural Park and is an avid traveler.

"To overcome the stigma of the 'redeemable child' label, the only thing I could do was take on all the dirtiest, toughest, and most dangerous jobs on the farm."

Yang Heping (b. 1953, rusticated from Meixian 1970–77) worked on Hainan Island as a telephone operator and then a broadcaster. After rehabilitation, she became a factory worker before joining Radio Guangdong as a photographer and editor. She has a number of photographic titles to her credit.

"What a twist of fate that after my rustication my life should once again have been bound up with broadcasting."

Yang Yanhui (b. 1953, rusticated from Jieyang 1971–1991) spent his twenty-year rustication on Hainan Island working on the rubber plantation and at the propagation center of the farm. He now runs his own business in plant propagation.

"Without my twenty years' hard work on Daling Farm, I wouldn't be the man that I am."

Zhang Cheng (b. 1953, rusticated from Meixian 1970–76) was assigned to work in a state factory after his rustication ended. He was made redundant in 2004.

Zhang Huixin (b. 1950, rusticated from Guangzhou 1968–1977) worked on Hainan Island as a farm laborer, cook, teacher, and propaganda officer. On completing her diploma, she was a factory worker and an accountant before being moved to a post in the Guangdong propaganda department in 1986.

"Whatever conclusions others might have drawn about rustication or their own experience of it, mine remains the most memorable period of my life."

Zheng Xiuhua (b. 1953, rusticated from Yangjiang 1969–1978) planted and cut rubber on Hainan Island while engaging in experiments on rubber plants. In 1973, she returned to Yangjiang to continue her rustication in a rural village. After rehabilitation, she worked in nursing, midwifery and pharmaceutical and administrative posts.

"I hope history will remember the zhiqing tribe. I hope we will be known and understood by more people."

Zhong Enming (b. 1949, rusticated from Guangzhou 1968–1976) was a laborer on Hainan Island before being assigned to a task force during a political campaign, and then to the job of tractor driver. He was a regular member of the propaganda troupe. After returning home, he was recruited by the Guangdong Hydroelectric Institute and ended his career with the Guangzhou Electricity Corporation.

Zhu Jianqiang (b. 1948, rusticated from Guangzhou 1969–1978) was briefly a farm worker and cook on Hainan Island. In 1971, he became a fixture of the Maoist propaganda troupe of the division and a year later was promoted to the army corps troupe as a composer and conductor. In 1986, he emigrated to New York to run a catering business. He is a member of the Chinese Music Ensemble of New York and promotes Chinese music.

Zhu Zhaoyu (b. 1950, rusticated from Guangzhou 1968–1973) organized night classes and led the Maoist propaganda troupe while working as a farm laborer on Hainan Island. In 1973, he was offered a place to study geology as a worker-peasant-soldier-student. After completing his PhD, he became a geologist and is now a professor.

"The stamina I acquired from the hardships of the farm helped me to become a geologist."

ACKNOWLEDGEMENTS

Our first thanks are due to Chen Zufu and Lin Yuhua, whose idea this book was and who gave it their full financial support. For their enthusiastic response to the project and willingness to share their stories, we must then thank the *zhiqings* who were rusticated to Daling State Farm. Without all these people there would be no book to celebrate, and we owe a particular debt to Chen Hongbo, He Qinghua, Peng Lijia, Zhu Zhaoyu, Mei Fuming, Fang Jinqi and Yang Heping, who were the leading members of our editorial board. Huang Shangli, former president of Guangdong Press, Zhan Xiumin, publisher, and Du Xiaoye, editor of Huacheng Publishing House, lent their valuable assistance to the project.

For the English edition of the book, we are grateful for the generous support of Hou Jingjie, another former *zhiqing* at Daling Farm, and to Dr Zhu Zhaoyu, who collaborated with the editors in drafting the maps. We must also express our warm thanks to two British scholars, Laura Maynard of the University of Sussex and Andrew Crisell, Professor Emeritus, University of Sunderland. Laura selected and translated our stories, Andrew helped her to prepare the English version of the manuscript, and together they secured an American publisher, Douglas Merwin. It is to him that our final thanks are due.

We dedicate our book to all those *zhiqings* whose stories have not yet been heard.

Ou Nianzhong
Liang Yongkang
Guangzhou, November 2014